REBEL SAINTS

GEORGE FOX

(After the Painting by Sir Peter Lely in Friends' Historical Library, Swarthmore College)

REBEL SAINTS

BY

MARY AGNES BEST

ILLUSTRATED WITH REPRODUCTIONS
FROM OLD PRINTS

Essay Index Reprint Series

BOOKS FOR LIBRARIES PRESS
FREEPORT, NEW YORK

First Published 1925
Reprinted 1968

LIBRARY OF CONGRESS CATALOG CARD NUMBER:
68-55839

MANUFACTURED
BY
HALLMARK LITHOGRAPHERS, INC.
IN THE U.S.A.

MOTTO

Revolt! and still revolt! revolt!
What we believe in waits latent forever through all the continents, and all the islands and archipelagos of the sea;
What we believe in invites no one, promises nothing, sits in calmness and light, is positive and composed, knows no discouragement,
Waiting patiently, waiting its time.

I say where liberty draws not the blood out of slavery, there slavery draws the blood out of liberty.
I say the word of the good old cause in These States, and resound it hence over the world.

Walt Whitman.

FOREWORD

It is the aim of *Rebel Saints* to tell the story of Quakerism in the light of romantic adventure. It was the peculiar fanaticism of the Quakers, that the pressure of existing wrongs pushed them into immediate resistance. Characterized by profound spiritual experiences, the early Quakers verified the Christian doctrine that all things are possible to him who believes, and illustrated it by incredible adventures. It is the nature of men to content themselves with mulling over the wrongs of the world; under the dynamic leadership of George Fox, it was the practice of the Quakers to react immediately to belief "so as to be ready to be its martyr." That a wrong had gone on forever was to them proof that it had gone on long enough. The world can be changed when the spirit of man wills it.

Their relation to the political state was anarchistic; their anarchy was successful inasmuch as they proposed to substitute a higher law for that against which they rebelled; and to this higher law they submitted themselves with a phenomenal self-discipline. They refused to walk the beaten track when they had discovered a better way, and, unlike the ordinary revolutionist who blindly beats out against the system that oppresses him, they patiently set out to lead men to the path which, though the longest way round, was the shortest way to permanent relief.

While the Christianity of their day was busy converting other believers and unbelievers, by no gentle means, the Quakers specialized in the conversion of Christians to Christianity. From the mountains of theology they dug out the buried ore of the gospel. Their religion, said William James, "in a day of shams, was a religion of verity rooted in spiritual inwardness. . . . So far as our Christian sects to-day are evolving into liberality, they are simply reverting in essence to the position which Fox and the early Quakers so long ago assumed."

Unfortunately, says Buckle in his *History of Civilization,* European governments are always meddling in matters with which they have no concern. The Quakers gave government a liberal education in minding its own business; government usurps power when the people abdicate. Their measure of success in converting Christians and enlightening governments entitles them to the grateful consideration of all who prize liberty. Whatever interpretation a materialistic age may put upon their beliefs and behavior, it cannot be gainsaid that they left an ineffaceable mark on the thought of mankind.

Readers who would inquire further into the secret of the power of these extraordinary revolutionists are referred to the readable works of Rufus M. Jones, president of the Quaker college of Haverford. Sharpless and Janney contribute history and biography, and a monumental work by Mrs. Hirst follows the movement down to the present day. The present writer gratefully acknowledges the patient consideration of the Quaker libraries of Haverford and Swarthmore, and the staff of the Newark Public Library.

CONTENTS

ILLUSTRATIONS

REBEL SAINTS

The World as the Quakers Found It

Reader, if you are not acquainted with it, I would recommend above all church narratives, to read Sewel's *History of the Quakers.* — CHARLES LAMB.

ONE hundred years before the English colonies of North America startled the Old World with their bold Declaration of Independence, an outlandish individual in circus rider attire, arrested under the sedition act, was sent to London by special escort to receive the personal scrutiny of the English Dictator, Oliver Cromwell, against whose life counter-revolutionary plots were hatching. History presents the Great Protector in a variety of characters, but never as an easy mark. Yet in a brief early-morning interview, the strange hobo preacher in leather breeches severely lectured the ruler of England, brought tears to the eyes of the man of iron, and finally was led from his presence, not back to a cell, but into the banqueting hall of the kings of England.

In answer to his astonished inquiries it was told him he was there by command of the Lord Protector, that he might dine with his gentlemen. With more force than grace, the man who but an hour before had been a prisoner under suspicion of treason declined the hospitality. The terror of Europe, he who had made kings class-conscious, fearful not only for their crowns but for the heads on which to wear them, on hearing this curt refusal, far from being offended was greatly pleased, for, said he: "There is a people risen that I cannot win with gifts or honors."

This brusque, picturesque crusader, resistant to the most subtle form of bribery, flouting the hospitality of the man who peremptorily warned the rulers of Europe when to watch their step, was George Fox, the first Quaker, and it was he, and not Thomas Jefferson, says W. D. Howells, who imagined the first of the self-evident truths of the Declaration of Independence.

Carrying their message of freedom and equality, Fox and his intrepid band of outlaws, without respect of person, held up and admonished czars, kings, and sultans, princes and prelates, convicts and pirates, within and without the law. The industrious and inquisitive Dutchman, Sewel, whose narrative Charles Lamb so earnestly recommended, was the Boswell of that movement. His two yellowed volumes, entombed on the library shelves, are filled with incredible tales of ecstatic vision and wild adventure, which he got hot from the lips of the valiant fighters who made his and a good deal of our history.

In its time the Quaker uprising was regarded as extreme left-wing radicalism, subversive of law and order, threatening the overthrow of government; and it was therefore considered a pious and patriotic duty to suppress it by fair means or foul. As their dangerous radicalism became to some extent the orthodoxy of later generations, the absent-minded average man faced the other way round, and thought of those early Quakers, if he thought at all, as well-meaning, more or less cowardly, and too good to know any better, leading lives as drab as their clothes, their chief activity going into the silence. Like many popular opinions, this is as far from fact as it is possible to get.

Compared with the primitive Quakers, the I.W.W. in the oil fields of Oklahoma lead a sheltered and protected life. Far from being drab, their lives were lurid. They reached out toward danger as plants toward the sun. They trekked the whole wide world, challenging all the autocratic powers and potentates of their time. They sailed the seven seas in leaky tubs, and ran afoul the Algerian pirates before Commodore Decatur was born or thought of; met the enemy, and he was theirs without violence or epigram. Laying the foundations of a mighty nation, they established great states and administered them, without once making the Sermon on the Mount a scrap of paper. To the enrichment of their queen and their enterprising fellow countrymen, they were sold into Barbados, where those who survived the terrors of the transports were fattened for sale in stockades. As slaves among the heathen in Africa, their lot on the whole was less bitter than as freemen in England. In Old and New England vivisection was practiced on them — tortures too brutal to repeat to sensitive modern ears. They glutted

English jails, and the convict ships on which they were deported afforded them hardly more than standing room only. Too frequently their sufferings were relieved by a martyr's death, and the history of their adventurous lives reads like an invasion of the realm of Teutonic legendary tales.

But beneath all the fanatical exploits, buried under mountains of obsolete religious phraseology and dogma, one great fact emerges: their fight was one of the most cruel and persistent wars in the records of our race, between intrenched authority and custom on the one side and individual liberty on the other. They enlisted for the duration of that war, and, so far as the English-speaking peoples are concerned, went over the top almost alone, with nothing to back them but spiritual force, unparalleled courage, and a mighty power which they called God.

To succeeding generations, heirs of their victory, some of their war-cries seem trivial, or even absurd, but if they had been hampered by the delusion that God willed them to be nourished on a diet of dried prunes, it would not have altered the objective of their dogged march toward free speech, free assembly, and the complete separation of Church and State.

It is only against the background of their time, however, that their seeming absurdities can be viewed in the proper perspective. In many cases these were the protective coloring by which their raids on the fields of tradition were made less conspicuous. The politicians would have us believe that only their specialized wisdom can unravel the tangled snarl of world affairs, making a proper understanding of history possible. But history, after all, is that bugbear of the comfortable conservative, the ceaseless overthrow of government by the free play of human emotions; and human emotions, though often involved, are limited in number. Any average intelligence equipped with a list of them, a knowledge of the multiplication table, and a hint of the subcutaneous kinship of Judy O'Grady and the Colonel's lady, can make a reasonable guess as to why crowns and thrones have perished, and systems rise and fall world without end.

No intelligent idea of the far-reaching significance of the Quaker uprising is possible, without a glance at the conditions out of which it rose. An airplane view of the social topography is sufficient for our purpose; a little authentic gossip, a few illuminating anecdotes, will often give a truer picture than an erudite array of historical "facts," which are frequently but masquerading fancies.

The hard-fighting days of the Quakers began toward the close of Oliver Cromwell's meteoric career, and continued till the last ill-fated Stuart wore the crown of England. During this stormy period, two highly respectable gentlemen on the inside circle of power kept their diaries, John Evelyn, a cultivated gentleman of the court and a founder of the Royal Society, and Samuel Pepys, Secretary to the Admiralty. These, with the Quaker chronicles, enable us to work up a fairly satisfactory picture of the times.

The two dominant powers of the day, Church and State, in spite of occasional misunderstandings, were so happily married as to be one; their mutual dependence was recognized by the Stuart king who declared, "One stone out of the Church is two stones out of the crown." The King was the head of the English Church; its high offices were frequently political jobs, and Mr. Pepys constantly reiterates the plaint that "the clergy are very high."

"To church and heard Mr. Mills preach upon the authority of the ministers upon these words, 'We are the Embassadors of Christ' wherein among other high expressions, he said, that such a learned man used to say, that if a minister of the word, and an angell should meet him together, he would salute the minister first, which methought was a little too high." Mr. Pepys makes it quite clear that, according to his rating, you would glance down the page for the clergy, considerably lower than the angels.

The clergy had their own courts and the power to levy taxes, and we gather that, when these were in arrears, the Church was not particularly squeamish in its methods of collection. Delinquent debtors often languished long in jail. An Englishman's house is his castle, but that stronghold was frequently stormed, beds taken from under the sick, cheeses and other edibles captured, and even, on one occasion, the "pannikin" containing the baby's "pap," emptied and carried off.

The notorious Vicar of Bray stands a monument to the morality of that time. Taunted with being false to his principles in continually shifting his politics and religion, he brazenly replied: "Not so neither; for if I changed my religion, I am sure I kept true to my principle; which is, to live and die the Vicar of Bray." A less famous contemporary, Bishop Kitchen, was even more versatile than the famous Vicar. He ran the whole gamut of sects under six successive changes in the State, giving occasion to a witty punster to remark that the reverend doctor "loved the Kitchen better than the Kirk."

Despotism in Church and State was dying, but the death was a long and painful one, for the most zealous baiters of privilege aimed not to destroy but to transfer it. Seceding from the "unerring dictatorship of Rome," the Church of England laid claim to that most important prerogative of the Roman Church. The Puritan secession in turn reached out greedily for it. The name of the warring sects was legion, their ambition one and everywhere the same — to make the world safe for God by destroying all his and their enemies.

On the Continent the Inquisition was flourishing. To save their souls, the Roman Church was torturing the bodies of rebels against its authority, and, where this method yielded unsatisfactory results in the way of salvation, whole populations were dispatched by the Church Militant, to face the vengeance of an angry God.

If these things were done in the green tree, what shall be said of the dry? The secular government kept step with the clerical in the matter of coercion; press gangs hunted husky Englishmen as slavers stalked the blacks in Africa, and kidnaped them into the navy. Mr. Pepys was troubled: "To the Tower several times about the business of the pressed men, and late at it till twelve of night shipping of them. But Lord! how some poor women did cry; and in my life I never did see such natural expression of passion, as I did in some poor women's bewailing themselves, and running to every parcel of men that were brought, to look for their husbands, and wept over every vessel that went off, thinking they might be there, and looking after every ship as far as ever they could by moone-light, that it grieved me to the heart to hear them. Besides to see poor patient laboring men and housekeepers leaving poor wives and families taken up on a sudden by strangers, was very hard, and that without press money, but forced against all law to be gone. It is a great tyranny."

When these same men returned and lay begging in the streets, literally dying of hunger, the noise of the weeping women changed to low growls of rage, and Mr. Pepys was not only grieved; as a high official of the navy he was so extremely nervous that he shrank from the gaze of the mob. He hesitated to send a highly esteemed venison pasty on its way to the bake shop, lest the enraged Amazons should fall upon it: "To the office; the yard being very full of women, (I believe about three hundred) coming to get money for their husbands and friends that are prisoners in Holland; and they lay clamoring and swearing and cursing us, that my wife and I were afraid to send a venison-pasty that we have for supper to-night, to the cook's to be baked, for fear of their offering violence to it."

Ragged nerves must have been the chronic condition of Englishmen for many years. A permanent feature of the scenery on the Thames was a ghastly picket fence, ornamented with the heads and quartered bodies of the opponents of the group that chanced to be temporarily in power. From the King down, everybody was venal and under suspicion; public offices were bought by crossing the palms of greedy and dissolute court ladies. The highest in the land perjured themselves lightly, and took an oath of allegiance to whichever seemed to be the winning side; those who were doubtful of being good guessers sold out to both sides, and betrayed the loser to the winner to save their own skins.

For a time the iron hand of Cromwell boldly grasped the English nettle, and although in retrospect he gives the impression of being rather hard-boiled, he was decidedly softer than his time; nor is it on record than any gentler spirit ever aspired to his job. His own head and the heads of his followers were in the ring, and keeping the enemy's heel out of that area has always been a serious consideration for the revolutionist. The beasts of the jungle are less savage than men deprived of power they have come to regard as a divine right; the knowledge of the fate that waits on failure would curdle the milk of human kindness in the breast of the most moderate rebel. As it was in the beginning, is now, and perhaps ever shall be, revolutionists and counter-revolutionists neither gave nor received mercy. National housecleaning is the most exhausting of all human undertakings — the whole national family is upset and inflamed; none but the stoutest hearts can see the work through, and these persistent ones, as a rule, are neither timid nor tender-hearted.

With Cromwell's directing energy gone, the English yielded to national weariness, and the King came back, but only to increase the disorder, for the Stuart family never could take a hint. When the first Charles confronted Oliver's grim jury, so deaf was he to the hoof beats of the Black Doom close upon him, that, accused of being faithless to the trust of the people, he replied in his courtly manner, "I have not been entrusted of the people, the people are mine inheritance." And small wonder he felt that way about it, for the doctrine of the Lord's Anointed died a slow death among the people themselves, saturated as they were in Old Testament literature.

In the reign of his son, the second Charles, after the

Lord Protector had demonstrated the easy detachability of the anointed head, a philosopher popular with the court published a book in which the whole duty of subjects was clearly defined. If, so he wrote, the King commands his subjects to become Papists, Mohammedans, or pagans, theirs not to reason why; unquestioning obedience was the one virtue demanded of their station.

The grandfather of the Stuart lads whose path the Quakers crossed, gave his name to a translation which has proved the best seller of all time, and being also of a religious turn of mind, his worthy grandsons seem to have familiarized themselves with the Book, to the extent of selecting as a model for their kingly behavior Solomon in all his glory. Not only the radical rebel group, but the old-guard stand-patters as well, were inclined to regard the model as antiquated. The English were king-loving, and long-suffering where their traditions were concerned, and the age was speedy following the swift pace set by the court; but England had a speed limit, and the inarticulate classes heroically but ineffectually endeavored to call the attention of the royal family to it.

Having some idle time on their hands during the religious holidays at Easter, the London Apprentices flung themselves on the notorious red light district, with an enthusiasm so great that not a house was left standing; the whole district was razed to the ground, including property belonging to the King's brother. The entire army, foot and horse, was called out against the rioters, and the battle waged for several days and nights. A sympathetic populace rose to reinforce the Apprentices, stoned the soldiers, even stormed one of the jails and released the prisoners who had been taken.

"And Lord!" Mr. Pepys gloats, "to see the apprehension which this did give to all the people of the Court . . . as if the French were coming into town. . . . But these idle fellows have the confidence to say that they did ill in contenting themselves in pulling down the little brothels, and did not go and pull down the great one at White Hall [the King's palace]. And some of them have the last night a word among them, and it was 'Reformation and Reducement.' This do make the courtiers ill at ease to see this spirit among the people, though they think this matter will not come to much: but it speakes the People's minds; and then they do say that there are men of understanding among them, that have been of Cromwell's army."

The royal brothers made "mighty merry" over the affair, and indulged in "insipid jests." Some of the Apprentices were hanged, and those in power regarded the episode as closed. But "ill at ease" is a very unfavorable symptom of national health, especially if it inclines to increase, as it did.

Mr. Evelyn, a truly devout gentleman, one to sink or swim, survive or perish with his class, became very ill at ease, as the prospect to swim and survive grew dubious. His diary records his gloom: "The Bishop of Rochester preached before the King, after which his Majesty, with his three natural sons, (sons of Portsmouth, Cleveland and Nelly) went up to the altar, the three boys entering before the King on the right hand, three Bishops on the left. The Bishops first received [the sacrament] then his Majesty."

And again a few days later the entry reads: "Dr. Dove preached before the King. I saw this evening such a scene of profuse gaming, and the King in the midst of his three concubines, as I have never before seen, luxurious dallying [licentiousness] and profaneness."

Mr. Pepys, on the other hand, was an opportunist, not unduly concerned either for his class or for his soul, but he was a responsible official of the navy, a fat political job, which he was ambitious to prolong and make the most of. Kidnaped men who had served in the navy were starving, with their wives and families, while money raised under the false pretense of war expenses was squandered by profligate women, who could afford to spend three thousand pounds for embroidering the coverings of one bed. Ill at ease, he, too, confides in his faithful diary:

"My Lady Castlemaine swears the King shall own it [her child] and she will have it christened at White Hall so and owned for the King's, as other Kings have done, or she will bring it into White Hall gallery and dash the brains of it out before the King's face. . . . The King and Court were never in the world so bad as they are now for gaming, swearing, women and drinking, and the most abominable vices that ever were in the world, so that all must come to nought."

Thus the gay life went on, embellished with the pomp and ceremony of the Church, of which the King was the head, the religious note running through it all.

Into this choppy sea of messy morals, class arrogance, and mass misery, Quakerism was launched by George Fox, the son of a weaver known far and near as Righteous Christer. Honesty was almost a vice in the north country people who first joined his crusade, simple souls, to whom it seemed dishonest and little short of sacrilege to bare the head and bow the knee to those in power, who by their conduct outraged decency, mocked God, and made constituted authority contemptible.

It requires very little stretch of the imagination to understand how Fox, when he retired into himself and the solitude to listen for the voice of revelation, heard a divine command to give battle all along the front, and to raze the country of shams. "Thee" and "thou" was common usage among common people, "you" in the singular an innovation to enable the lowly to show proper respect to their superiors. God was no respecter of persons; by humbly aspiring to that Godlike attitude, the Quakers sidestepped the humiliating hypocrisy of showing less respect to their useful and industrious neighbors than to their idle, useless, and often vicious superiors. One form of address for all men was their leveling slogan, and they chose the old familiar one.

The oath, so lightly regarded that it had become a byword, was an insult to a Christian, who, if sincere, could not be a liar. The early Christian fathers held swearing in any form to be a sinful disobedience of their Lord's command. Fox and his following indorsed that view; they would solemnly affirm, but would swear not at all.

Fox could not discover that it was agreeable to the Divine Will that a "hireling priesthood," neither preaching nor practicing the teachings of Christ, should be allowed to extort a forced tribute from His followers; it was the duty of all true Christians to resist such levies. Fox preached that obedience to God meant resistance to tyranny, and in his day such teaching was revolutionary propaganda, properly so regarded by the authorities.

The Quakers might have slipped by with some of their heretical doctrines; the rub came with their attack on the Church revenues, which roused the clergy to a frenzy of animosity, resulting in reprisals so violent and brutal as to lend color to the Quaker preachment that the clergy were antichristian, and to stiffen the resistance to their authority. The civil power supported its ally, the Church, in contending for the special privileges at which Fox was hacking away. In every age the specially privileged have had the will and the power to put up a good fight to retain their privilege. These rebels, too, believed that a man should fight for the little things he cares about; though in matters of conscience, conformity to a disapproved standard has never been regarded as a little thing by those encumbered with a conscience.

That the real issue was conformity to an imposed standard, Pepys makes quite clear. "I saw several poor creatures carried by, by constables, for being at a conventicle. They go like lambs without any resistance. I would to God they would either conform, or be more wise and not be catched." The uneasiness of this worldly-wise man was a justification of the other worldly wisdom of the poor creatures; squirming at their plight, he prophesied their ultimate triumph.

For these rebels against ecclesiastical authority regarded themselves literally as soldiers, enlisted under the banner of the Prince of Peace to war against the powers of darkness. The severe army test was unconditional surrender of life and possessions. From the intrenchments of established order, church and state trained on them the machine guns of law and gospel. At every trial magistrate and priest shot at them the apostolic dictum: "The powers that be are ordained of God. Let every soul be subject to the higher powers." The rebels freely acknowledged the apostolic authority, but were never diffident in pointing out to all and sundry, beginning with the King himself, that where earthly power was abused, it was noticeable that the Supreme Power usually ordained a change.

Led as lambs to the slaughter, as sheep before their shearers, the Quakers were seldom dumb, always ready to give a reason for the faith that was in them. They counseled wisdom in the use of power with such unflinching audacity as to become a public nuisance. By scriptural command they were to fear God and honor the King, duties which often conflicted. They therefore gave the fear of God precedence, and took the King's punishment, submitting with unswerving patience to the aberrations of worldly power.

Of all the absurd labels which men in their ignorance have affixed to one another, passive resistance as applied to the Quakers is the most ludicrous; their untiring active resistance knew no bounds short of physical violence. "Your principle is passive obedience and nonresistance," said a bromidic New England magistrate to a Nantucket Quaker. On the contrary, he promptly came back, "Our principle is active obedience (to God) and passive suffering."

"We who do not fight with carnal weapons," was the plea of Thomas Story, an apostle to the American colonies, "meddle not with you who do, other than to persuade you to leave them off, and be enlisted under the saving banner of the Prince of Peace, to come out of the spirit of this world in which is all trouble, into the spirit of the Kingdom of Christ in whom is perfect peace. If you will not do this we must leave you to fight with one another until you are weary, and have the recompense of it in the natural consequences of that destructive evil, with this caution of the apostle, nevertheless, 'That if ye bite and devour one another, take heed lest ye be devoured.' Against the enemy of our souls we find warring sufficient, and fighting enough daily, though we war not among you to destruction, nor with one another to a breach of the peace."

The Quakers declared the war; it was their adversaries who dictated the rules of the warfare; there was to be no quarter given to the enemies of society. The stubborn moral resistance of the rebellion was met by the unrestrained violence of the authorities. History is the continued story of the leavening power of personality on the apathetic mass, and the Quaker revolt was rich in personality. Their missionaries wandered over the world, voices in the wilderness, proclaiming liberty throughout the lands, to all the inhabitants thereof. It was a Quaker who put that inscription on the great bell in Philadelphia which pealed out the news of American independence.

No amount of antiquated theological patter, nor the occasional indecorous behavior of a few of the wilder spirits of the Society of Friends can obscure the fact, that, whatever their beliefs, they bought with their blood the right to hold them, a right which they passed on to us. As the Chinese reverence the memory of the benefactors of their race, we may invigorate our souls by glancing at the portraits in the Quaker hall of fame, burning incense before the tablets of these pioneers of our freedom.

George Fox—in Europe One Free Man, and Thou Art He

The key to the age may be this or that or the other, as the young orators describe; the key to all ages is imbecility, imbecility in the vast majority at all times, and even in heroes in all but certain eminent moments; victims of gravity, custom and fear. This gives force to the strong, that the multitude have no habit of self reliance or original action. — EMERSON.

GEORGE FOX, general-in-chief of the Quaker revolt, looms upon the horizon of his generation as a man of self-reliance and original action. His vigorous personality, like a powerful current, charged thousands of his contemporaries with an energy which he directed against the giants of gravity, custom, and fear. For centuries the Roman Church had ruled by the authority of tradition; the Protestant rebels fell back on the authority of the sacred writings as interpreted by themselves. Fox directed all men everywhere to the authority of divine revelation in their own souls.

As he listened to a sermon on the infallibility of the Scriptures, by which, said the preacher, all doctrines, religions, and opinions were to be tried, "the power of the Lord was so mighty upon me, that I could not hold, but was made to cry out and say, 'Oh, no; it is not the Scriptures!' and I told them what it was, namely the Holy

Spirit, by which holy men of God gave forth the Scriptures, whereby opinions, religions and judgments were to be tried; . . . the Jews had the Scriptures, and yet resisted the Holy Ghost, and rejected Christ. . . . They persecuted Christ and His apostles, and took upon them to try their doctrines by the Scriptures; but they erred in judgment, and did not try them aright, because they tried without the Holy Ghost. As I spoke amongst them, the officers came and took me away, and put me into a nasty stinking prison; the smell whereof got into my nose and throat that it very much annoyed me."

Has the creative energy ever revealed itself to man? Fox inquired of all his adversaries. All creeds were based on that assumption, their exponents admitted. Then, argued Fox, that revelation is still going on; it is not conceivable that it should be limited to a few prophets and apostles long since dead. In his age that doctrine was blasphemy, and the penalty for blasphemy was death.

Fox formulated no creed, he appealed for the life approved by the conscience of the race; his aim was to awaken into that life every soul he could touch. Not to convert to a dogma, but to convince men of the reality of the spiritual life; not to rubber-stamp opinions on his followers, but to stir that life into action. William Penn, a court-bred young dandy when he came into the Quaker fold, delighted to wear a sword, for he had served in the army. As the Quaker conception of Christianity gradually unfolded, he began to entertain doubts as to the propriety of this decoration, and appealed to his leader for light.

"Wear it as long as thou canst," was the cryptic reply.

Meeting Friend Penn a few weeks later, the great voice of Fox boomed out:

"William, where is thy sword?"

"I wore it as long as I could," was Penn's laconic response.

Fox might have lived in history as a military leader; so magnetic was the power of his utter fearlessness that on one occasion, while he was a prisoner, his soldier guard clamored to have him made their officer. Army officials, finding recruiting increasingly difficult, proffered him the command. He scornfully turned down the offer, accepting the alternative of a loathsome dungeon. "I told them I was come into a covenant of peace which was before wars and strifes were. That I lived in the virtue of that life and power which took away the occasion of all wars. I told them I knew whence all wars arose, even from the lusts, according to James' doctrine."

"Clense your hands, ye sinners," he admonished, "and purify your hearts ye double minded."

"Then their rage got up, and they said, 'Take him away, jailer, and put him into the prison amongst the rogues and felons.' So I was put into a lousy, stinking place, without any bed, amongst thirty felons, where I was kept almost half a year; yet at times they would let me walk in the garden, believing I would not go away."

In his history of England, Macaulay pauses to hurl a few epithets at the Quaker leader, an unsympathetic subject to the author of the most stirring war lyrics in our language. "He was," says Macaulay, "a youth of pure morals, grave deportment and a perverse temper, with the education of a laboring man, and an intellect in that most unhappy of all states, too disordered for liberty, and not sufficiently disordered for Bedlam." Macaulay makes no allowance for youth, and fails to mention that Cromwell's "glance of genius," which engages his admiration, approvingly scanned the Quaker on various occasions without apparently detecting any mental malady. A leader with nothing to offer his followers but torture, imprisonment and death, able to enlist thousands of shock troops, can hardly be swept into Bedlam by the paragraph of a temperamental historian.

Assuming the correctness of the judgment that Fox barely escaped Bedlam, a perusal of Macaulay's own account of the time leads to the conclusion that his unhappy state would hardly have distinguished the Quaker among his contemporaries. The aggressive and boisterous religionists of all denominations in those days seem to have had more affinity with Bedlam than with the Christianity they professed.

When the Puritans in the name of their crucified Master drove out the established Church of England, they regarded capital punishment as an all too merciful sentence for traitors who dared to use the Book of Common Prayer. Returning again to power, the grave and reverend Lords spiritual handed over the Solemn League and Covenant of their foes to the public hangman to be ceremoniously burned. Fox was branded as a fanatic; if it be conceded that he was a fanatic for peace with freedom, it is certain that his adversaries were even more fanatical for compulsion with violence.

Notwithstanding his whole-hearted worship of his great hero, Cromwell, Carlyle's interest was arrested by the sincerity and courage of Cromwell's Quaker critic, and he was impelled to contribute a wreath to the memory of Fox, while taking a fling at Macaulay and other contemporary historians. He says: "Perhaps the most remarkable incident in Modern History is not the Diet of Worms, still less the battle of Austerlitz, Waterloo, Peterloo, or any other Battle; but an incident passed carelessly over by most Historians, and treated with some degree of ridicule by others; namely George Fox's making to himself a suit of Leather. This man, the first of the Quakers, and by trade a Shoemaker, was one of those, to whom under purer or ruder form, the Divine Idea of the Universe is pleased to manifest itself, and across all the hulls of Ignorance and earthly Degradation, shine through in unspeakable Awfulness, unspeakable beauty on their souls, who are therefore rightly accounted Prophets, God-possessed. . . . Mountains of encumbrance, higher than Aetna had been heaped over that Spirit; but it was a Spirit, and would not lie buried there. . . . That Leicester shoe-shop, had men but known it, was a holier place than any Vatican or Loretto-shrine. Often has it seemed to me as if such first out-flashing of man's Free will, to lighten more and more into Day, the Chaotic Night that threatens to engulf him, were properly the only grandeur there is in History. . . . Stitch away, thou noble Fox; every prick of that little instrument is pricking into the heart of Slavery, and World worship, and the Mammon-god . . . every stroke is bearing thee across the Prison-ditch, within which Vanity holds her workhouse and Ragfair, into the lands of true Liberty; were the work done, there is in broad Europe one Free Man, and thou art he."

Whichever view may be taken of Fox's powers, of his mental and educational limitations, whether he was prophet or moron, the fact remains, that he succeeded in hurling thousands of the canniest of his hard-headed countrymen against the prevailing violence of his age, inspiring them with a faith immune to every form of fear — "Most Enfeebler of the passions" — fear of others or public opinion, fear of poverty or personal disaster, and fear of man's last invincible enemy. In their exalted state of freedom, he pressed his followers to the attack on clerical tyranny intrenched in gravity and custom.

"I showed them that God was come to teach His people by His Spirit, and to bring them off from all their old ways, religions, churches and worships, for all their religions, worships and ways *were but talking with other men's words;* but they were out of the life and spirit which they were in who gave them forth."

With consummate generalship he rallied his band of outlaws, invaded the palatial churches, and heckled the temporally powerful but spiritually impotent clergy. God does not dwell in your brick and mortar "steeple-houses," he thundered, but in the hearts of those who love and serve Him. "Now that which made them the more afraid was this: when I was in the steeple-house at Oram . . . there came a professor, who gave me a push on the breast in the steeple-house, and bade me get out of the church. 'Alas, poor man!' said I, 'dost thou call the steeple-house the church? The Church is the people, whom God hath purchased with His blood, and not the house.'" A few such thunderclaps of the gathering storm, and it was not necessary to be especially weather-wise to predict that the signals would soon be hung out for tempests and high galcs.

"The step from knowing to doing," says our American philosopher, "is rarely taken. 'Tis to step out of the chalk mark of imbecility into fruitfulness." This one step, and that elusive personal quality which attracts a following, marks the great leader. In the days of the Great Rebellion, the brutal violence of authority forced men everywhere out of their natural apathy into some degree of mental exertion. Little futile grumbling groups were welded together by the strong men who offered them direction. The revolt against the civil power was directed by Cromwell, a believer in physical force, who wielded it to such purpose that every throne in Europe felt the impact. It was the gossip throughout the Continent that the powerful Cardinal Mazarin feared Oliver with his Ironsides more than he feared the devil.

Fox with his militant army of peace lovers was no less terrifying to the English clergy. Scorning carnal weapons, with an unquestioning faith in the omnipotence of spiritual power, and the inevitable triumph of right when backed by that power, he harried the clerical oppressors. When these twain met, the two most forceful personalities in England confronted one another. There is room for the suspicion that, wearying of the tyranny of the populace, of which he was both master and slave, the leader whose trust was in chariots and horsemen regarded with a sort of pathetic envy his fellow revolutionist, who alone, with God on his side, was sure of a majority.

With the flaming sword of his faith and personality, Fox fired the smoldering discontent against the ecclesiastical power; that the resulting conflagration was considerable we may judge by the drastic methods used to smother it. "The Lord said unto me [Fox] that if but one man or woman were raised up by his power to stand and live in the same spirit that the prophets and apostles were in who gave forth the scriptures, that man or woman should shake all the country in their profession (Christianity) for ten miles round." Fox stood and lived, and shook the country round far beyond the ten-mile limit; the rumblings were felt beyond the seas.

Carlyle and Macaulay view Fox as an appearance in history; to William Penn he was an intimate and beloved friend, "of an innocent life, no busy-body nor self seeker, neither touchy nor critical. So meek, contented, modest, easy, tender, it was a pleasure to be in his company. He exercised no authority but over evil, and that everywhere and in all; but with love, compassion and long suffering. A most merciful man, as ready to forgive as unapt to take or give offense. Thousands can truly say he was of an excellent spirit and savour among them, and because thereof the most excellent spirits loved him with an unfeigned and unfading love. . . . As he was unwearied so he was undaunted in his service for God and His people; he was no more to be moved to fear than to wrath."

With keen sympathetic insight, Carlyle discovers the source of Fox's power to be his trust in the divinity of man and the omnipotent power of love. "He looks Heavenward from his Earth, and dwells in an element of Mercy and Worship, with a still Strength, such as the Cynic's Tub [Diogenes] did nowise witness. Great, truly was that Tub; a temple from which man's dignity and divinity was scornfully preached abroad; but greater is the Leather Hull, for the same sermon was preached there, and not in Scorn, but in Love."

Glancing through Fox's interminable sermons and wearisome doctrinal debates, one might incline to differ with William Penn as to the pleasurableness of his society. The theological "mountains of encumbrance" must not be forgotten, the creeds in which Christianity had so long lain fossilized. For ages the laity, held in spiritual servitude, had been denied the right to think or speak on matters of religious faith. When the release came, they went in for doctrinal discussion with an eagerness that amounted to obsession. Fox came preaching no doctrines, but a life motived by love to God and man. In the field of discussion where so much was being threshed out, he was revered as a teacher and leader; he was loved as a man who lived the self-effacing life of fearless honesty which he preached.

"I was sorely exercised in going to their courts to cry for justice, in speaking and writing to judges and justices to do justly. . . . In fairs also, and in markets, I was made to declare against their deceitful merchandise, cheating and cozening, warning all to deal justly, to speak the truth, to let their yea be yea, and their nay be nay, and to do unto others as they would have others do unto them. . . . The earthly spirit of the priests wounded my life; and when I heard the bell toll to call people together to the steeple-house, it struck at my life; for it was just like a market bell, to gather people together, that the priest might set forth his ware for sale. Oh, the vast sums of money that are gotten by the trade they make of selling the Scriptures, and by their preaching, from the highest bishop to the lowest priest! What one trade in the world is comparable to it."

Many leaders and geniuses have absolved themselves, and have been absolved by others from ordinary human obligations, an absolution which Fox never claimed, even when his work was most absorbing and exhausting. While wrestling with the Lord for new life, he was mindful of the anxiety of his parents. Always with troubles enough of his own, he was never so preoccupied with them but that he was ready to break a lance, even in the cause of the most humble of the ungodly.

"While I was in prison there was a young woman in jail for robbing her master. When she was to be tried for her life I wrote to the judge and jury, showing them how contrary it was to the law of God in old time to put people to death for stealing, and moving them to show mercy. Yet she was condemned to die, and a grave was made for her. And though they had her upon the ladder, ready to be turned off, yet they did not put her to death, but brought her back to prison."

Cruelty and injustice to whomsoever, Fox made his own personal concern.

After all the testimony is in, Fox is his own best interpreter. Of all the Quaker journals, his own is by far the most racy, livened with a dry, astringent humor, and flavored with his unique personality — a personality which runs like a bright thread through all the other

Quaker biographies. Dramatic adventures are recorded with a poverty of detail somewhat irritating to the worldly-minded; nevertheless, we get a remarkable silhouette of the man who knew no rest while there was a wrong to be righted. His autobiography has been read by the wisest of men since his time, as a thrilling chapter in the history of our journey up toward freedom, and all have paid their profound respect to his achievement for human liberty.

Fox makes short work of his significant genealogy. "My father's name was Christopher Fox, and he was by profession a weaver, an honest man, and there was the seed of God in him. My mother was an upright woman, and of the stock of the martyrs. As I grew up my relations thought to have made me a priest [clergyman] but others persuaded to the contrary; whereupon I was put to a man who was a shoemaker by trade, and dealt in wool. He also used grazing and sold cattle, and a great deal went through my hands. I never wronged man or woman in all that time. While I was in that service I used in my dealings the word, Verily, and it was a common saying among those who knew me, 'If George says Verily, there is no altering him.'"

Even as a prisoner his judges confirmed this reputation for veracity: "If he promises, you may take his word for it." And Fox and his Friends, to save expense, were sent on long journeys from one prison to another, without a guard.

The tender age at which his relations considered him sufficiently mature to assume the responsibilities of business life we do not learn, but in his twentieth year, he abandoned that life forever, " for this poor Cordwainer, as we said was a Man; and the Temple of Immensity, wherein as a Man he had been sent to minister, was full of holy mystery to him."

As Fox himself puts it: " At the command of God in the ninth of the seventh month [1643] I left my relations and broke off all fellowship with young or old. As I travelled through the country professors sought to be acquainted with me, but I was afraid of them, for I was sensible *they did not possess what they professed.* Sometimes I kept myself retired to my chamber, and often walked solitary in the Chase, to wait upon the Lord. So I was brought to call to mind all my time that I had spent, and to consider whether I had wronged any. I went to many a priest for comfort, but found no comfort from them. Some tender people would have had me stay, but I was fearful and returned home into Leicestershire, having a regard upon my mind to my parents and relations, lest I should grieve them, for I understood they were troubled at my absence. I continued in great sorrow and walked many nights by myself."

A serious youth, of the order of mystics, with a highly sensitized social conscience, sorrowing for a suffering and confused society, he was not only willing but eager to be guided by his pastors, masters, and teachers. With a child-like faith in his spiritual guides: "I went to another ancient priest. But he was ignorant of my condition. He bade me, take tobacco and sing psalms. Tobacco was a thing I did not love, and psalms I was not in a state to sing. I could not sing."

This "jolly old clergyman, of the Anglican communion" evokes Macaulay's delighted approbation, but on the suffering young soul in spiritual distress his joviality missed fire. "I heard of another priest living about Tamworth who was accounted an experienced man, but I found him an empty hollow cask. . . . After that I went to another, Macham, a priest in high account. He would needs have given me some physic, and I was to have been let blood, but they could not get one drop of blood from me either in my arms or head (though they endeavored to) my body being as it were dried up with sorrows, grief and troubles. . . . I could have wished that I had been born blind, that I might never have seen wickedness or vanity, and deaf, that I might never have heard vain and foolish words."

Scouring the countryside for a priest to afford him guidance, Fox gave the old system every possible chance, before taking the turn to the left, the path of revolt. As he was walking in the fields on a first-day morning, "The Lord opened to me that being bred at Oxford or Cambridge was not enough to fit and qualify men to be ministers of Christ, and I wondered at it, for it was the common belief of the people."

This revelation moves Macaulay to derision. Fox was only twenty, an unlettered boy, agonizing over the orgy of violence and dishonesty all about him, the result of futile, endless fratricidal wars. Honor and glory, dominion and power belonged to the Church as the strong right arm of the civil government. The clerical caste, supreme in a worldly way, was powerless to relieve the spiritual distemper. The only remedies it could suggest to this troubled soul were song, tobacco, physic, and blood-letting. The boy turned on the blind leaders of the blind and branded them as Scribes, Pharisees, and hypocrites, who exacted an exorbitant toll from the simple for a guidance they were utterly incompetent to give. Once again the senility of the old order was driving youth into rebellion.

Cut adrift from the old moorings, Fox "now wandered up and down as a stranger on the earth. For I durst not stay long in one place, being afraid both of professor and profane, lest being a tender young man, I should be hurt by conversing much with either. . . . Seeking heavenly wisdom and getting knowledge from the Lord alone . . . I regarded priests less and looked more after dissenting people . . . among whom I saw there was some tenderness. . . . But as I had forsaken priests, so I left the dissenting preachers also, for I saw there was none among them that could speak to my condition. When all my hopes in them and all men were gone, so that I had nothing outwardly to help me, then, oh then, I heard a voice which said, 'There is one even Christ Jesus that can speak to thy condition.' . . . And when I heard it, my heart did leap for joy. . . . Christ Jesus who enlightens and gives grace and faith and *power*. And this I knew experimentally."

Confident that he had tapped the boundless deep of spiritual power, Fox went about earnestly persuading men to enjoy that power with him, and to prove it experimentally. Wandering over the country without stave or script, he "convinced" many that Christ and His Apostles meant neither more nor less than what they said; that Christianity was a life, and that those who lived that life should know the doctrine. Within six years he had gathered a group of young enthusiasts known as the Valiant Sixty, and "if blood be the price of admiralty" these valiant spirits paid the price in full. Making sorties through the country, within eight years from the time of Fox's call to arms, he had in battle formation an army fifty thousand strong; this in spite of the fact that he and his Valiant Sixty spent a considerable portion of their time in jail. These early Quakers were no "pale pacifists"; many of them were stout Cromwellian soldiers, some had been officers. Weary and disheartened by the utter futility of the long reign of violence, they were lured from disillusionment by Fox's gospel, and fell into rank.

Fox preached peace the more earnestly for being deprived of it; his life was the life of abuse and hardship which the ignorance and apathy of the mass of mankind has forced on the innovator in all ages. The prisons into which he was thrown were so incredibly vile that, even in that unsanitary age, humane magistrates had the courage to say they would not use such places as kennels for their dogs.

It is not to be wondered at that the common people heard Fox gladly; there was no aloofness of leadership, no arrogance of superior power; the power which he possessed was free to all who yielded to it. He was the servant of all, and ready to enter the lists against injustice wherever he encountered it, whether the oppressed were godly or ungodly. Stopping at an inn, he heard that eight miles distant a committee of judges was sitting to fix the wages of servants. "I ran thitherward as fast as I could. When I was come to the house where they were, I exhorted the justices not to oppress servants in their wages, but to do that which was just and right to them, and I exhorted the servants to do their duties, and to serve honestly."

Fox made a tour of America, sailing in a ship which "was very leaky, so that the seamen and some of the passengers did, for the most part, pump day and night." In spite of this and other perils which made ocean travel at that time an exciting adventure, they reached land in safety. Here Fox led an amphibian life, wading streams, or making progress in open boats drenched to the skin, or when fortune favored him, seeking shelter among the

Indians. Even with his oxlike constitution he admits to being often overweary. Never so weary, however, as to refuse the plea of a despairing wife for her sick husband, for it was well known that he had power to heal the sick. After a long and exhausting meeting, he mounted his horse and rode off to restore the invalid to health.

While he was traveling through Virginia, preaching the universality of the Divine Light, an argumentative doctor denied that the light had ever penetrated to the Indians. "Whereupon I called an Indian to us, and asked him whether when he lied, or did wrong to any one, there was not something in him that reproved him for it. He said there was such a thing in him, that did so reprove him; and he was ashamed when he had done wrong or spoken wrong. So we shamed the doctor."

Even for the brute creation Fox was unsparing of himself. He tells of a long and tiresome journey when finally "we came to a little alehouse, where we thought to have stayed and baited, but finding we could have neither oats nor hay there, we travelled all night." And again at another inn: "I but turned my back to the man that was giving oats to my horse, and looking around again, I observed he was filling his pockets with provender. A wicked thievish people, to rob the poor dumb creature of his food. I would rather they had robbed me."

Times without number Fox was shut up in prison, often for long periods. In his intervals of freedom he was beaten by mobs, so severely at times as to be temporarily crippled, attacks which were frequently instigated by the clergy. Dragged through the streets covered with mire and blood, he escaped as if by miracle the death with which he was continually threatened. Less sturdy and less fortunate, many of his comrades yielded up their lives in the black holes of England. Undaunted and undeterred, others stepped in to fill the gaps. Thousands of Quakers glutted those terrible English prisons, the birthplace of many of our liberties. The story of their martyrdom fills many huge volumes. Their zeal was at times fanatical; only a fanatical courage could have made the attempt to grapple with the arrogance of authority.

Fanaticism was universal, the outgrowth of the political and religious conditions of the time. It was not alone the Quakers who were harried; confidence and security were unknown in the land, each faction busily plotting the destruction of the others. From the security of his shelter in France, Charles Stuart, Defender of the Faith, "on the word of a Christian King," caused to be secretly circulated an offer of five hundred pounds to the brave man who should succeed in jostling Oliver Cromwell from his tight-rope eminence by any means, poison specifically mentioned. His good intention was an open secret to the revolutionary government, which found its own safety a more immediately pressing concern than the popular liberty it was fighting to usher in. All public meetings, including religious gatherings, were ruthlessly suppressed, excepting those of the dominant orthodox dissenters; for many religious sects were more prone to the use of cold steel than to the sword of the spirit.

The Quakers maintained a strict political neutrality, having reached the conclusion that politics and the Christian life were incompatible. A power which they recognized as higher than the state had commanded them not to forsake the public assembly for worship; they therefore ignored the government prohibition of their meetings. It was the performance of this duty of civil disobedience that resulted in introducing Fox to his fellow revolutionist, Cromwell.

"At this time," Fox writes, "there was much noise of a plot against Oliver Cromwell. There came seventeen troopers of Colonel Hacker's regiment . . . and took me up before meeting. I told the marshall he might let all the Friends go; that I would answer for them all. Therefore he took me and let all the Friends go. . . . At night they had me before Colonel Hacker, his major and captains, a great company; and we had a great deal of discourse about the priests. . . . Then Colonel Hacker said I might go home, and keep at home, and not go abroad to meetings. I told him I was an innocent man, free from plots, and denied all such works.

"His son said, 'Father, this man hath reigned too long; it is time to have him cut off.'

"I asked him, 'Whom have I wronged? I was bred and born in this country, and who can accuse me of any evil from childhood up?'

"Colonel Hacker asked me again if I would go home and stay at home. I told him if I should promise him this, it would manifest that I was guilty of something, to make my home a prison. Therefore I told him I should go to meetings as the Lord should order me, and could not submit to their requirings; but, I said, we were a peaceable people.

"'Well then,' said Colonel Hacker, 'I will send you to-morrow morning by six o'clock to my Lord Protector by Captain Drury, one of his life guard.'"

Fox had ruled that it was the Christian duty of the Quakers to refuse obedience to laws discriminating against their peaceable assembly, but there must be no evasion; the laws must be openly violated until the authorities were moved to repeal them, and the punishment for disobedience must be patiently suffered. Other religious groups met persecution with subterfuge, and continued the proscribed worship secretly, a practice which the Quakers regarded as treason to the cause.

Pepys puts in an occasional sly good word for the decency of Oliver's stern soldiers; Colonel Hacker's military tribunal certainly conducted Fox's trial with patience and restraint; religion with them was a serious concern, but so also was the revolution. Colonel Hacker, like his chief, was a jump beyond his time in toleration. In the day of his own doom, he was visited in the Tower by Margaret Fell, Fox's wife, who offered him consolation, and no doubt stressed the superior efficacy of non-violent resistance, for the Colonel's own head, alas, was destined to be added to that weird anatomical collection on the banks of the Thames.

In the custody of Captain Drury, Fox was passed on to Cromwell. The good-natured Captain pleaded with his prisoner to change his mind, go home, and keep out of trouble, but was unsuccessful in thrusting liberty on Fox on any but his own terms. "I told him I could not submit to that, but must have my liberty to serve God and go to meetings." The Captain indulged in some ribald pleasantries at the expense of Quakerism; nevertheless he respected his prisoner, and showed him every possible consideration, allowing him to stop at the prisons on the way to London, to console and strengthen the Friends who filled them.

Arriving in London, Captain Drury lodged his charge at the "Mermaid," and went off to take his orders from the Protector. His report on his prisoner must have been favorable, for "when he came back he told me that the Protector required that I should promise not to take up a carnal sword or weapon against him or the government as it then was, and that I should write it in what words I saw good. . . . I said little in reply to Captain Drury."

We may be sure that Fox was holding himself in for the encounter with the Big Man, eager to match the power of God against the Commander General of the English army. "I was moved of the Lord to write a paper to the Protector Oliver Cromwell, wherein I did in the presence of the Lord God, declare that I denied the wearing or drawing of any carnal weapon against him or any man, that I was sent of God to stand a witness against all violence, to turn people from darkness to light, and to bring them from the causes of war and fighting to the peaceable gospel. I set my name to it and gave it to Captain Drury to hand to Oliver Cromwell, which he did."

The Protector was interested, and sent for Fox; he must judge for himself what manner of man this was, this fellow rebel, who above the tumult of violence and strife boldly proclaimed a gospel of peace and good will. In the morning, before Cromwell was dressed, the Quaker in leather breeches was ushered in. Like Socrates, Fox claimed a spirit of discernment, and as he entered the Protector's chamber, he tells us, "I was moved to say, 'Peace be in this house.'" Certainly a discerning prayer for the man who was to know peace neither in life nor in death; whose long last rest was to be disturbed by his enemies, for they pried him out of the quiet of Westminster Abbey, where he had been laid away with regal pomp, ignominiously hanged his dead body on the gallows, dismembered it, and scrapped his bones in the Potter's Field.

These strange revolutionists, differing in many things, spoke a common dialect. "I spoke to him much of truth," continues Fox, "and much discourse I had with him about religion, wherein he carried himself very moderately. But he said we quarrelled with his priests whom he called ministers. I told him I did not quarrel with them, but that they quarrelled with me and my Friends."

It is recorded of Oliver that in moments of extreme irritation he characterized the clergy as wolves; that he often found it necessary to seek patience from the Lord to endure the intolerance of the saints. He had found it less difficult to instill the fear of God in the hearts of the corulers of Europe, than toleration in the hearts of his coreligionists. Free from the political trammels which hindered the Protector, Fox was attempting that task, and as the old soldier listened, we can imagine him suppressing a twinkle, and wishing the Quaker joy of an undertaking which had proved too much for himself.

" I showed him," says Fox, " that the prophets, Christ and the apostles declared freely (without money) and against them that did not declare freely, such as preached for filthy lucre, and divined for money . . . and were covetous and greedy, and could never have enough. . . . As I spoke he several times said that it was good, and it was the truth . . . but people coming in I drew a little back. As I was turning, he caught me by the hand, and with tears in his eyes said, ' Come again to my house, for if thou and I were but an hour of a day together, we should be nearer one to another; ' adding that he wished me no more harm than he did his own soul. I told him if he did he wronged his own soul; and admonished him to hearken to God's voice, that would keep him from hardness of heart, but if he did not hear God's voice, his heart would be hardened. He said it was true. Then I went out; and when Captain Drury came out after me, he told me the Protector said I was at liberty and might go where I would."

Fox was much too wary to be caught in the most ingeniously baited trap. "I was brought into a great hall, where the Protector's gentlemen were to dine. I asked them what they brought me thither for. They said it was by the Lord Protector's order, that I might dine with them. I bid them let the Protector know that I would not eat of his bread or drink of his drink. When he heard this he said 'Now I see there is a people risen that I cannot win with gifts or honors, offices or places; all other sects and peoples I can.'"

Whatever Cromwell's shortcomings, he loved England with a great pride. His sun was setting, his hard fight for a freer world nearly ended. Behind the Quaker's ungracious message he saw an incorruptible courage; the solacing conviction that a hardy breed of rebels would survive his passing, tipped the scales against any affront to his personal dignity.

We gather from these recorded interviews with Colonel Hacker and the Lord Protector, that unfavorable comment on the clergy was a conversational perennial of the time. Fox was the preacher of a Christian love which was illimitable. "Whereas Major Porter saith I am an enemy of the King, this is false, for my love is to him and to all men, even though they be enemies to God, to themselves, and to me." His love for the clergy, however, admitted of extreme frankness in stating the truth as he saw it, "for I was brought into the deep, and saw all the religions of the world, and the people that lived in them. And I saw the priests that held them up; who were a company of meneaters, eating up the people like bread, and gnawing the flesh from their bones."

Avarice and cowardice were the most obnoxious vices on Fox's list, and it was with these that he charged the clergy. Worldly ambition was the root from which their cowardice sprang, evidenced in the case of one Britland, who "saw beyond the common run of priests, and had spoken much for truth before he was priest at Chesterfield, but when the priest of that town died, he got the parsonage, *and choked himself with it.*"

Fox now had the ear of the Dictator of England, and chance gave him opportunity to pour into it the Quaker grievances against the Puritans. Mounted on his steed, he was passing through Hyde Park, when he spied the Protector riding in state surrounded by his Life Guard, at which sight he was immediately moved of the spirit to give chase. Cantering through Hyde Park, the Quaker must have presented a spectacle not unlike an Indian warrior in an Easter Day parade. There is no hint that he attempted singularity in his attire, nor any doubt that he attained it.

Committed to a life of poverty, wandering from John o' Groat's to Land's End in all weathers, traveling sixty miles or more to hold a meeting, sheltering himself from snow and rain beside haymows in the open fields, he must needs have serviceable raiment. None more suitable could be found than his leather breeches and umbrella hat. For his long hair he may have had equally good reason, and he was quite unperturbed by the amusement it afforded to fashionable ladies, or a "silly young priest who desired to cut off my hair, which was then pretty long, but I was not to cut it off, though many were offended by it. I told them I had no pride in it, and it was not of my own putting on."

It was this extraordinary figure in leather breeches, broad-brimmed hat, and Mexican cowboy haircut, that charged into Cromwell's Life Guard, which naturally hastened to intercept him. "But he forbade them. So I rode by his coach declaring what the Lord gave me to say to him, of his condition, and of the suffering of Friends in the Nation, showing him how contrary this persecution was to the words of Christ, and His apostles, and to Christianity. When we came to James' Park Gate I left him, and at parting he desired me to come to his house.

"Next day one of his wife's maids came to see me at my lodgings and told me that her master came to her, and said he would tell her some good news, 'George Fox is come to town.' She replied, 'That is good news indeed,' (for she had received the truth), but she said, she could hardly believe him, till he told her how I had met him and rode from Hyde Park to James' Park Gate with him."

Aside from the admonitions recorded in his journal, Fox refrains from any comment on Cromwell's character; there is little doubt that he classed him with the renegade Christians whose lives did not square with their professions. Yet Carlyle in his most extravagant eulogies has left no such likable picture of his great hero as the one Fox so unwittingly throws on the screen.

The rumor that Cromwell was to be crowned king stirred Fox again to remonstrance, notwithstanding his denunciation of political meddling. He is silent as to the grounds on which he based his protest. "There was some talk now of making Cromwell king; whereupon I was moved to go to him and warn him against accepting it; and of divers dangers which, if he did not avoid them, would bring shame and ruin on himself and his posterity. He seemed to take well what I said and thanked me."

Fox had been astonishingly successful in rousing men from their lethargy, and once aroused, unity of spirit and purpose gave impetus to his group. Cromwell, scaling the same "mountains of encumbrance," was hampered in his climb by the necessity of holding in leash men of inflamed passions, with conflicting interests and prejudices. He could lead his horse to the water, but even he could not force it to drink. The Quaker, in his unequivocal disapproval of violence and his distress for the sufferings of his band under the power of Puritan bigotry, made scant allowance for the difficulties of Cromwell. In George Fox's philosophy of life and action there was no place for an insuperable obstacle.

As the Protector was laying down the heavy burden of greatness, Fox entered his last protest. "I met him riding in Hampton Court Park, and before I came to him, as he rode at the head of his Life Guard, I saw and felt a waft of death go forth against him, and when I came to him he looked like a dead man. After I had laid the sufferings of Friends before him, and warned him, according as I was moved to speak to him, he bade me come to his house. So I returned to Kingston, and next day went to Hampton Court, to speak further with him. But when I came he was sick, and Harvey, who was one that waited on him, told me the doctors were not willing I should speak with him. So I passed away, and never saw him more."

So parted the two great revolutionists of their time, dauntless and courageous both, who fought each in his own way, that liberty might have a little wider breathing space. Meeting violence with violence, one taught kings to be a little more careful. Opposing unyielding moral force to clerical tyranny, the other taught ecclesiastics to be a little less "high" than Pepys had found them. If these two autocracies "by divine right" were not immediately divorced there was at least an estrangement that weakened the strength of their union. From that time to this both have walked more circumspectly all their days.

LINTON'S PORTRAIT OF CROMWELL

(*From the Print Collection, Metropolitan Museum of Art*)

Margaret Fell — The Lady of Swarthmore

He's truly valiant that can wisely suffer
The worst that man can breathe, and make his wrongs
His outsides, to wear them like his raiment, carelessly,
And ne'er prefer his injuries to his heart,
To bring it into danger. — SHAKESPEARE.

The great hope of society is individual character.
— CHANNING.

MARGARET FELL was the angel of the Quaker band of fighters; she was the Red Cross, the commissary department, and the emergency corps. When little Elizabeth Fletcher was wounded in the battle, it was to Margaret Fell the appeal came for some woman to go to her relief, a call for a volunteer for dangerous service. She was kept fully informed of the way the fight was going in the different sectors. Francis Howgill, who later died in the service, writes to headquarters at Swarthmore Hall: "Thy letters I have received; those to Oliver Cromwell are both delivered into his hand. He is full of subtlety and deceit, will speak fair, but hardens his heart, and acts secretly underneath. Most of our army is scattered and broken and cast into prison." The Quakers fully realized that they were at war with the spirit of the time, and knew from experience that "war is hell."

Margaret Fell was endowed by nature with a pleasing personality, a combination of vigor and serenity that makes for perennial youth. Even in middle life, she is described by the sober Quakers as beautiful, and her sweet voice elicited pleasurable comment from all who heard it. In her early years of Quakerism she was not free to leave her large family, to go into the highways and hedges; she was a home-body and a home-maker, not only for her own family, but for the whole family of wandering homeless Quakers. It was the assertion of her right to entertain these Friends and to live her own life within her own four walls that brought her into conflict with the state.

Margaret was born and bred a lady, "so called" as the Quakers would say, descended from a knight who had accompanied Henry VIII to the Field of the Cloth of Gold, and who was enriched by that monarch with valuable estates wrested from the Church. One branch of her family had produced a woman who suffered martyrdom at the stake in the reign of Bloody Mary; with all her good looks and polite breeding that martyr strain was conspicuous in Margaret.

At the age of seventeen Margaret Askew married Judge Fell of Swarthmore Hall, a man of wealth and position, twice her age, circuit judge for North Wales, a member of Parliament, and vice chancellor of the Duchy of Lancaster. "He was," she says, "a tender loving husband to me, a tender father to his children. He was much esteemed in his country, and valued and honored in his day by all sorts of people for his justice, wisdom, moderation and mercy." All rare traits in his day.

Judge Fell and his extremely prepossessing young wife kept open house at Swarthmore Hall, a fine old Elizabethan manor house, extending their hospitality to friend and stranger, especially to traveling clergymen. "In this," writes Mrs. Fell, "I hoped I did well, but often feared I was short of the right way. After this manner I was inquiring and seeking about twenty years." Until one winter day George Fox, with two other Friends, turned up to claim the hospitality of Swarthmore Hall.

Judge Fell was off on legal business at the time; his wife was out for the day; in the absence of their parents, the daughters of the house made welcome the man whose fame had spread over the land. The parish clergyman dropped in, in the course of the day, and did not hit it off well with Fox. When Mrs. Fell returned in the evening, she was grieved as a good churchwoman to hear of a heated controversy between the two men. As Fox expounded his doctrines, however, like so many others, she felt that she was close to what she had been seeking for twenty years, and made him a welcome guest.

"Soon after," Fox writes in his Journal, "a day was to be observed for humiliation, and Margaret Fell asked me to go with her to the steeple-house at Ulverstone, for she was not wholly come off from them." Fox preferred to wander in the fields by himself, where he heard the command: " Go to the steeple-house after them." At the close of the service he asked and was granted permission to speak; his discourse proved objectionable to a magistrate who was present, who ordered him to sit down. Mrs. Fell interposed. " Let him alone. Why may he not speak as well as any other? " she demanded.

Returning to Swarthmore Hall, Fox held a meeting for the family and servants, gathering in a rich harvest; not only the under servants, but the steward, housekeeper, and governess, " were all generally convinced," says Mrs. Fell. " But I was stricken with such a sadness I knew not what to do, my husband being from home. I saw it was the truth and I could not deny it. . . . Any may think what a condition I was in, that either I might displease my husband or offend God."

Mrs. Fell's neighbors were actively displeased; they hastened out on the road to meet Judge Fell returning from his circuit, and break the cheering news that three fanatical Quakers had invaded the Hall and seduced his entire household. He reached his home in a disturbed state of mind, but, says his wife: " After his talk with the two Friends, the Judge sat pretty moderate and quiet, and his dinner being ready, I went and sat me down beside him. Whilst I was sitting there the power of the Lord seized upon me, and he was stricken with amazement, and knew not what to think; but he was quiet and still. . . . At night George Fox arrived, and after supper when my husband was sitting in the parlor, I asked if he might come in. My husband said: 'Yes.' So George walked into the room without any compliment. He spoke very excellently as ever I heard him."

From his subsequent behavior, we may infer that this quiet and prosperous lawyer found the fanatics much less wild than popular opinion represented them. Judge Fell was distinguished in his profession, a moderate man of judicial temper, with no urge toward martyrdom. He sat tight, kept his position and estates, no mean achievement in that day, and undoubtedly was of greater service to his family and the Friends than if he had joined their ranks. Although he shied at martyrdom, he came out strong for civil and religious liberty; when the Quakers could find no meeting place, he said, "You may meet here if you will," and for many years the great dining hall of his spacious mansion was the Quaker meeting-house, which during his lifetime none had the hardihood to disturb. Probably with an eye to the legalities, Judge Fell never sat in the meeting, but in his study adjoining the dining-room, he listened to all that went on; it was not long before he gave up attendance at the established church.

In the exercise of his legal authority, he was able to help his wife's Friends out of many an unpleasant scrape. When a mob fell upon the Quakers and manhandled them unmercifully, it was customary to fine and imprison the victims for starting a riot; this never happened within the jurisdiction of Justice Fell, without effective action on his part. George Fox, the storm center of one of these "riots," was attacked with "pitchforks, flails and staves to keep him out of the town, the mob crying, 'Kill him; knock him on the head.' . . . G. Fox went to a ditch of water and washed himself from the blood and dirt. . . . Margaret Fell the next day hearing what had befallen G. Fox, sent a horse for him; but he was so sore and bruised that he was not able to bear the shaking of the horse without much pain. When he came to Swarthmore the justices gave forth a warrant against him, but Judge Fell coming home made it ineffectual, and sent out warrants to apprehend all those riotous persons; whereupon some of them fled the country.

"Judge Fell now desired of G. Fox a relation of what had befallen him; but he was backward, and said, 'that those people could not do otherwise in the spirit they were in; and that they manifested the fruits of their priests' ministry'; which made the judge afterwards say to his wife, 'G. Fox spoke of the things as a man that had not been concerned.'"

Secure in her husband's support, Margaret Fell threw herself into the cause. The mother of seven daughters and a son, all of whom she raised to maturity, she left the preaching to others while her family were in need of her care, giving shelter to the "public" Quakers when they were wounded in the fight — Swarthmore Hall was a sort of military hospital, where the wounded Quakers came to receive attention. Judge Fell had some qualms, and feared they would be eaten out of house and home, but his wife persuaded him that they would be blessed in their giving.

In 1658 Judge Fell died, and the hostility he had held at bay came full force against his widow. Among her many activities, she kept up a running fire on the higher-ups. Cromwell had heard from her when his dour Presbyterians and Independents violently assailed the Friends, and when, after the restoration, in violation of King Charles' Declaration of Toleration from Breda, the Episcopalians carried on even more harshly, Mrs. Fell advised his Majesty, "not to heed the Bishops, for it was their counsel was the ruin of thy father." Freedom of speech seems to have been much less upsetting to the temper of the King than to many of the lesser majesties.

Within two years after her husband's death, the authorities decided that Mrs. Fell should have no more prayer meetings in her house, and soldiers were sent to put an end to them. George Fox was captured, a military feat which greatly elated the soldiers, who said, "they had not thought a thousand men could capture him." To make certain of their victory, sixteen men guarded him, the soldiers sitting in the fireplace to prevent a miraculous flight up the chimney, "such dark imaginations possessed them," says Fox.

Margaret Fell, "considering what injury was offered her by hauling G. Fox out of her house," made a vigorous protest to the magistrates, and went down to London to see the King. Justice Porter, who had ordered the arrest, made the same journey, to be on hand to justify the proceedings. Unfortunately for his side of the case, he ran across several noblemen whose houses he had plundered during the late unpleasantness, who frankly reminded him of his participation in the thefts, and he retired discomfited. Margaret Fell had the support of Anne Curtis, whose father had been hanged before his own door by Justice Porter's party, for allegiance to the King.

Mrs. Fell had a long head as well as a pretty face, and quickly took the King's measure. Charles had made some pretty promises of toleration from Breda — Stuart promises. "The man is moderate," Mrs. Fell writes, "and I do believe he hath an intent in his mind and a desire to do for Friends, if he knew how, *and not to endanger his own safety.* He is dark and ignorant of God, and so anything fears him." At any rate, he was not insensible to Margaret Fell's charm of manner and person, nor to Anne Curtis' claim on his favor, who had lost a father in his behalf, and ordered that Fox be sent on to London for trial. Fox's indictment charged him with embroiling the nation in blood, yet in spite of the highly treasonable nature of the charge, to save the expense of a guard, he was allowed to go to London, a journey of three weeks, on his own recognizance. This illogical procedure Fox used as an argument in his defense; if he had been such a character as the indictment described, he would hardly have been trusted to carry it to London alone, a distance of two hundred miles, but

"I had need to have been guarded up with a troop of horse."

"Being satisfied of G. Fox's innocency," the King signed an order for his release. He had now been a prisoner for nearly half a year, and was urged by some to bring an action against Justice Porter and others for false arrest, "but he said, he should leave them to the Lord; if the Lord did forgive them, he should not trouble himself with them."

Margaret Fell kept up the fight by approved Quaker tactics, and "with unwearied Application procured [from the King] a Proclamation, prohibiting Officers and Soldiers from entering houses without a legal warrant." This proved of little value to her; her prayer meetings were regarded as "an affront to authority," and it was a simple matter to obtain legal warrants for their suppression. George Fox was again taken and sent to Lancaster jail, and Mrs. Fell herself was brought to trial. The punishment for holding religious meetings was heavy, but not sufficiently heavy to satisfy the magistrates. The one law with real teeth in it was the law made for dealing with those who refused to take the oath of allegiance, an oath which many were as ready to break as to take; offenders against this law were to lose their real and personal property, and to suffer imprisonment for life, or at the King's pleasure. The Quakers were technical offenders only, they were quite willing to solemnly affirm their allegiance; it was against the swearing that they balked, and in order to bring them under the extreme penalties of the law, magistrates insisted on that legal formality.

Mrs. Fell's judge had the effrontery to tell her that, if she would promise to hold no more Quaker meetings, he would not insist on the oath. She seems to have been equal to conducting her own defense: "I answered, they knew I could not swear, and why should they send for me from my own House, when I was about my lawful Occasions, to ensnare me, what had I done? They said, If I would not keep Meetings at my house, they would not tender the oath. I told them that I should not deny my Faith and Principles for any Thing they could do against me, and while it pleaseth the Lord to let me have an House, I would endeavor to worship him in it." The blood of the Askew martyr who was burned at the stake was up.

Margaret Fell came into Court accompanied by four of her grown daughters, leading her youngest child by the hand. In deference to her social position, Judge Twisden called for "a cushioned seat for Mistress Fell," and invited the four older girls to a seat by himself. Judge Twisden, it will be remembered, at the trial which sent Francis Howgill to his death, made the brilliant plea that in the olden times they were heathen that persecuted, "but we are Christian magistrates."

Arguing in her own defense, Mrs. Fell said: "I was sent from my own house, from amongst my Children and Family, when I was about my outward Occasions, when I was in no Meeting, neither was it Meeting Day; therefore I desire to know what this Foundation and Matter of Fact was, for there is no Law against the innocent and Righteous, and if I be a Transgressor, let me know wherein."

JUDGE: You say well; the Law is made for Transgressors: But Mistress, do you go to Church?

MARGARET: I do go to Church.

JUDGE: What Church?

MARGARET: The Church of Christ.

JUDGE: But do you go to Church along with other People? You know what I mean.

MARGARET: What dost thou call a Church, the House or the People? . . . I was separated from the general Worship of this Nation, . . . and was persecuted by that Power that then was, (the Parliament) and suffered much Hardship; and would you now have us deny our Faith and Principles, which we have suffered for so many years, and turn to your Church contrary to our Conscience?

JUDGE: We spend Time about these Things; come to the matter in hand: What do you say to the oath and the indictment?

MARGARET: I do not deny this oath because it is the Oath of Allegiance, but I deny it because it is an Oath. If I might gain the whole world for swearing an Oath, I could not, and whatever I have to lose this Day for not swearing an Oath, I am willing to offer it up.

JUDGE: What say you to the Indictment?

MARGARET: I am clear and innocent of wronging any Man upon this Earth, as my little Child that stands by me: and if any have any Thing to lay to my charge, let them come down and testify it before you, and if I be clear and innocent, you have no Law against me.

Then Colonel Kirby and the Sheriff whispered to the Judge, whereupon she spoke to the Colonel:

MARGARET: Let us have no whisperings; if thou hast any Thing to lay to my charge, or to speak against me, come down here, and testify against me.

JUDGE: Jury take notice, she doth not take the Oath.

MARGARET: This matter is weighty to me, whatever it be to you. I stand here in obeying Christ's Commands. . . . If I obey this law and King Charles' Commands, I defile my Conscience. The cause and Controversy in this Matter, that you are all here to judge this Day, is betwixt Jesus Christ and King Charles.

The jury found the verdict for King Charles. It may now seem far-fetched for the Quakers, who had no scruples against affirming allegiance to the King, to balk at the oath. It was much farther fetched for magistrates, who had themselves taken and broken oaths of allegiance to each faction in succession, to insist on administering the oath to those who had conscientious scruples against swearing. Fox called attention to the absurdity: "I told the Judge that I had never taken an oath, covenant or engagement in my life, but my yea or nay was more binding to me than an oath was to many others; for had they not had experience how little men regarded an oath; and how they had sworn one way and then another, and how the justices and court had foresworn themselves now? I told him I was a man of tender conscience."

Margaret Fell asked for a delay of sentence till the following morning, that she might bring in an Arrest of Judgment.

JUDGE: You shall have it — Mrs. Fell, you wrote me concerning the badness of your Prisons, that it rains in, and that they are not fit for People to lie in.

MARGARET: The Sheriff knows, and has been told of it several Times, and now it is raining, if you will send, you may see whether they be fit for People to lie in or not.

In the opinion of Colonel Kirby, no place was so vile as to be unfit for housing Quakers; he spoke up in defense of the prisons.

MARGARET: If you were to be in it yourselves, you would think it hard, but your Mind is only in Cruelty to commit others, as William Kirby here has done, who hath committed ten of our Friends, and put them in a cold Room, where there was nothing but bare Boards to lie on, where some have lain several Nights, some of them above three score years of age and known to be honest Men in the Country where they live, and when William Kirby was asked, Why they might not have Liberty to shift for themselves for Beds? he answered, They were to commit them to Prison, but not to provide Prisons for them. And being asked, Who should do it then? He answered, The King.

JUDGE: You should not do so: They ought to have Prisons fit for Men.

Prison reform was a side issue of the Quaker fight. George Fox, who suffered imprisonment at the same time as Margaret Fell, has left a description of the lodging provided by the State: "The smoke of the other prisoners came up so thick it stood as dew upon the walls, and I being locked under three locks, the under jailer, when the smoke was great, would hardly be persuaded to come up to unlock one of the uppermost doors for fear of the smoke, so that I was almost smothered.

"Besides, it rained in upon my bed, and many times, when I went to stop out the rain in the cold winter season, my shirt was as wet as muck with the rain that came in upon me. And the place being high and open to the wind, sometimes as fast as I stopped it the wind blew it out again.

"In this manner I lay all that long cold winter, in which time I was so starved, and so frozen with cold, and wet with the rain, that my body was greatly swelled and my limbs much benumbed."

Many died in these prisons; how so many delicate women managed to stick it out will always remain a mystery.

To return to Margaret Fell. She had conducted her case with so much keenness that the judge feared the effect on the jury of her "everlasting tongue." But she got no arrest of judgment; the staggering sentence of praemunire was passed upon her; her property forfeited, herself imprisoned for life, or at the King's pleasure, she was out of the King's protection, whatever that might signify. "But," she says, "the Great God of Heaven and Earth supported my Spirit under this severe sentence, that I was not terrified, but gave this answer to Judge Turner, Although I am out of the King's protection, yet I am not out of the Protection of Almighty God." This, her first imprisonment, lasted four and a half years; even if by her "unwearied application" and her "everlasting tongue" she succeeded in getting a rain-proof cell, the prisons at best were damp, unheated, and usually filthy.

Half of her period of widowhood Margaret Fell spent in jail; when she was released, eleven years after the death of Judge Fell, she married George Fox. Serious beyond her years, at seventeen she had married a man sixteen years her senior; youthfully enthusiastic and vital at fifty, her second husband was ten years her junior. Fox's Journal gives an account of the courtship: "I had seen from the Lord a considerable time before, that I should take Margaret Fell to be my wife . . . yet I had not received a command from the Lord for the accomplishment of it then. Wherefore I let the thing rest, and went on in the work and service of the Lord as before . . . traveling up and down in this nation and in Ireland. But now being at Bristol and finding Margaret Fell there . . . after we had discoursed the matter together, I told her if she also was satisfied with the accomplishing of it now, she should first send for her children. . . . I asked both them and her sons-in-law if they had anything against it, or for it; and they all severally expressed their satisfaction therein. I asked them whether, if their mother married they would lose by it. . . . The children said she had answered to them, and desired me to speak no more about it. I told them I was plain, and would have all things done plainly; for I sought no outward advantage to myself. . . . We stayed about one week in Bristol, and then went together to Oldstone; where, taking leave of each other in the Lord, we parted, betaking ourselves to our several service, Margaret returning home to the North, and I passing on in the work of the Lord as before."

After this brief honeymoon, Fox fell into a state of depression; he was in great bodily weakness as the result of his imprisonment and the buffetings of the mobs, and was also "warring in spirit with the evil spirits of the world." It was, he says, "a bloody persecuting time. . . . Some sober people of other professions would say, 'If Friends did not stand, the nation would run into debauchery.' The remainder of Margaret's honeymoon she spent in jail, where she was laid by for another year. Her husband suffered too much from prison sickness to move about, but he got Margaret's daughters to go to the King,

SWARTHMORE HALL, A QUAKER SHRINE

(*From a Photograph by Albert G. Reckitt*)

who finally came over royally, and gave an order "to clear both her and her estate."

The release came just in time to enable her to see her husband off to America, where the service now called him. On land or sea life was a succession of thrills for the Quakers: the vessel on which Fox took passage was so leaky that the passengers were pressed into the work of pumping day and night. "One day they observed that in two hours' time she sucked in sixteen inches of water." To add to the excitement they were chased by a man-of-war, "But Friends were well satisfied, having faith in God, and no fear upon their spirits." Fox believed he had assurance from the Unseen that they would not be taken.

"I sat up in my cabin, and, looking through the port hole I saw them very near us. I was getting up to go out of the cabin, but remembering the word of the Lord, that His Life and power were placed between us and them, I lay down again. . . . A fresh gale arose, and we sailed briskly on and saw them no more." After nearly two months of these adventures, the leaky ship made port in Barbados. It was on this tour that Fox initiated his antislavery movement: "I desired that they would deal mildly and gently with their negroes, and not use cruelty toward them, and *that after certain years of servitude they would make them free.*"

A brief note to his wife reads, in part:

My Dear Heart,

To whom is my love, and to all the children . . . I have undergone great sufferings in my body and spirit, beyond words; but the God of Heaven be praised, His Truth is over all. I am well now.

On his return voyage Fox landed in Bristol, where he was welcomed by his wife with her daughters and sons-in-law, the William Penns and other prominent Friends. Hunted as they were, the ties of friendship and consanguinity meant much to the Quakers, and were religiously strengthened by them. After some work in London, Fox had a visit with Penn at Rickmansworth, which, as elsewhere noted, probably resulted in transforming a castle in the air into the Province of Pennsylvania.

Fox was on his way to his aged mother, then on her deathbed, but "at night as I was sitting at supper, I felt I was taken (a prisoner); yet I said nothing to any one of it. . . . Next morning we travelled . . . to John Halford's at Armscott, where we had a large and precious meeting in his barn. . . . Henry Parker, a justice . . . and the priest plotted together to break it up and apprehend me. . . . They did not come till the meeting was over, . . . yet Henry Parker took me and Thomas Lower for company with me; and though he had nothing to lay to our charge, sent us both to Worcestershire jail."

Fox wrote his wife (their twenty-two years of married life was matrimony chiefly by correspondence):

Dear Heart:

Thou seemedst to be a little grieved when I was speaking of prisons, and when I was taken. When I was at John Rous's I had a sight of my being taken prisoner; and when I was in Oxfordshire as I sat at supper, I saw I was taken, and I saw I had suffering to undergo. But the Lord's power is over all.

There was no legal charge against Fox, and the clergyman proposed the tried and true method, tendering the oaths of allegiance and supremacy, which the prisoner, in spite of " a fit of sickness, which brought me very low and weak in my body," refused to take.

Margaret Fox went to the King in person, and found him very friendly; " but," says Fox, " the King could not release me otherwise than by a pardon, and I was not free to receive a pardon, knowing I had done no evil. . . . The King . . . told Thomas Moore that I need not scruple, being released by a pardon, for many *a man that was as innocent as a child had had a pardon granted him;* yet I could not consent to have one. For I would rather have lain in prison all my days, than have come out in any way dishonorable to the Truth; therefore I chose to have the validity of my indictment tried before the judges."

Fox was successful in having his case brought before the King's Bench Bar.

" Some of my adversaries moved the judges that the oaths might be tendered again to me, telling them I was a dangerous man to be at Liberty. Chief Justice Sir

Matthew Hale said he had heard such reports, but he had also heard many more good reports of me; and so he and the rest of the judges ordered me to be freed *by proclamation.* Thus after I had suffered imprisonment for a year and almost two months for nothing, I was fairly set at liberty, . . . without receiving any pardon, or coming under any obligation at all."

It is evident that between the cause and the clergy, the comforts of home played little part in the married life of the Foxes. There were, however, many affectionate interchanges by letter. While undergoing this imprisonment at Worcester, Margaret sent her husband some money to ease his condition. He commissioned a Friend to purchase "a piece of black Spanish cloth for a gown," writing her, "it cost a great deal of money, but I will save it." It would be interesting to know where he made the cut in his expenses, his diet often consisting of bread and water. One of his jailers refused to allow beer to be brought in to him, the sale of beer to prisoners being a graft of the warden, which yielded him a handsome profit. Rather than submit to extortion, Fox steeped wormwood in his water, and went without his beer.

Margaret Fox seems to have made no effort to divorce her husband from his spectacular leather clothing, nor did he endeavor to reduce her to Quaker drabness. With wifely concern Mrs. Fox sent her husband money to buy a warm coat. He bought instead some "crimson cloth for a mantle," which in his judgment she needed more than he needed a coat. Perhaps she thought crimson rather gay for a grandmother, for she writes:

Dear Love —

Glad am I to hear that the Lord preserves thee in health and capacity to travel in his work and service. . . . We hope and expect He will draw thee homeward. Thou art much expected and longed for here, but we must all submit to the Lord's will and time. I received thy kind token by Leonard. . . . I thought to have sent something by Mary Fell to thee, but I considered thou would only buy something with it for me, as thou used to do, which caused me to omit it. I perceive thou hast sent things to the children by Leonard, he hath not yet delivered them; but thy company would be more and better to us than all the world; but only for the Lord's truth and service, we would not exchange it for all beside.

From thy endeared and loving wife.

M. F.

The insistence on uniformity in color and dress got no support from Fox or his wife. The more austere sisters endeavored to bring Margaret into line, but she put her foot down firmly; her life and property were freely given to the cause; her dress was her own personal concern, and she frankly refused to be browbeaten into uniformity: "Legal ceremonies are far from being gospel freedom. . . . It is a dangerous thing to lead young Friends much into observation of outward things, for that will be easily done, for they can soon get into an outward garb to be all alike outwardly, but this will not make them true Christians. It is the spirit that gives life."

Few of the years of Margaret's married life were spent with her husband; six months before his death, she journeyed to London to be with him. Persecution was hot, and Fox spent his time "visiting Friends in prison . . . encouraging them in their sufferings, and exhorting them to stand faithful and steadfast in the testimony, which the Lord had committed them to bear. Sometimes I also visited them that were sick and weak in body, or troubled in mind, helping to bear up their spirits from sinking under their infirmities."

Imprisonment wrought great havoc on the health of those who stood steadfast in the testimony; Fox himself had gone through sufferings that would have killed an ox, beatings and prison sickness which in time wore down his marvelous constitution, and made his last years of labor among other sufferers painful and difficult. He died as he had lived, in harness.

Margaret praises the Lord, "who gave me strength and ability to travel that great journey, being seventy-six years of age, to see my dear husband . . . for he lived but half a year after I left him." Fox had preached "a long and powerful sermon," and when he had ended, he felt the chill of death "strike to his heart." Knowing that his end had come, he said: "I am glad I was here. Now I am clear, I am fully clear."

It was William Penn who broke the sad news to his wife, and after the Quaker custom, wrote a "testimony" to his friend. "In all things he acquitted himself like a man, yea a strong man, a new and heavenly minded man. Civil beyond all forms of breeding in his behavior; very temperate, eating little and sleeping less, though a bulky person. As he lived so he died, feeling the same eternal power that had raised and preserved him in his last moments; . . . as if death were hardly worth notice or mention."

Margaret lived on for twelve years, and while she lived she worked. "And at length after a laborious and godly life, she piously departed hence in a great age (eighty-eight years) having uttered in the time of her sickness many excellent sayings, by which it appeared that she was prepared for death and longed to be dissolved."

Thomas Lurting — An Able-Minded Seaman

The Quaker testimony against bloodshed was practical, as such testimony can still be when men will. Their principle of equality as well as their practice of it was their legacy to our people, and now remains all that differences us from other nations. It was not Thomas Jefferson who imagined the first of the self-evident truths of the Declaration of Independence, but George Fox. — W. D. Howells.

Thomas Lurting's unique exploits were undertaken without the orchestral accompaniment of cannon; he had no support from the pomp and panoply of war. Even among Quakers of this generation his name is unfamiliar. Under the title "A Fighting Sailor Turned Peaceable Christian," the Quakers of his own time published a tract recording the sensational incidents of his career. To his ultimate peaceableness must be attributed Lurting's obscurity, for as the historian of the Decline of Rome points out, "men are ever more ready to glorify their destroyers than their benefactors."

At a time when aged women and young girls were done to death for the crime of holding a religious meeting, this bold sailor man, "in obedience to the promptings of the Holy Spirit," opposed his individual conscience to the might and majesty of the English navy, declared a strike on war on the eve of battle, took pirates captive, rebuked his King, and in spite of all continued to live happily ever after.

Curiosity as to the secret of this disarming personality will find little gratification in the Quaker records, which ascribe all victories to the Lord. We infer, however, that this human agent of the Lord must have been a likely creature physically, for he was only fourteen when he arrested the appraising eye of the press gang, and remained ever after the victim of their flattering approval, and a justification of their efficiency. Impressment was the synonym for shanghaiing men into the army and navy for involuntary servitude, often without pay, and under armed guards. The old pagans frankly called such service slavery, a word abhorrent to Christians, and embarrassing to men boasting that they "never, never, never shall be slaves."

In time the boy was shifted from the army to the navy, and we learn that when the celebrated Admiral Blake "ruined the Admiral and Vice Admiral of the Spanish Galleons," Lurting was chosen for the perilous honor of firing the enemy ships. In a pinnace with seven men he passed under the fire of the Spanish fort, turned his trick neatly, and returned unhurt, though two of his men were killed and one shot in the back. The pamphlet published by the Society of Friends at the time of his "convincement" puts the soft pedal on the prowess of Thomas the fighter, and emphasizes the valor of Thomas the Christian. Friend Sewel got hold of Thomas, and succeeded in extracting from him further details of his adventures, which he preserved in his "History of the Quakers." Both narratives have the stamp of truth, the simplicity of the Gospels, and the fantastic unreality of fairy tales; by reinforcing one with the other, we come to the whole story.

The courage of the youth had brought him to the rank of boatswain's mate of the frigate *Bristol*, with two hundred men under his command. Among other duties it fell to him to enforce attendance at divine worship, as by law established. "I was diligent in the performance of that service," he says, "and when any refused to obey my command I endeavored by force to compel them. But then neither was I a Quaker, nor were there any of the people so-called on board our ship. Now I shall hint at the first rise of the Quakers in our ship."

It fell to the *Bristol* to transport a company of soldiers, among them a young lad who had been infected with Quaker principles in Scotland. With the racial passion for proselyting, the young Scot communicated the infection to the sailors of the *Bristol*; the first symptoms were refusal to attend compulsory worship, and to doff caps to officers. A few were ripe for the disease and it spread, to the consternation of the captain, and the increased severity of discipline. The captain, in his leisure moments a Baptist preacher, was just then commander of a battleship, and naturally "he was sore troubled." Bluff and blustering, but not ill-disposed, he commissioned the chaplain, "a cruel and bitter man," to put matters right with the assistance of the sturdy boatswain's mate.

The good man appealed to Thomas: "Oh Thomas, an honest man and a good Christian, Here is a dangerous people, a blasphemous people, denying the ordinances and word of God." With a mandate from both law and Gospel to go the limit, Thomas admits he was as cruel and bitter as the priest: "I gave them many a heavy blow, and I was violent upon them. But the Lord so wrought upon me that in a little time I could no more beat any of the Quakers. And very soon the Lord gave me a true sight of the priest, for when I could not do his work, and beat and abuse them, I was accounted neither an honest man nor a good Christian. So I separated myself from all sorts of professors [Christians] except one Roger Denis whom I entirely loved. In all my cruelty I never struck him, *for he had a check upon me, though he spoke never a word*." The quiet wordless Quaker, Roger Denis, possessed the mysterious force which arrests violence in man or beast. In later life Thomas wrote that, "as silence is the first word of command in martial discipline, so it is in spiritual; for until that is come unto, the will and mind of God concerning us cannot be known, much less done."

The silent power which Thomas could not subdue was conquering him; his sympathy for the Quakers made him an object of derision among his mates of the *Bristol*, and jeering parties from sister ships of the fleet came aboard to ridicule him. He still retained the shape of a man, they assured him, but he looked like a dumb saint. Now Thomas was a social creature, a good mixer, an upstanding and outstanding figure. The man who had faced the gunfire of the Spanish forts flinched before ridicule; fervently he besought the Lord that it might not be required of him to cast in his lot with a despised sect, mocked of all men. " For the reasoning part got up. What, to such a people that both priests and professors are against? What, to such a people that I have been so long beating and abusing, and that without just cause? Death would be more welcome." Alas for his peace of mind, Thomas already belonged with the minority, and his conscience was putting pressure on him to make a public acknowledgment.

Finally, " after many a bitter sigh, I took up this resolution by the assistance of the Lord, whether Quaker or no Quaker, peace with God I am for. . . . I could contain no longer but gave up and went to my friend Roger Denis and said, I would speak with thee. . . . He spake only a few words, but they were in great humility and tenderness toward me, hitting the mark to a hair's breadth. I had great satisfaction, being quiet in my mind, and we parted in great love."

There was no quiet for the captain's mind; twelve boys aboard that fighting frigate were now meeting unmolested by the mate, to meditate on those things which are eternal. The captain and the priest called Thomas above to reason with him, "and when they had done I went to my Friends in great peace, telling them that when I went to the Captain I was scarce half a Quaker, they have made me almost a whole one."

These unruly Christians, it would seem, enjoyed the good will of their shipmates, for the captain impressed men from other ships to flog them. Even these strangers balked before the patient obstinacy of their victims, and at this acute stage of hostilities, Providence interposed an armistice in the form of an epidemic. "About this time we had a great sickness on board. We took great care of one another, so that nothing was wanting amongst us; but what one had was free for all of us. I have heard men say when upon a languishing pillow and death bed, 'O carry me to the Quakers, for they take great care of one another, and they will take some care of me.'"

The missionary soldier from Scotland had left the Bristol sailors in ignorance of the full program of the Quakers; they knew nothing of the war on war, nor had they as yet fully grasped the implications of the Quaker principles. They had got as far as to interpret the command "Thou shalt not steal" to mean that they could take none of the plunder of war, which left their share to be divided among their mates, and gave them some popularity. The captain grew calmer as he discovered no abatement of their fighting spirit, and fell into the habit of saying, "Thomas, take thy friends and do so and so." "And I took my Friends and did it far beyond his expectation, by which he got great credit. As yet we were not brought to testify against fighting, but we would take none of the plunder, and in all our desperate attempts we received no hurt, though others were killed and wounded. . . . The Captain would often say to other captains, He cared not if all his men were Quakers for they were the hardiest men on his ship."

The captain's boast was premature; Thomas felt in his bones that a storm was brewing, "For what was done in pretended friendship was but to serve their own ends. I expected a time would come to try all our foundations, which it accordingly did, and drove every man to his own." That time came when Thomas got to the point of interpreting another command, Thou shalt do no murder.

The *Bristol* was ordered to demolish a castle in Spain, a very substantial one. "And we Quakers fought with as much courage as any, we seeing then no further. I was stripped to the waist, and every one of us being in fighting habit, we went at it in earnest." The Scotch soldier had started the *Bristol* sailors with the fundamental and most subversive of Quaker principles, that in every one of His creatures the Creator has implanted the Divine spark; to this extent all men are equal. That premise inevitably led to the question, Dare any man by violence snuff out a life which shelters that spark?

The answer came to Thomas at this very inopportune moment; the ship was in action, and with all diligence he was sighting the guns, when "He that hath all men's hearts in His hand so far changed my heart, that whilst a minute before I was setting all my strength to kill and destroy men's lives, but a minute after I could not kill a man if it were to gain the whole world. As I was coming out the forecastle door to see where the shot fell, the word of the Lord ran through me, How if I had killed a man, and it was with such power that for some time I hardly knew whether I was in the body or out of it. I turned and put on my clothes and walked on deck in great exercise of mind. Some one asked me if I was hurt. I answered, No, but under some scruple of conscience on account of fighting. *Although I had not then heard that Quakers refused to fight.*"

The sudden defection of the mate escaped the watchful eye of authority, the naval engagement ended; but the battle in the soul of Thomas continued to rage. "Full well ye reject the commandments of God that ye may keep your own traditions," was the accusation of the most subversive of great teachers. Tradition had not sterilized the mind of Thomas; after a period of gestation an idea had been born to him, and he was not the man to strangle it. He called a Quaker meeting and presented his idea to his Friends. All expressed profound disgust with the atrocities of war, and delivered themselves of the ancient and honored platitude, that if the Lord got them well out of this one, they would never go to it again. This was not enough for the mate, in whom belief was immediately converted into action. "If I stood honest to that which is of God in my own conscience," he told his Friends, "and if we came to it to-morrow, I would bear my testimony against it, for inasmuch as we had been so great actors in it, now we must bear our testimony against fighting." Courage begets courage, one of the young comrades immediately sought out the captain to acquaint him with the weight on his conscience. "He that denies to fight in the time of engagement," roared the exasperated officer, "I will put my sword in his guts." More calmly the Quaker came back, "Thou wilt be a manslayer, and guilty of innocent blood."

As a Baptist preacher, the captain doubtless had a disturbing fear that these troublesome Quakers interpreted the Christian teaching correctly, though inconveniently; as a naval officer, loving enemies was an absurdity. In his mental conflict he hit upon an ingenious scheme for reducing the friction on his conscience while performing his whole duty as commander of a warship. Notices were posted up giving any of his crew the privilege of killing a shipmate who proved delinquent in time of battle. For all his blustering, this Cromwellian captain showed no eagerness to plant his own sword in the bowels of a fellow Christian.

And now, says Thomas, came a time "to prove everyone's foundation." A strange ship was sighted and the *Bristol* cleared for action; for Thomas the time had come to stand honest to that which was of God in his own conscience, and he told his Friends so, "but I lay not this as an injunction upon any, but leave you to the Lord." Those who were prepared to stand with him, however, must take no devious course which would leave the captain in the lurch: "I must tell you that the Captain puts great confidence in you. All that are of my mind let us meet in the most public place upon the deck in full view of the Captain, that he may not say we deceived him in not telling him that we would not fight, so that he might have put others in our place."

To a man the twelve Quakers followed their leader; the distracted captain, when he saw them, drew his sword "in as much fury and indignation as ever I saw a sword drawn. No sooner was his sword drawn than the word of the Lord ran through me like fire: 'If he will have a sacrifice proffer it him,'" and Thomas, advancing "in great dread of the Lord," "fixed his eye with great seriousness" on his chief. It was not the mutineer but the captain who flinched; "his countenance changed pale," and he passed his sword to his man.

At this moment of high tension the stranger ship was discovered to be no enemy, but a friend. When the captain had cooled off, he sent the chaplain to Thomas to ask forgiveness for his passion, "but I bid him tell the Captain to have a care of such passion, for if he had killed a man in his passion, he might seek for a place of repentence and not find it. Ever after this the Captain was very kind and respectful to me."

To this preacher captain, an infusible mixture of warrior and Christian, the Lord was as real as to the Quakers. If the rebels had been cowards he could, and probably would, have killed them. But he knew these followers of his Lord to be men of intrepid courage, the most engaging and disarming of human attributes. We are not told what disposition he made of the mutineers; as he was unable to cure them, and loath to kill them, in all probability he relieved his ship and his conscience of the impossible crew at the first opportunity.

Thomas's life was now filled with "exercises" and "concerns." His pacifist protestations were unheeded by his admirers, the ubiquitous press gang; he was "a powerful man," they said, and into the navy he must go. He was repeatedly captured and forcibly installed on various ships of the line. Any of the captains with whom he debated might have sent him to join the noble army of martyrs, but he led a charmed life. He was reasoned with, cajoled, bribed with offers of command, and threatened with death, but not a hair of his head was injured.

Even Captain Jeremiah Smith, "a loose and wicked man, a very furious man and frequently in drink," fell under his spell. Thomas turned a deaf ear to the captain's offer of a command, and of various occupations which would involve no actual killing. The captain had a brilliant idea, an employment "which will be a great piece of charity, thou shalt be with the doctor; and when a man comes down that hath lost an arm or a leg, to hold him while the doctor cuts it off. This is not killing, but saving men's lives."

"But I will not do that," said the inflexible Thomas, "for it is all an assistance." Then said the loose and furious captain, "I will send thee ashore to prison."

Thomas answered: "I am in thy hands. Thou may do with me what thou pleases."

The captain pleased to accuse Thomas of an attempt to starve himself, for he had eaten no food for five days. "Not so, said I, for I have money in my pocket. And if thou wilt sell me victuals I will eat before thee."

"I cannot sell the King's victuals," said the captain.

"Nor can I do the King's work, therefore I cannot eat the King's victuals."

Sent ashore as he supposed to prison, Thomas discovered that even this furious captain had given him his liberty. He promptly sought a berth on a merchant vessel, but again the attentive press gang waited to welcome him, and he was assigned to a captain "who appeared like a madman, swearing and cursing against Quakers, often swearing that if he did not hang me, he would send me to the Duke of York and he would." When the captain had "tired himself with scolding," Thomas still remained silent.

"What," shouted the angry captain, "dost thou say nothing for thyself?"

"Thou sayest enough for thee and me, too," was the reply.

With a good prospect of hanging, Thomas lay peacefully asleep on the deck between two guns; the captain was wakeful and troubled. At midnight he had the Quaker routed from his slumber and got rid of him. "And this was the man," comments Thomas, "who said hanging was too good for me, and in six hours time was so weary of me that he could not take his natural rest whilst I was on board."

After many such adventures, Thomas at last succeeded in eluding the vigilance of the press gang, and slipped off to sea as mate aboard a merchantman, under a Quaker skipper, destined for the most thrilling adventure of his turbulent life. He had outwitted the pressers only to fall into the hands of the Barbary pirates, who captured the English vessel as she was returning from Venice with a cargo.

Thomas had a premonition of their fate. "We heard that many Turkish men-of-war were at sea, . . . and it was much on my mind that we should be taken. I was very much concerned as well for the men as for myself; at which I went to the Master and desired him to go to Leghorn, and to stay for a convoy, agreeing that during such a time we would have no wages. The Master would not agree to this, but kept out to sea, contrary to our minds."

The master was between two horns of a dilemma — as a good Quaker he could not accept assistance from the navy, nor on the other hand could he force others to act according to the dictates of his conscience. Thomas had no criticism for the master's choice of duty, which resulted in their capture by the Turk.

The Turks removed the English captain with four of his men to their own ship, placing fourteen of their own men aboard the prize to guard the remainder of the crew, including Thomas. "The Mate," Sewel quaintly records, "was under great exercise of mind, the rather because the Master with four of his men were then with the Turk, and those that were left were somewhat unruly. In this concern, however, he believed it was inwardly told him by the Lord, 'Be not afraid for thou shalt not go to Algiers,' for having formerly great experience of the Lord's deliverance, he had learned to trust in God almost against hope. . . . All fear was removed from him, and going to the ship's side to see the Turks come in, he received them as if they were his friends, and they also behaved themselves civilly. He said to his men, 'Be not afraid, for all this we shall not go to Algiers; but let me desire you, as ye have been willing to obey me, be as willing to obey the Turks.'" Kings, naval commanders, able-bodied and unruly seamen were all one to Thomas, all in the day's work.

"The Turks seeing the seamen's diligence grew more careless and favorable to them, some went again to their own ship and eight staid with the English. Then the Mate began to think of the Master and the four that were with him on the Turk's ship; as for himself and the others that were with him he had no fear at all; nay he was so far from it that he said to one of his men: Were but the Master on board and the rest of our men, were there twice as many Turks I should not fear them. By this he encouraged the seamen, who not being of his persuasion thought much otherwise than he, and would have been ready enough to kill the Turks if they had seen opportunity. Meanwhile the Mate's earnest desire to the Lord was that He would put it into the hearts of the Turks to send the Master and the four others back, and his desire was answered. . . . Then all manner of fear concerning Algiers was taken from him.

"Now the English being all together except the Master, he said to them, 'What if we should overcome the Turks and go to May-York (Majorca)?' At which they were very much rejoiced, and one said, 'I will kill one or two,' and another said, 'I will cut as many throats as you will have me.' But at these sayings the Mate was much troubled, for he intended not to hurt any, and therefore told the men: If I knew that any of you would touch a Turk at that rate, I would tell the Turks myself. But, said he, if ye will be ruled I will act for your delivery as well as my own, if not I will be still. They seeing he would not suffer them to take their own course agreed to do what he would have them. Well, said he, If the Turks bid you do anything, do it without grumbling and with as much diligence as ye can, for that pleases them, and will cause them to let us be together."

Having brought the seamen into line, Thomas turned his attention to the master, and takes up his own narrative: "Then I went to our Master who was a Friend, and a bold spirited man, and told him of our intention, whose answer to me was: if we offered to rise and they overcame us, we had as good be burned alive, the which I knew very well. But I could get him no way to adhere to me, in that he was fearful of bloodshed, for that was his reason, insomuch that at last I told him: We were resolved, and I questioned not but to do it without one drop of bloodshed; and I believed the Lord would prosper it, by reason that I would rather go to Algiers than kill one Turk. So at last he agreed to this, and let me do what I would, provided we killed none. There being two Turks lying in the cabin with him, he was still to lie in the cabin, that by his being there they would mistrust nothing. And having bad weather and lost the company of their man-of-war (which thing I much desired) the Turks seeing our diligence grew careless of us."

For all his confidence in the Lord, the mate was not one to expect God to do for him that which he could very well do for himself; on the contrary, he made good use of the excellent headpiece with which the Lord had endowed him. With tact and patience he managed to steer the Turks into separate cabins, and while they slept the more serenely for an imperfect estimate of their Quaker prisoner, the English disarmed them and turned the key, all done, Thomas assures us, "by fair means and persuasions."

With the master resting quietly in his cabin, and their captors secured under lock and key, the mate was free to make terms with the restive seamen. "Then I said to the men of our vessel, Now we have the Turks at our command, no man shall hurt any of them, for if you do I will be against you; but this I will do, now they are below deck we will keep them so, and go to May-York. My orders were: if any offered to come out, not to let above one or two at a time. And one came out expecting to have seen his own country, but on the contrary, it was May-York."

Thomas, with the assistance of Providence, having securely bolted every door of hope against the Turks, "instead of rising they fell to crying, for their courage was taken from them, and they desired they might not be sold, which I promised them they should not." Thomas was unmoved by the consideration that the Turks would have sold him; they might follow what code they would, he was a Christian.

"And when he had appeased them," with nothing to conceal from his scrupulous superior officer, "I went into the cabin of our Master, he not knowing what was done, and he told their captain that we had overcome his men, and were going to May-York. At which unexpected news he wept, and desired the Master not to sell him, which he promised he would not."

Majorca, whither they were bound, was a Spanish port. An extensive acquaintance with Christianity, as interpreted by the Spaniards, aroused great fear in the Turks and no little concern in the minds of the two Quakers. Therefore "we told the captain that we would make a place to hide them where the Spaniards would not find them, at which they were very glad, and we did accordingly."

The master went ashore at Majorca, returning with an acquaintance, another English captain. The Quaker captain was naturally gratified by the bloodless victory of his Quaker mate; under solemn promise of secrecy, he confided to his English friend the whole story of the concealed pirates. That enterprising gentleman was appalled by the mere thought of abandoning riches so providentially cast upon the waters; he offered to purchase some of the Turks himself on speculation. "Whereat the Master and I told him, that if they would give many thousands they should not have one, for we hoped to send them home again."

So great was the English captain's disgust with the vagaries of the Quakers, that his promise of secrecy quite escaped his mind; going ashore, he conspired with the Spaniards to steal a march on his fanatical friends, and salvage their valuable cargo. Crafty as he was, he was no match for the wary Friends, who suspecting his design took the Turks into their confidence, and with the assistance of the enemy, without waiting for legal formalities, glided swiftly out of Spanish waters, headed for England and fresh trouble.

In defending the Turks from the slave hunters, the Quakers were chancing recapture, for pirates were numerous; their own pet pirates, moreover, grew restless and nervous when they discovered they were on the way to England. The courage which had ebbed through fear, returned in their greater fear of England; the eye of a vigilant Christian detected an approaching squall. On deck with only a helmsman, the English crew asleep below, Thomas noticed with alarm that the Turks had surrounded his captain.

"Their countenances began to look very sourly. A great weight fell upon me. How if they should lay hold upon the Master and heave him overboard, they being ten strong men, and he a small man. My weight increasing I started up and stamped my foot." With a rush the English sailors responded, seizing workmen's tools as they ran, for Thomas had cautiously sequestered the Turkish weapons. "So when I heard them threaten the Master I said, Let us have them down; we have given them too much liberty. But turning to our men, Lay down the crow and axe, and every man of you what you have provided to hurt them; they are Turks and we are Englishmen; let it not be said we are afraid of them. I will lay hold of the captain. So I laid hold of him and said he must go down, which he did very quietly and all the rest followed him."

Having so easily persuaded the pirates, Thomas now faced a new perplexity presented by his unpersuadable conscience. There was no blinking the fact that the terror of the Turks was not unreasonable; they had the same good grounds for dreading England that the English had for dreading Algiers; capture in either case meant slavery and loving enemies had no vogue either with heathen or with Christian. Nor was Thomas unmindful of his responsibility for the safety of his English crew, and the consciences of those sturdy seamen were untroubled by anxiety for the welfare of Turks. They were hard sayings, those commands laid on Christians, but for Thomas Lurting there could be no halfway allegiance; he would be "clear" only when he had set the Turks down within sight of home and safety. The vessel was ordered right about.

"Some of his men grumbled and said he had more care for the Turks than for them, to which his answer was that they were strangers and he must treat them well. . . . The Mate saw well that he being the man who had begun this business, it would be his lot to bring it to an end."

His surmise was correct, and, though his men grumbled, they fell in behind his quixotic plan; for although to them his ideas seemed rather wild, it was his courage and sagacity which had rescued them from Algeria and slavery. As they neared the perilous pirate coast, Thomas's perplexities increased; he loved his enemies but was not unmindful of their limitations. If he gave them a boat they might easily return with reinforcements and overpower the English. On the other hand, landing ten able-bodied Turks in a small boat manned by a few unarmed sailors was an undertaking which excited no enthusiasm in his men.

Thomas proposed to the captain to give him a small boat, and, with three volunteers to accompany him, he hoped to make a permanent parting with their guests. "The Master, relying perhaps on his Mate's conduct, consented to the proposal, though not without some tears dropped on both sides. Yet the Mate taking courage said to the Master, 'I believe the Lord will preserve me, for I have nothing but good will in venturing my life, and I have not the least fear upon me, but trust that all will do well.'"

Thomas now called for volunteers; of the three who responded one thought better of it. "Then I went to another and said to him, Thou and I have been good friends. Wilt thou venture to go with me? He answered, Yes if the Master will give me leave." The volunteers were much disturbed by the looks of their charges, and suggested that the Turks be bound, but the projects of Thomas were always well reasoned out. He had considered the possibility of a parting from the Turks so sudden that they would make the home stretch by swimming, and for this he desired to leave them free.

"I answered I was not afraid, and to bind them would

but exasperate them. Now they are quiet let us keep them so. Come, let us hoist out the boat." Cheering on his uneasy helpers, Thomas adroitly packed his Turks in layers. Their captain was the strong man of the party; him he placed in the stern of the boat, with another in his lap to hold him down. The others were disposed of in like manner, an insurance against too much liberty of action; the weapons went in the bow, out of reach of the strong man. "And when our men saw how I had placed them, they were willing to go without binding them."

It was then agreed to by all, that in case of resistance, no violence should be offered to the Turks until Thomas signified he could do no more, in which case every man might defend himself according to his own light. Then the eccentric boatload shoved off, five Turks securely holding down the other five, three Englishmen and a boy, armed with a carpenter's adz, a cooper's heading knife, an ax, and a boat-hook, the weapons of the Turks securely tied for delivery to the owners, Thomas "not being willing to keep anything of theirs."

Thomas's companions were very jumpy: "Every rock they made out to be a boat," and nearing the shore they cried out, "Lord have mercy on us there are Turks in the bushes." "They speaking so positively it seized me that I was possessed with fear. And as soon as the Turks saw that I was afraid, they all rose in the boat at once. This was one of the greatest straits that ever I was put to — not for fear of the Turks in the boat, but for fear of our men killing them, for I would not have killed a Turk or caused one to be killed for the whole world."

As his men hastily jumped to the conclusion that Thomas could do no more, he gave orders to take up such arms as they had. "Then I said to them, I would have you be as good as your word, for you promised you would do nothing till I said I could do no more. Now I desire you to keep to that. For there was nothing lacking but my word to kill the Turks."

Then "seeing there were no men in the bushes, that it was only imagination," he thought within himself, "It were better to strike a man than to cleave a man's head." With this happy and humane reflection "all fear was taken away, and life arose and courage increased again. I struck the captain a smart blow and bid him sit down, which he did instantly, and so did all the rest, without any more blows.

"Then I stepped forward and said to our men, Now you see what it is to be afraid; what shall we do now?"

Thoroughly unnerved, his men were for putting back to the ship. "Not so, said I, God willing I will put them on shore, for if we carry them on board there will be nothing but rising. For if it were my own case, I would rise ten times, and so will they."

So the crazy little craft steered toward the shore, put in not too close, and, within wading distance of the land, unloaded its inflammable freight into the cool water. "With signs of great kindness they took leave of us and jumped out not very wet. Then we put our boat close in and gave them about a hundred of bread and some other things, and hove all their arms ashore to them. (They were not above four miles from two towns, and forty from Algiers.) They would gladly have had us gone with them, telling us there was wine and many other things, and as far as it concerned myself I could have gone with them. So we parted in great love, and stayed till they had all gone up the hill. Then they shook their caps at us and we ours at them."

Thomas had given his conscience a loose rein, Providence had favored him with a clear track, the goal was made. The English crew turned joyfully homeward, devoutly praying that no further "concerns" would exercise the conscience of their intrepid mate. Rumors of these strange happenings blew into England before them, and "when we were coming up the River Thames, some boats went ahead of us, and King Charles and the Duke of York and many of his Lords being at Greenwich, it was told them that there was a Quaker ketch coming up the River, that had been taken by the Turks and had redeemed themselves, but had never a gun. As we got near to Greenwich, the King came down to our ship's side and discoursed the Master, and the King and the Duke of York asked me many questions."

The royal brothers were an unlikely pair to appreciate the Quaker scruples; King Charles had piously plotted the assassination of Cromwell; the Duke of York, when he came to the throne, allowed his queen to increase her pin money by the sale of Quakers and other undesirables. It was natural that they should stress the Quaker folly, rather than the pluck which had brought ship, crew, and cargo safely into port.

"You have done like a fool," the King frankly told the Quaker captain, "for you might have had good gain for them." And turning to Thomas, the real culprit, "You should have brought the Turks to me." The man of many conflicts was no more to be intimidated by a King than by a pirate. "I answered that I thought it better for them to be in their own country, at which they all smiled and went away. So I rest in that which can do good for evil, which should be the practice of all true men."

Here the Quaker chronicle drops Thomas; against all odds he had carried the Christian banner to victory, and justified the ways of God to man; there was no more to be said.

"In the meanwhile," we are told, "the name of Quakers came to be known at Algiers, as a people that might be trusted beyond others." A few years later we learn "concerning Quakers in Algiers, that were slaves there, they were suffered to go loose through the town; liberty was allowed them to meet for religious worship (a liberty denied them at home); their patrons themselves would sometimes come and see what they did; and finding no images as Papist slaves made use of, but hearing from their slaves that they reverently worshipped the living God, Creator of Heaven and Earth, they said it was very good and they might freely do so."

The word had been passed along through the bazaars that the Quakers were to be trusted, and they made many converts. These Christian soldier-slaves were invading the enemy country with the assistance of the enemy; King Charles's fools scored a great strategic triumph. Thomas Lurting was after all a practical idealist.

Mary Fisher—A Religious Maiden

Even in war, moral power is to physical as three parts out of four. — NAPOLEON BONAPARTE.

IN the way of Quaker audacity, Thomas Lurting might be supposed to have uttered the last word, a prerogative usually conceded to womankind. The Turks thrust themselves upon Thomas, and he was able to give a good account of himself; Mary Fisher, a Quaker girl, footed it across Europe alone, to confront an army of fifty thousand of them, the Sultan himself in command.

Mary was the product of the policy of George Fox, to whom the modern women's movement, if indeed it is modern, has yet to make proper acknowledgment of a great debt. The outstanding teaching of the Quaker heresy was the divine potentiality of every human soul, regardless of race, color, sex, or condition of servitude. If women manifested ability to minister to the growth of the divine life, let them minister, said Fox. Obviously the gifts of the spirit were impartially bestowed, and it was not for man to question the wisdom of his Maker, nor to bind what he had loosed.

Fox's radicalism went even further than the admission that women had spiritual gifts; he was willing to give them an equal chance with men for their development:

"I advised the setting up of a school for teaching boys; and also a women's school to be opened at Shacklewell for instructing girls and young maidens in whatsoever things were civil and useful in the creation."

In his stand for the rights of women, he went far beyond the spirit of his time, for he tells us he met "with a sort of people that held women have no souls, (adding in a light manner), No more than a goose. But I reproved them, and told them that was not right; for Mary said, 'My soul doth magnify the Lord.'" Some of his followers decided for schism, rather than follow their leader in his advanced views: "We met with much opposition from some who set themselves against women's meetings; which I was moved of the Lord to recommend to Friends, for the benefit of the Church of Christ, that faithful women being made partakers of the same precious faith, and heirs of the same everlasting gospel of life and salvation with men, might in like manner come into the possession and practice of the gospel order; so that all the family of God, women as well as men, might know, possess, perform and discharge their offices and services in the house of God."

In his pamphlet, "An Encouragement to All the Women's Meetings in the World," he brings the Old Testament to the support of his position: "In the time of the law, there were the assemblies of the women that were wise of heart to help in the work of the tabernacle, and Moses and Aaron and the seventy elders did not say to them: 'We can do our work by ourselves, and you are more fitter to be at home to wash the dishes,' or such like expressions; but did encourage them in the work and service of God."

On this question Fox, with his usual tenacity, stood his ground, with his back to the wall, defending the principle of equality before the Lord. In their meetings for worship and the exchange of spiritual experience, every Quaker, young or old, man or woman, master or servant, was at liberty to rise and let the Light shine. It was frequently necessary to exercise patience toward the faithful, and occasionally remonstrance or even discipline was considered expedient, but to none was the right of expression denied. In due time one whose ministry proved edifying to his own Meeting, was given a certificate of ministry, and as the ability to edify was the gift of God's free grace, the possessor looked for no other reward than the approval of the Giver.

A minister who was moved to carry his message further afield laid his "concern" before the Meeting; if it met with approval, he was given a certificate to other Meetings. All such ministers were received gladly by Friends everywhere, who provided for their entertainment.

The clergy, trained in the schools of theology, were scandalized when untrained and unpaid men presumed to invade their province. When the women followed, the scandal became insupportable. Vituperation was poured out upon the "she preachers." Neither comeliness, nor youth, nor extreme age, saved the women from the roughest usage, nor did rough usage save the clergy from their missionary zeal. Fox had no reason to regret his championship of the women; they proved the most adventurous and enduring of his fighters. Now after three centuries the wisdom of his policy is dawning upon civil governments.

Mary Fisher, "a religious maiden," entertained the ambitious idea of carrying the Christian gospel of peace and good will to the embattled Turks at Adrianople; no adventure was so daring as to be rejected by the Quaker mind. Like the Apostles, they believed in the imminence of God's universal Kingdom upon earth. Fearlessness and trust was the slogan of their band; under the command and direction of Omnipotence, as they believed themselves to be, they recognized no finite barrier to their activity.

It was their strategy to attack the powers of darkness in their strongest positions, and throughout Europe the reputation of the Turks was of the blackest; of all heathen powers they were the most obnoxious, for, in addition to being heathen, they possessed a very efficient military organization, with the will and skill to use it. Already Europe was glaring with covetous eyes at the wealth of the East; already the Turk was a problem, and all Christian countries maintained a propaganda against him.

It is one of the staggering curiosities of history that in France, where seventy thousand Huguenots were put to the sword overnight, and forty thousand more fled, leaving all their worldly goods behind in their haste to escape indiscriminate slaughter; and in Spain, where, for some slight deviation from the accepted creed, men were tortured and impaled on spikes to prolong their dying agonies, the popular imagination could always be fired by tales of the heathen cruelties of the Turk, and Christian armies raised to exterminate them.

Mary Fisher no doubt believed the worst of these tales, a belief which decided her to do something about it; her scheme met with the approval of the Society of Friends. For although a young woman, and, as we infer from the casual remark of the experienced Turkish Emperor, with no small degree of feminine charm, Mary was a veteran who might have worn the Distinguished Service Medal, if her sect had countenanced such vain and worldly honor. A year and a half of her youth had been passed in a Yorkshire jail, and as a prison sentence too often amounted to a death sentence, her survival implied the necessary qualifications for hard service.

Persecution only hardened Mary's moral fiber; she left prison determined to attack that most impregnable fortress of learning and tradition, Cambridge University. Accompanied by a sober woman of fifty, Mary endeavored to direct the attention of the students to the disparity between their unseemly behavior and the conduct becoming to professing Christians.

"Whereupon the Scholars began to mock and deride

them. The women, observing the Froth and Levity of their Behavior, told them they were antichrist, and that their College was a cage of Unclean Birds and the synagogue of Satan. Such severe Reprehensions are usually most offensive to those who most deserve them."

The reprehensions were very offensive to the students, who complained to the Mayor of their outspoken critics, and the women were jailed. The Mayor himself was not above using plain language and calling a spade by name when occasion required. "He demanded their Husbands Names: They told him they had no Husband but Jesus Christ, and He sent them. Upon this the Mayor grew angry and called them Whores, and issued a warrant to the Constable to whip them at the Market-Cross till the Blood ran down their Bodies. The Executioner commanded them to put off their clothes, which they refused. Then he stript them naked to the Waste, and put their Arms into the Whipping post, and executed the Mayor's Warrant far more cruelly than is usually done to the worst Malefactors."

Beaten and bloody though they were, they were by no means deprived of the use of speech, nor frightened into silence. "As they were led back to the Town, they exhorted the People to fear God, not Man, telling them that this was but the beginning of the Sufferings of the People of God. They were thrust out of the Town, no Man daring to show them any Countenance, or give them any Relief, for though many did secretly commiserate their Case, yet none had the Courage to oppose the Current of popular Prejudice, and the misapplied Power of the Magistrate."

Mary had the courage which is nourished on opposition; her thoughts now turned to New England, where the pious Puritans were reveling in misapplied power, and exhibiting to the world an excellent imitation of the tyranny which had driven them out of England. There were no Quakers in New England when Mary invaded the sacred pale of Puritanism, then under the sway of the vindictive and implacable Governor Endicott; there were, however, some who held views not unlike the Quaker principles. Anne Hutchinson had already been driven out of the colony for expressing opinions disapproved by the ruling theocracy, leaving behind her many intimidated sympathizers, a condition of affairs which attracted the notice of the Quakers.

In company with Anne Austin, Mary landed in New England, or rather her vessel anchored there, but that was as far as she got; before their feet touched the Land of the Free, they were taken into custody and hustled off to prison. The window of their cell was boarded up, that none might be contaminated by speaking to them; heavy penalties were imposed on any who should so much as attempt to communicate with them. Although they had been arrested on board the ship that carried them, before they had opportunity to utter a word, they were charged with holding "dangerous, heretical and blasphemous opinions," so extremely dangerous in fact, that the custodians of the New England conscience ordered that "none be admitted to Communication with them without Leave of the Governor . . . to prevent their spreading their corrupt Opinions," until such time as opportunity offered to transport them as far as possible from the "Holy Land of New England."

Meantime, pending deportation, certain officials obtained leave to be admitted to their cell, who stripped the women quite naked, and searched for marks of witchcraft with such indecency "that modesty forbids to mention it." It was their good fortune, however, that Governor Endicott had gone off on a journey to Salem, an absence which he very much regretted, for said he, "If I had been there, I would have had them well whipped." Alas, poor Endicott! There was thundering in England, and the lightning was soon to strike him.

According to the Body of the Liberties of the Colony: "No man's life shall be taken away, no man's honor or good name shall be stained, no man's person shall be arrested, restrained, banished, dismembered, nor any ways punished; . . . no man's goods or estate shall be taken away from him, nor any way indamaged under color of law or countenance of authority, unless it be by virtue or equity of some express law of the country warranting the same, established by the General Court . . . *or in case of a defect of a law in any particular case, by the word of God.*"

The Mosaic law, the Word of God, allowed its Puritan interpreters a wide margin for severity.

An order in council was issued as a warning to ship captains:

"Whereas there are several Laws, long since made and published in this jurisdiction, bearing Testimony against Heretics and erroneous Persons, yet notwithstanding Simon Kemthorn, of Charles-Town, Master of the ship Swallow of Boston, hath brought into this Jurisdiction . . . two women . . . Anne, the Wife of one Austin, and Mary Fisher, being the Sort of People commonly known by the Name of Quakers, who upon Examination are found not only to be Transgressors of the former Laws, but do hold very dangerous, heretical and blasphemous Opinions, and they do also acknowledge that they came here purposely to propagate their said Errors and Heresies, bringing with them, and spreading here sundry Books, wherein are contained most corrupt, heretical and blasphemous Doctrines, contrary to the Truth of the Gospel professed among us,

"The Council therefore, tendering the Preservation of the Peace and Truth enjoyed and professed among the Churches of Christ in this Country, do hereby order,

"First, That all such corrupt Books . . . be forthwith burned and destroyed by the common Executioner.

"Secondly, That the said Anne and Mary be kept in close Prison and none admitted to Communication with them . . . until such Time as they be delivered aboard some Vessel to be Transported out of the Country.

"Thirdly, That the said Simon Kemthorn is hereby enjoined, speedily and directly to transport . . . the said Persons from hence . . . he defraying all the Charges of their Imprisonment, and for the effectual Performance hereof, he is to give Security in a Bond of one Hundred Pounds Sterling, and on his Refusal to give such Security he is to be committed to Prison till he do it."

This order in Council was effective, in so far as it related to ship captains; no Quaker would deny his religion, and no captain would carry one who acknowledged it. The Quakers were obliged to land as far south as Virginia and walk up to Massachusetts.

In the background of the Quaker stories, we usually find some courageous figure, hazily sketched in. In this case one Nicholas Upshall, "an old inhabitant of Boston, and a member of their church there," was the untrammeled spirit who braved old Endicott's rage, set at naught the penalties of the Court, and slipped the jailer five shillings a week, for the privilege of getting enough food in to the prisoners to ward off starvation. We shall have the pleasure of encountering Nicholas again, on his way out of Massachusetts.

The first outgoing vessel carried the blasphemous heretics back to England, via Barbados, minus their personal effects, which the jailer retained for his fees. Only for the moment was the theological purity of New England safeguarded from Quaker error; within the week after the deportation of the women, nine others landed to carry on.

Forced to relinquish to others the task of overcoming Puritan reluctance to the Light, Mary now turned to the darkness of the Near East. Her experience with the tender mercies of the righteous may have made the infidel Turkish terror seem rather faded. At any rate, the indefatigable young woman now heard the call of God, or as Sewel cautiously puts it, "so she believed," to deliver to the Turks the Divine message scornfully rejected by the Christians. In her former campaigns Mary had the support of a companion, on this most venturesome of all, she went alone.

Less than a year after Mary had been shipped out of Boston, we find her at Zante with a party of three men and three women. The division of their forces is unexplained, and may have been due to consular interference, for the missionary enterprise of the Quakers made that branch of the English government an active service in the Orient, if we may judge by the wails of the embassy at Constantinople: "Nor are all our troubles from without us: some are, as I may say, from amongst and within us, occasioned by a generation of people crept in unawares called Quakers, three whereof not long since arrived here from Zante by way of Morea. I friendly warned them to return, which the two women did quietly, but John Buckley refusing, I was constrained to ship him hence upon the *Lewis*."

Whatever the reason, Mary started off alone for an interview with the Sultan. Her onward march as a Christian soldier was rudely interrupted at Smyrna by the vigilance of the English consul, who regarded with extreme disfavor conferences between religious maidens and heathen potentates; consuls in heathen lands had no intention of adding the quibbles of Christianity to the perplexities of diplomacy. Mary was led to a ship headed west, and went quietly; as he wished her *bon voyage*, the consul washed his hands of the affair with a sense of duty well performed.

He had incorrectly taken the measure of the docile Quaker lady. Cut off in her approach by sea, Mary decided to execute a flank movement by land, and persuaded the captain to set her ashore at the first port he touched. From this point it was six hundred miles to Adrianople where Sultan Mahomet IV lay encamped with his great army, six hundred miles over the mountains and wild lands of Greece and Macedonia! Neither distance nor obstacles could stay a messenger of the Most High, before whose faith mountains at command must be removed into the midst of the sea.

Alone and afoot, without a word of the language, Mary blithely started off. Unfortunately, there is not a line in the voluminous Quaker records relating to the adventures of that journey. Mary was under orders; she carried them out and made a safe return, to the glory of God; further details were superfluous. As the records are usually Histories of Sufferings, it may be assumed that her journey was uneventful in that respect.

Mahomet IV was in the field with the army, but that luxurious potentate was not roughing it. Surrounded by his great nobles and councilors, he was camping in oriental splendor. Mary tried to persuade some of the citizens of Adrianople to keep her company to the camp of the Sultan, but found none with sufficient courage to venture. She was obliged to go alone, "and procured information to be made to the Grand Vizier's tent, that there was an English-woman who had something to declare from the Great God to the Sultan, who sent her word that she should speak with him the next morning."

The Grand Vizier was renowned for his opposition to petticoat influence in the affairs of his master, the petticoats to which he objected being no doubt of another color than Quaker gray. There is no explanation of Mary's mysteriously quick conquest of the great man's prejudices; all we learn is, that a religious maiden, carrying a message from the Lord, met with much gentler treatment from the Turks than from the New England Christians. The girl with a lingering memory of the Christian courtesies of Massachusetts, and whose body was still scarred from the wounds inflicted by the students in the Battle of Cambridge, must have been overcome with astonishment at the kindness and respect shown her by the infidels.

One would like to know how Mary managed to make a presentable appearance at that splendid court after six hundred miles of rather rough travel. We do know that, fresh and alert after her long tramp, the Quaker girl came into the imperial presence, and was received by the Sultan with the ceremony accorded to an ambassador of a king, all the Turkish nobility in attendance.

"The Sultan asked her, Whether it was so as he had heard, that she had a message from the Lord? She answered, Yea. Then he bade her speak on (having three interpreters by him) and when she stood silent a little, waiting on the Lord when to speak, he supposing she might be fearful to utter her mind before them all, asked her, Whether she desired that any of them might go out before she spake? She answered, Nay."

The young woman who had so often stared death out of countenance was not at all abashed in the presence of the mighty Sultan. The scriptural frugality of her speech, which he so mistakenly attributed to the natural timidity of her sex, was merely the mental poise of the Quaker before the verbal leap; once started Mary held her high record for volubility.

"Then the Sultan bade her speak the word of the Lord to them, and not to fear, for they had good hearts and could bear it, and strictly charged her to speak the word she had from the Lord, neither more nor less, for they were willing to hear it, be it what it would."

Quaker missionaries, spreading their unwelcome doctrines over the world, were always prepared for the worst. The pleasant surprise of a reception so free from suspicion, and these agreeable encouragements, doubtless limbered up Mary's tongue, and evoked her most effective oratory. Before the assembled magnificence of the Turkish Empire, she spoke, and "all gave diligent attention with much gravity and seriousness till she had done, and then the Sultan asked her, Whether she had anything more to say. She asked, Whether he had understood what she said. He replied, Yes, every word: Adding that it was the truth, and desired her to stay in that country, saying, that they could not but respect such a one as had taken so much pains to come to them so far as from England with a message from the Lord."

When Mary had fully unburdened herself, the Turks were given a chance, and questioned her as to what she thought of their prophet Mahomet. Considering the treatment she had received from his followers, it seems likely that she suddenly thought better of him; certainly she could not meet such unaccustomed courtesy with rudeness: "She answered warily that she knew him not, but Christ that enlightened every man who came into the world, Him she knew. . . . And concerning Mahomet she said, they might judge him to be false or true according to the words and prophecies which he spake. The Turks confessed this to be true." Mary was a diplomat as well as a soldier.

Her mission so successfully accomplished, it was her

desire to be off to Constantinople, and the Sultan ordered a military escort to conduct her on her journey, "which she not accepting, but trusting to the arm of the Lord, who had brought her safe hither, to conduct her back again, he told her, It was dangerous travelling, especially for such a one as she, and wondered she had passed safe so far as she had, saying, It was respect and kindness to her that he offered her a guard, and that he would not for anything she should come to hurt in his dominions."

Nor did she, for "having performed her mission, she departed from the camp to Constantinople, without a guard, whither she came without the least hurt or scoff, the Turks in this behalf receiving her message with far more respect and civility than she had often met with from those who covered themselves with a profession of Christianity. And so she returned to England."

It is interesting to note that, in Quaker biographies, the Turks appear at no moral disadvantage in comparison with the Christians of their time. Generally speaking, the Quakers seem to have fared better in heathen than in Christian lands, which no doubt confirmed their belief that there was no darkness to which the True Light had not penetrated.

We should like to follow Mary's subsequent career, but the details of her later life are meager; it seems to have been one of approved domesticity, varied by persecution, in which her husband shared. On her return to England she married William Bayley, a seafaring man and a Quaker preacher of her own stripe. Bayley accompanied George Fox on his missionary tour of the American colonies, and while her husband went forth battling for the Lord, Mary busied herself with her young brood.

Bayley died at sea, desiring those about him, " to remember my love to my dear wife; she will be a sorrowful widow. But let her not mourn too much, for it is well with me." Not for long did Mary remain a sorrowful widow; some years later she became the happy wife of John Crosse, and with husband and children emigrated to America. Others of her sect had meanwhile brought the New England theocracy to terms, and Mary was " clear " to settle down in peace in South Carolina. Notwithstanding the extreme hardships they endured, many of the Quaker Amazons lived to a great age; Mary was seventy-four when she was gathered to her reward. It is supposed that her mortal remains rest in the Quaker cemetery at Charleston; it is to be hoped that, in her descendants, her free and unconquerable spirit goes marching on.

Katherine Evans and Sarah Chevers

The tale is one of an evil time,
When souls were fettered and thought was crime,
And heresy's whisper above its breath
Meant shameful scourging and bonds and death!

Oh woman, at ease in these happier days,
Forbear to judge of thy sister's ways;
How much thy beautiful life may owe
To her faithful courage thou canst not know,
Nor how from the paths of thy calm retreat
She smoothed the thorns with her bleeding feet.

— WHITTIER.

KATHERINE EVANS and Sarah Chevers, a pair of respectable wives and mothers, contribute a twin biography to the Quaker Chronicle of Sufferings. These women had no occasion to look about for a moral substitute for war; the temper of their time supplied it, and they acquitted themselves as good soldiers.

A brief mention of the first campaign of this pair occurs in Sewel's History: "I find that Scotland was early visited by Katherine Evans and Sarah Chevers, two eminent women, of whom something extraordinary is to be related in due time." The dour Scotch Calvinists put up a stout resistance to the Quaker invasion, and the two women were therefore well seasoned soldiers when in 1658 they heard the East a-calling.

"Having drawings in their minds to travel to Alexandria," they took ship, and after a month of tempestuous tossing on the sea arrived in Leghorn, where they were refreshed among English Friends. In whatever quarter of the world they were called to fight, the Quakers invariably found a detachment of their own troops; their morale was strengthened by the congenial association of spiritual kin, among the best things that life has to offer.

Taking leave of their good Friends in Leghorn, the two women embarked on a Dutch boat bound for Alexandria, but it was not destined that their Light should be kindled in the darkness of Egypt. The vacillation of the Dutch captain resulted in their being set down in Malta, a citadel of the Roman Church, where it was their misfortune to fall into the hands of that power.

Premonition or prevision was commonly claimed by the early Quakers, and as the coast of Malta was sighted, Katherine was seized with such anguish that she cried out: "Oh we have a dreadful cup to drink in that place." And standing on the deck of the ship, and looking upon the people who stood upon the walls she said in her heart, "Shall ye destroy us? If we give up to the Lord then He is sufficient to deliver us out of your hands; but if we disobey God, all these could not deliver us out of His hand. So all fear of man was taken from them."

On landing they made the acquaintance of the English consul, a timorous, uncertain soul, who does not present a very heroic picture. Full of fear and encouragement to caution, he warned them that the dreaded Inquisition was in eruption. This information was far from producing the desired effect on his countrywomen; they saw only the hand of Providence diverting them from Alexandria, that the Light might flash in the greater darkness of Malta, and, against the trembling entreaties of the consul, the torch bearers sallied forth.

In the northern countries through which the Reformation had run like wildfire, the Pope rivaled the Turk for first place among national hatreds. The hatred of the Papacy combined the venom of political and religious animosity; for the Pope was not only the head of an aggressive religious organization which contested every inch of ground, he was a temporal sovereign as well, and a dreaded political power, during the period of the fiercest struggle for political freedom.

So the two Friends found themselves in the heart of the enemy country, and the plucky pair, in the hardihood of their faith in an invincible God and "the power of an endless life," determined to give battle. Heedless of the consul's protests, they set out to exhort the Islanders to repentance and Christian charity. Under the very eye of the Inquisition they distributed their literature, protesting against persecution, and giving arguments for the faith that was in them, bestowing their tracts, which were printed in many languages, impartially on the English consul, the nuns in the convent and the man in the street.

The Governor of Malta inclined to befriend the

strangers; he had a sister, a nun in the convent, he said, who desired to speak with them. With characteristic reticence, our chronicle gives no hint of the motive of the nun, nor of the result of the interview. That there was no sinister design on the part of the Governor is certain, for when the English consul, terrified for his own safety, suggested that his zealous visitors be safely jailed, the Governor would not hear of it. "They are honest women," was the reason he gave for leaving them at large.

No plea can be made for the decorum of the two women, the situation called for courage rather than etiquette, and with this they were abundantly supplied. Their methods would now be classed as disorderly conduct, if noticed at all, punishable with a small fine, or at most a few days' imprisonment. At that time their crime was heresy and sedition, punishable with torture and death.

For a time the Holy Office was nonplused; accustomed to hunt down heretics, they were at a loss how to take this pair of weak women who so deliberately thrust their heads into the noose. Not peace, but a sword was the Quaker contribution to the life of that quiet town; great was the furore as the sympathies of the populace divided, many favoring the disturbers, while others cried, "Fire, fire!" signifying the stake. The Holy Office was compelled to take the disturbers of the peace into custody on a charge of sedition; for in that day not the State but the Church was the sacred abstraction, and opposition of the individual conscience to the omniscient decrees of power is always and everywhere sedition.

Considering his calling and the clerical behavior of that time, the Lord Inquisitor does not on the whole appear to have been a bad sort, but rather decently humane, the victim of his organization. As the more bloodthirsty monks of the Inquisition pointed out, his failure to deal properly with heretics would have cost him his own head, which he quite naturally had no desire to part with.

The Quaker trials are all tragically amusing, with a lesson for fundamentalists, which they little like to take to heart; old Father Time has a limbo into which he has swept many fundamentals. The die-hard fundamentalist of today would hardly venture to disturb the peace by raising the question, Did Mary the mother of Jesus remain a virgin? After the lapse of time it is hardly credible that the good monks were vitally interested in the answer; the real issue, for which all the babble was but a smoke screen, was the right of the ecclesiastical organization to dictate belief, and to enforce submission to its dictates on pain of death. The Quaker insistence on the immediate relation of the individual soul to its Maker was a blow at the organization; the ecclesiastics, acting as intermediary between God and man, finding their power both pleasant and profitable, were loath to relinquish it.

In the case of these women, the Inquisition moved with unusual caution. It may be that the pious and immortal memory of the Great Protector was still potent, or that the tolerant Governor was only one of a strong moderate party which the Church had no desire to rouse, or that the steady supply of Jews and Turks was sufficient to feed the fires and demonstrate the awful power of the Church. Whatever the restraining influence, the women escaped the rack and the stake, though constantly threatened with both. The Lord Inquisitor seemed desirous of making the easiest terms possible to be rid of them; any act symbolizing submission to the Papal power, kissing the cross, or receiving the Holy Sacrament as the real body of Christ, and the prison doors would be opened. Resistance to compulsion in spiritual matters, however, was the whole aim and object of the Quaker war, submission to dictation meant defeat; the women refused to lower their colors. "You may kill us," was the war-cry of their band; "the truth you shall never conquer."

As mothers of young families, Katherine and Sarah did not rush toward the fires of martyrdom with undue haste, nor as advance guards of the truth did they strain the detective abilities of their judges. Freely and boldly they proclaimed their beliefs and insisted on their right to hold them.

"If ye would do but a little," mourned the friars, "ye would be set at liberty; but you will do nothing at all, but are against everything." In answer to which they expressed a willingness to do anything that might tend to the glory of God.

"You are possessed," cried the monks in despair.

"We are," they admitted, "by the power of an endless life."

One imaginative brother had the happy thought that they were obstinate from fear, and to help matters along, suggested that they might make an outward show of their national religion, while secretly remaining Catholics. If they had required proof that they were in the toils of the painted Babylonish woman, this ill-advised brother supplied it.

The pious monks seem to have found endless satisfaction in predicting their eventual and eternal fate as heretics, while the women extracted such gratification as the circumstances afforded by entangling the brothers in their own admissions. Cross examination and discussion they welcomed as opportunities for putting over Quaker propaganda.

"Make yourself a Catholic, and have freedom to go where you will," one was urged.

"Thou hast Catholics enough already," was Katherine's retort. "Endeavor to bring some of them to the Light in their own consciences, that they may stand in awe, and sin not." The monk would willingly lose one of his fingers, he said, if she and Sarah would become Catholics. "Then she told him, it was Babylon that was built with blood, but Zion was redeemed by judgment."

It was generously admitted by the monks that their prisoners were possessed of all the virtues. "Ye are good women, but there is no redemption for you except ye will be Catholics."

"When told that we were Heretics and Heathens, we said, 'They were Heretics that lived in sin and wickedness, and such were Heathen that knew not God.'

"One said he would give me to the Devil. I said I did not fear all the Devils in Hell, and that though he had the Inquisition with all the countries round about on his side, and I was alone by myself, I did not fear them."

Repartee, however, only occasionally lightened the terrible sufferings of the four years of imprisonment. In an airless room, in that unaccustomed hot climate, "we were fain to rise often out of Bed, and lie down at a Chink of the Door for Air to fetch Breath, and with the fire within (fever) and the Heat without, our Skin was like Sheep's Leather, and the Hair did fall from our Heads. We desired to die, but Death fled from us. We did eat our Bread with Weeping, and mingled our Drink with our tears."

Death seemed so near that the prudently feminine Sarah "did dress her hair as she would lie in the grave." Still there was no visible progress made in the taming process; they wrote to the Inquisitors, "If it was our blood they did thirst after, they might take it any other Way, as well as smother us up in that hot room." The punishment for this presumption fitted the crime; their writing materials were taken from them, their copies of the Bible having already been confiscated, a book, it was claimed, that had sent thousands to hell.

Gnats added their small but effective contribution to the discomforts of the prison, and Katherine's face became so swollen from the stings that the monks spied an evil spirit in it. They were further convinced that the women "corrupted each other"; they were separated and condemned to the most dreaded of prison punishments, solitary confinement, and subjected to every trick of the third degree; each was told that the other had "confessed all." They had little faith in the veracity of their jailers; Katherine was so frequently moved to tell the monks they were lying, that they assumed she possessed occult power, and declared her a witch. In the good old days it was dangerous to be less stupid than one's neighbors.

Katherine was prostrated by a fever which dampened even her proselyting ardor and disabled her ready tongue. An amiable brother coming into her cell and finding her so strangely dumb inquired: "Is the devil so great in you that you cannot speak?" She mustered up sufficient strength to retort: "Depart from me, thou worker of iniquity." The first impulse of the good man was to seize his crucifix to strike her on the mouth; on second thought he went instead to Sarah to complain of the insult to his cloth, that her fellow heretic had called him a worker of iniquity.

"Did she?" inquired Sarah. "And art thou without

sin?" He believed he was. "Then," said Sarah judicially, "she hath wronged thee."

The story offers an interesting study in the variety and eccentricity of human behavior; priests who without a scruple would have led their prisoners to the stake, were sincerely grieved when they could not persuade them to share a fat hen or a bottle of wine, or otherwise indulge in the fleshpots of Egypt. It might be they desired to crucify the flesh, the brothers reasoned, and willing to encourage the laudable intent, one offered to lend the whips with which they drove out their sins. "They said they did whip themselves till the blood came. But we said, That could not reach the Devil, he sat upon the Heart." To four years of incessant pleading the women returned but one answer: they could not change their minds "if they would burn us to ashes, or chop us as Herbs for the pot."

The most human of the weird aggregation of pious men was the Lord Inquisitor himself. When the physician announced that the women were dying for want of fresh air, the Lord Inquisitor gave orders that their cells be opened for six hours daily. When the indignant monks ran to report to him the pert replies of the women, he laughed; and at the final parting his behavior was extremely courteous.

From the cruelty of religious bigotry, one turns with relief to a pleasanter picture of the human animal. At great risk to themselves, the poor workmen who were enlarging the Inquisition prison did many kindnesses to the Friends, constantly smuggling letters between them. In one of these Katherine put Sarah on her guard against the wiles of the harsh English friar, painting his character in no bright colors. As it happened, he himself intercepted the letter; in his wrath he went to Katherine's cell and confronted her with it, asking her if she could read it.

"Yea," said she calmly, "I writ it."

"Oh, did you indeed," said the friar, "and what is it you say of me?"

"Nothing but the truth," was the frank reply.

"He said I must tell what Man it was that brought me the Ink, or else I should be tied with chains presently. I told him I had done nothing but what was just and right in the Sight of God, and what I did suffer would be for the Truth's sake, and I did not care: I would not meddle nor make with the poor Workmen."

Then there were the bluff English ship captains, not themselves Quakers, but unfailingly friendly to them, and with stiff backbones to oppose injustice. One came into port with an Irish friar, who went beyond the safety line to put his shoulder to the wheel of the Inquisition, probably on the theory that one good turn deserves another, for in the cruel Irish wars the impartiality of Quaker philanthropy was well known. The captain and the friar did their unavailing best, "but the Captain saw it was a very hard Thing, so that it grieved him to the

Heart. He prayed God to comfort us, and went away, and we do beseech God . . . to never let him go without a Blessing from Him for his Love. He did venture himself exceedingly in this Place."

But the palm is borne away by "a poor young Englishman," who had been captured by the Turks, and recaptured by Christian soldiers. Confronted by his last captors with the alternative, "Our religion or your life," he expediently became a good Catholic, for all religions by that time must have looked alike to him. His chivalry was stirred by the sad plight of his countrywomen; on the forlorn hope of rendering some assistance, he scaled their dungeon walls and succeeded in communicating with them before he was detected and assigned to a cell himself. With their usual gloom the monks dropped in on the women to speculate on the probable fate of their brash young friend; burning at the stake was the most hopeful outlook they had to offer. Fortunately, they were but indifferent prophets; the young man was soon released. Sarah prayed that the Lord for his love would preserve him to everlasting life, and every heart that lifts to a gallant deed will heartily say, Amen.

Finally the scene was enlivened by the presence of one Daniel Baker, a fighting Quaker. By the ever watchful eye of diplomacy, Daniel, too, had been frustrated in his ambition to enlighten the Turks. He with another Friend came to a halt at Constantinople, for, says our narrative:

"This testimony of theirs, however *christian*, meek, humble and inoffensive, as was also their Behaviour and Deportment, was received with Scorn and Indignation, especially by the Professors of *Christianity* in those Parts (for the Turks, Jews and Greeks, did not appear altogether so ill affected toward them). A Message was forthwith sent from Smyrna to Constantinople, to the *English* Ambassadour, beseeching him to expel them out of *Asia*, with which he complied, as appears by the following Warrant.

"*To our Loving Friend*, Anthony Isaacson, *Esq;* Consul *for the* English *Nation* at Smyrna.

"'Whereas we are informed that there is lately arrived with the Zant Frigate one Daniel Baker with his companion, commonly called Quakers, with intention to come to this port, and because we sufficiently have had Experience that the Carriage of that Sort of People is ridiculous, and is capable to bring Dishonor to our Nation, besides other Inconveniences that may redound to them in particular, and to the *English* in general.

"'We therefore will and require you to give a Stop to the said *Quakers* from proceeding any farther in their Journey, either to *Constantinople* or the present Court of the grand Seignior (*viz.* the great Emperor of the *Turks*) or to any other Place where our Authority extends, shipping them away either directly for *England*, or any other Port for which they shall chuse to embark.

"'And we do hereby require all Officers and Members of the Fraternity, and Masters and Officers of Ships, to be aiding and assisting you herein: And for so doing this shall be your Warrant.

"'Given under our Hand and Seal at our Court at *Pera* of *Constantinople*, the 19th Day of July 1661

"'*By his Excellency's Command.*

"'PAUL RICOAT, *Secretary.*'"

By his Excellency's command, therefore, Daniel was marooned on the Island of Zante, where it was hoped that his ridiculous carriage would give the least trouble. "But during his stay in that place, he inwardly felt drawings toward Malta, to try whether he could be helpful to Katherine and Sarah that were prisoners there."

Into the lion's den at Malta Daniel walked boldly, not as a suppliant, and confronted the Lord Inquisitor in excellent Italian, crowding his whole story into one meaty sentence: "I am come to demand the just liberty of my innocent Friends, the two English-women in prison in the Inquisition."

By reason of much importunity the Lord Inquisitor had become peevish; he longed to be rid of a white elephant, and was willing to compromise on a pecuniary basis, but "they should lie in prison till they died," he said, "unless some English merchants who were able would give obligation for three or four thousand dollars that they would never return thither." English mer-

WILLIAM PENN AT THE AGE OF 22

chants who were able were more considerate of their money than the poor young Englishman of his life; nor would any Quaker pledge his word to restrict his activity to places where he was welcome; nor would Daniel or his two Friends agree that one penny of tribute should go into the coffers of Babylon.

Mystical as to religion, Daniel was canny enough in the management of mundane affairs. During his short stay he succeeded, in spite of inquisitorial vigilance, in getting letters through to the prisoners, and receiving in return letters for their Friends in England and Ireland. Some of these "were intercepted, and communicated to the *Popish* Lord Inquisitor, who forthwith sent for *the English Consul*, and charged him to get them copied out. The Consul was very angry with the said *Daniel Baker* about it; but to pacify him, *Daniel* proposed to him, that *if he thought the copying of them too much trouble, he would copy them truly for him*, which the Consul agreeing to, the said *Daniel* transcribed fair Copies of them, which he delivered to the Consul's Hands for the Lord Inquisitor, *and kept the original Papers himself*, which he brought over with him to *England*." A triumph of the terrible meek.

He also succeeded in communicating personally with his Friends "both to comfort and exhort them to steadfastness, . . . and for a time as they stood at the prison gate, he being come in their sight saluted them in these words, 'The Holy Body of God's elect, right dearly beloved, own your testimony, and ye are a sweet savour unto the Lord and His people.' "

Daniel had one last try at the Lord Inquisitor, a proposal that his life be taken, and the two mothers sent home to their families. His Lordship hoped it would be his lot never to encounter a Quaker again, and would listen to no terms but a bond guaranteeing him relief for the future. Daniel had spent three weeks in Malta. " He frequently visited the Prisoners with the Hazard of his Life . . . and although he was daily threatened with the Inquisition, and followed to and fro by their Officers, yet . . . he was preserved out of their Hands, and afterward returned to *England* where we find him imprisoned for his Testimony among other Friends in Newgate."

Katherine and Sarah were now left to the cheerful society of the monks. Meanwhile, George Fox had been busy in England; encouraging his followers to the supreme sacrifice, which he himself was always ready to make, Fox was no advocate of martyrdom for its own sake. While the least of the brethren suffered slavery in freedom's cause, Fox was untiring in his efforts for their release. Unalterably opposed to the principles of the Roman Church, the Quakers vigorously opposed the persecution of its members; they were willing to give the toleration they demanded. Moreover, a dead Catholic could not be " convinced "; while there was life there was argument. Relying on their clean record for fair play all round, Fox appealed to Lord d'Aubigny, an English

Catholic nobleman with influence at Rome, to cut the red tape of the Inquisition and set his Friends free. Incidentally he took the occasion to air his views: "G. Fox had now opportunity to reason with this Lord (who was a Roman Catholic priest in orders) about religion, and brought him to confess that Christ enlightened every man that cometh into the world with His spiritual light. Then G. Fox asked him what the Romanists would do with all their relics and images, if they did own and believe in this light? He answered that those things were but policies to keep the people in subjection."

In spite of religious differences, the obliging Lord d'Aubigny got the word through to Rome, which was relayed to Malta, to the great relief of the Lord Inquisitor, who was instructed to set his captive Quakers free.

So ended the long imprisonment — nearly four years — with good will all round. In gratitude for many kindnesses, the women divided what money they had with the poor workmen. The Inquisitor waived payment of prison fees, which were then customary: "He took leave very courteously of them and wished them a prosperous return to their own country; so did likewise the magistrates and inferior officers." With flying colors and all the honors of war, the two prisoners marched out of jail, and made the homeward journey in the manner of a triumphal procession.

"At length came one of the King of England's frigates

called the Sapphire, commanded by Captain Titswel, who took them in, together with some Knights of Malta, among whom was the Inquisitor's own brother."

After four years of captivity these women had earned a furlough; they might well have called it a successful campaign and let it rest at that, but that thought never occurred to them.

"Departing from Malta they came to Leghorn, where the merchants showed them great kindness, and sent them wine and other things for their refreshment, proffering them also money, but they were unwilling to accept it.

"From thence they came to Tangier. This place was at that time besieged by the Moors, yet Katherine and Sarah entered the town, and many came flocking into the house where they lodged, for they boldly exhorted the people to depart from wickedness. They also went to the Governor, who was courteous to them, and took their admonitions in good part, and promised to follow their counsel. And he would have given them money, but they took none, though they accepted his love; for he commanded that none of the garrison should abuse them in word or deed.

"They being *inclined to go out to the Moors*, desired the Governor to let them go forth, but he told them that they must expect from that savage people nothing but cruel death or bonds forever; and though they signified to him that they believed the Lord would preserve them, yet the Governor in a friendly manner withheld them from going. Being thus stopped, they believed the Lord accepted of their good will."

He, at any rate, made no further test of their courage either by Moorish armies or by Roman Inquisition. The Inquisitor's brother, who had embarked on the *Sapphire* at Malta, showed them much friendly attention, and " spoke often to the Captain that they might not want for anything that was in his ship, and told them that if they came to Malta again they should not be persecuted so. And to the Captain he said, ' If they go to heaven one way and we another, yet shall we all meet together at last.' " Which was rank heresy and sedition in the very household of faith; their accusers said well, they were dangerous women; into the established order of Malta they had forced the thin edge of the wedge of a new order.

William Penn—An Undesirable

To be ignorant of the lives of the most celebrated men of antiquity is to remain in a state of childhood all our days.

— Plutarch.

The way to fame is like the way to heaven — through much tribulation.

— Sterne.

By the whimsy of a humorous and ironical Fate, the only authentic portrait of the great pacifist statesman, the most celebrated of all the Quakers, represents the Founder of Pennsylvania as an aristocratic youth, of rather saintly countenance, heavily armored in a coat of mail. It is a relic of Penn's unregenerate soldier days, before he joined the sect which frowned on war and on portraiture of the creature.

The Quaker ranks were principally recruited from the sturdy homespun class, for they naturally rise against an irksome social system who find the sitting least comfortable. The most romantic figure in the romantic era of Quakerism was not born to the homespun; the heir of the wily and prosperous Admiral Sir William Penn opened his infant eyes on fabrics of purple and fine linen, and fed from a silver spoon.

As a child he cried unto the Lord, and before he was twelve he believed that a voice in his own soul had answered that cry. Loyal and affectionate as a youth, he nevertheless blazed for himself an independent spiritual trail, which he followed with the immovable obstinacy of the gentle, to the disgust and disappointment of the imperious and ambitious Admiral, his father.

When William had come as far on his way as Oxford University, he discovered that his trail was not the path to favor with the conservative faculty of that stronghold of tradition. His chosen companions, a small unpopular minority of independent youths, thought to roughly jostle the University out of its rut. The attempt was unsuccessful, and although young Penn disclaimed any part in the rowdyism of his set, the faculty seized on a convenient excuse for relieving Oxford of his undesirable presence. They intimated to the Admiral their willingness to have his son continue his education elsewhere. The parting was mutually satisfactory; in his earliest break into authorship, Penn characterized universities as "signal places for idleness, profaneness, prodigality and *gross ignorance.*"

A worldly, showy, ambitious gentleman was Sir William Penn, and no mean diplomat withal. Favored by Cromwell with the command of the English fleet in the West Indies, he managed to continue in favor when the exiled Stuart prince ascended the throne of his fathers, and made short work of Cromwellian favorites. Admiral Penn buttered his bread on both sides.

The expulsion of his young son from Oxford stirred the father to a more or less tempered exasperation with the boy, rather more tempered than his regard for the clergy who were responsible for it. William got a generous caning, and was hustled over to France to be polished off, for he was destined by his father for the gay life of the court.

William took the polish easily — having always a taste for the ornamental side of life, he was presented at the French court, and had the *entré* to the upper circle of the gay life of the capital. The polish was overlaid on a rather stiff course in theology under an eminent Calvinist divine. Returning to England, he was appraised by Mrs. Pepys as "a modish person and a fine gentleman." Admiral Penn decided to send the young man to Ireland to manage the family estates.

In Ireland young Penn served in the army under the Duke of Ormond, commander of the Irish forces. Well pleased with his youthful aide, the Duke wrote to the Admiral, at that time commander of a troop of horse, that if — as he had already hinted — he cared to resign, the command would be given to his son. This brought a letter from the Admiral to Son William, expressing paternal solicitude, "lest your youthful desires mayn't outrun your discretion." With exemplary discretion Admiral Penn clung tenaciously to his post.

A short service in the navy was the beginning of William Penn's lifelong friendship for James, Duke of York, successor to the throne. Popular with his superiors, he seemed about to be lifted on the waves of circumstance and inclination into a life of military pomp and distinction, when a strong undercurrent carried him far off.

Some years before a traveling Quaker preacher, Thomas Loe, had stirred the imagination of the youth. During one of Penn's visits to Cork, where his father had an estate, it so happened that Thomas Loe was preaching there, and gorgeously appareled as any gay young gallant of the time, he dropped in on one of the meetings, to listen to his old friend. It further happened that this meeting was raided, and along with others Penn was marched off to jail.

When it became known that he was the son of Admiral Penn, William was offered his liberty, and indignantly refused it on such grounds. This encounter with the authorities did not increase the young man's reverence for justice as administered, nor lessen his esteem for the hunted Quakers. By taking thought no better plan could have been devised for driving a high spirited youth into open rebellion. Thomas Loe, when arrested, was preaching on the faith that is overcome by the world, and the faith which overcomes the world. Then and there William Penn decided for overcoming the world, and made his life surrender to the Quakers.

The distress of the elder Penn may be imagined, when his heir — a handsome youth of twenty-two, trained for life at court, popular in the highest circles, and with every prospect of military preferment — reluctantly broke the news that he had cast in his lot with that notorious aggregation of jail birds derisively called Quakers.

Properly reared seventeenth century sons uncovered and knelt in the paternal presence, a custom in high esteem with seventeenth century fathers. Thomas Ellwood, when sufficiently mature to support himself as secretary to the poet Milton, felt the weight of his irate father's hand when, on turning Quaker, he was constrained to omit that filial ritual. To argue the same point with his wayward son, Admiral Penn used his fists vigorously, and when a good trouncing failed of persuasion, young William was set adrift without a penny. The Admiral was willing to compromise, if William would agree to remove his hat in the presence of the King, the Duke of York, and himself; William's Quaker principles would admit of no such distinction of the creature.

Cut off by his father, he soon discovered that overcoming the world could be accomplished on less than his accustomed allowance, for much of his time was spent in the seclusion of Newgate prison. The Quakers, though a poor and pilfered people, religiously cared for their prisoners for "truth," and Penn's Dutch mother succeeded in slipping a little across to keep her son going while his father's wrath was cooling.

Those patriots who hysterically, if somewhat vaguely, invoke the memory of the Founders, would doubtless be aghast to learn how much of his time Founder William Penn spent behind the bars. On one occasion, after an examination in the Tower, he was sentenced to Newgate, and the commander called for a military escort.

"No, no, send thy lacquey," said Penn cheerily, "I know the way to Newgate."

A wordy, rancorous, religious battle of the day was the cause of his imprisonment. A violent Presbyterian divine had shouted from the pulpit that "he would as lief his hearers should go to a baudy house as to frequent Quaker meetings," and as for himself, he "would rather drink poison than suck in their damnable doctrines." The Quakers rushed to the defense of their heresies, and many hitherto ignorant of what the disturbance was all about, heard and eagerly lapped up the damnable doctrines, bolting in large numbers to the insurgent party.

The bomb which Penn threw into the fray, a pamphlet, "The Sandy Foundations Shaken," would now be a fundamentalist's delight, soporifically orthodox to modernists. The bomb-throwing led to Penn's retirement in the Tower. Secretly proud of his handsome, fearless boy, Admiral Penn was supposed to have connived at his imprisonment, in fear of a worse fate.

In jail or out, a worse fate seemed not improbable. "Prison shall be my grave before I will budge a jot, for I owe my conscience to no mortal man," was Penn's defiance to the Bishop of London's resolve that the young man "should publicly recant or die in prison." With an iron will and a splendid physique, Penn did neither, though his prison was the death house of many a young

Quaker. One less vigorous fellow convict did succumb, and a coroner's jury was empanelled. Ellwood, one of the Quaker prisoners, writes: "The manner of doing it is this. As soon as the coroner is come, the turnkeys run into the street, and seize upon every man that passes by, till they have got enough. It so happened that they lighted on an ancient man, who was trudging through the gate in great haste. He begged and besought them to let him go, assuring them he was going on very urgent business, but they were deaf to all entreaties. When they were shut in together, the others said to this ancient man, 'Come father, you are the oldest, you shall be our foreman.' When the coffin was uncovered that they might look upon the body, the old man said, 'To what purpose do you show us a dead body? How shall we be able to judge how this man came by his death, unless we see the place where he died, and where he hath been kept prisoner?'

"This much displeased the keepers, and they began to banter the old man, thinking to beat him off. But he stood up tightly to them: 'Come,' said he, 'though you made a fool of me in bringing me hither, ye shall not find me a child now I am here; for I understand my place and your duty; and I require you to conduct me and my brethren to the place where this man died. Refuse at your peril.' They now wished they had let the old man go about his business, rather than by troubling him have brought this trouble on themselves. . . . As soon as they were come to the door (for within there was scarcely room for them to come) the foreman lifting up his hands said, 'Lord bless me, what a sight is here. I did not think there had been so much cruelty in the hearts of Englishmen to use Englishmen in this manner. We need not now question how this man came to his death; we may rather wonder that they are not all dead. If it please God to lengthen my life till to-morrow, I will let the King know how his subjects are dealt with.'"

The sinister shadow of this Newgate death-house failed to reduce Penn's ebullient enthusiasm; as soon as he regained his liberty he took the shortest cut to fresh mischief. Several hundred Quakers who had met for religious worship, which was often silent, were forcibly driven from their meeting house by soldiers. Contesting the right of the civil or military authority to interfere with their peaceable assembly, they continued their worship in the street outside. Here Penn addressed them, and with one William Mead was arrested and charged with conspiracy. The authorities and the Quakers have handed down conflicting versions of this memorable trial, memorable inasmuch as the vibrations were felt long afterward in far-away New York.[1]

The Quakers insist that "in the beginning of September of this year was a remarkable struggle between the efforts of arbitrary Power in the Magistrates of this City,

[1] Don C. Seitz has collected the records of the trial in *The Tryal of William Penn,* a little book well worth reading.

and the just and ancient Liberties of the people of England, notably defended in the following Trial, *viz.* the Trial of William Penn and William Mead, at the Session House in Old Bailey, London."

The other side tells a different story, the legal jargon of the indictment obviously embellished by imaginative fear. It asks us to believe, "That William Penn, Gent, and William Mead, late of London, Linen Draper, with divers other persons to the jurors unknown to the number of three hundred, on the 14th day of August . . . about eleven of the clock in the forenoon . . . *with force of arms* . . . unlawfully and tumultuously did assemble . . . to the disturbance of the Peace of the said Lord the King; and the aforesaid William Penn, by agreement between him and William Mead (conspiracy), then and there in the open street did take upon himself to preach and speak . . . by reason whereof a great Concourse and Tumult of people in the street aforesaid, then and there a long time did continue, in contempt of the said Lord the King, and of his Law, to the great Disturbance of his Peace, to the great Terror and Disturbance of many of his Liege People and Subjects, *to the ill example of all others in like case offending*, and against the Peace of the said Lord the King, his Crown and Dignity."

A fascinating picture this, of the great city of London, patrolled by the military, and terrorized by a Quaker prayer meeting.

The trial was a racy one, the prisoners far from tractable. Whatever the effect of Penn's street preaching on others of his Majesty's liege people and subjects, it is obvious that he was a terror and disturbance to his judges. Among them sat Alderman Richard Brown, "Master of Misrule," the judge who in his own court had jumped from the bench to knock down and kick helpless Quaker women. Alderman Brown had gone over to the Cromwellian faction when the tide turned in their favor; to atone for that apostasy, and ingratiate himself with the restored episcopacy, he was bringing forth fruits meet for repentance in his furious persecution of the Quakers. To the son of the Admiral his behavior was more circumspect, indeed almost courteous; none more keenly aware of the sudden shiftings of power than Alderman Brown, and he was not the man to take chances.

Other judges were much irritated by the turbulent conduct of the young prisoner, for Penn not only routed the clergy with the Scriptures, he routed the lawyers with the statutes. His legal points were met with irrelevant assertions; he was a saucy fellow, an impertinent fellow, and was constantly urged to silence, an advice which he as constantly ignored.

It may be noted in passing, that the method of relieving Quakers of that treasure which moth and rust doth so easily corrupt was amazingly simple. As the prisoners entered the court their hats were removed by an officious attendant. A judge angrily ordered them replaced, inquired severely if they knew where they were, and fined them forty marks each for having them on.

The court tried intimidation on the jury, including personal threats, while Penn pleaded with them for an honest and just verdict. After some deliberation, the foreman came in with the verdict, "Guilty of meeting in Gracious Street," which in the opinion of the court was as good as no verdict at all. The mayor thought matters might easily be smoothed out by the interpolation of two simple words, "unlawful assembly"; the foreman thought not, the jury had rendered a verdict; the court could take it or leave it.

Thereupon the court became abusive; one Bushel, whose light was not concealed under his name, was suspected of being the trouble-maker, and for him the court predicted an extremely unhappy future. Mr. Bushel was mild, even conciliatory, and wholly unmoved. The required verdict was outlined by the court, and the jury dismissed to bring it in. Again with extraordinary effrontery the foreman came back and announced, "Guilty of meeting in Gracious Street." The court completely lost its temper and declared the jury should be locked up without bread or water, tobacco or fire, and in modest Quaker phraseology, "without means to exonerate nature," until a verdict satisfactory to the judges was forthcoming.

For four days the court stormed and threatened, while the fasting jury monotonously repeated those six infuri-

THE TOWER OF LONDON, WHERE WILLIAM PENN WAS IMPRISONED

(*From the Print Collection, Metropolitan Museum of Art*)

ating words. Change the verdict or starve, was the ultimatum to the famished twelve, and having gone as far on the road to starvation as seemed prudent, they decided to change. Retiring for the last time, they were warned that each juror would be called on individually for his verdict, a threat which proved a boomerang; every last man as his name was called answered, "*not guilty.*"

During the long struggle, the recorder had been moved to the extra-judicial comment, "Till now I never understood the reason of the Policy and Prudence of the Spaniards in suffering the Inquisition among them, and certainly it will never be well with us till something like the Spanish Inquisition be in England." Toward a consummation so devoutly to be desired, the patriotic recorder took one sturdy stride. With the dignity of outraged authority confidently wresting victory from defeat, he turned to the hungry, thirsty, unwashed jury:

"I am sorry, gentlemen, you have followed your own Judgments and Opinions rather than the good and wholesome advice that was given you. God keep my life out of your hands, but for this you are fined Forty Marks, and imprisonment till paid."

Penn quickly rose to a point of disorder, "I demand my liberty, being freed by the jury."

MAYOR: No, you are in for your fines.

PENN: Fines, what fines?

MAYOR: For contempt of Court.

PENN: I ask if it be according to the fundamental laws

of England that any Englishman should be fined or amerced, but by the judgment of his peers or jury, since it expressly contradicts the 14th and 29th Chapter of the Great Charter of England, which says, "No Freeman ought to be amerced but by the oath of good and lawful Men of the Vicinage."

RECORDER: Take him away. Take him away. Take him out of the court.

PENN: I can never urge the fundamental laws of England but you cry, Take him away. But it is no wonder, since the Spanish Inquisition hath so great a place in the Recorder's heart.

When power and prejudice agree, fundamental law is likely to remain in its proper place — on paper. The stubborn twelve and the prisoners they had acquitted all adjourned to Mr. Penn's more or less permanent quarters in Newgate prison, while the authorities continued to puzzle over the strange increase of Quakers.

"Thus," runs the Quaker record, "ended that Memorable Trial, wherein the ancient and just Liberties of the People were notably asserted against the arbitrary Proceedings of Men in Power, who would have made their Wills a Law, according to that saying of Juvenal, sic volo, sic jubeo, stat pro Ratione voluntas."

Thus the trial did not end; nearly a century later when the powerful Justice De Lancey would have coerced a jury in the interest of Governor Cosby of the Province of New York, Andrew Hamilton, lawyer for the defense, declared that Penn's jury had established as a precedent for all time the right of juries to find their verdict regardless of the opinions of the court.

In Hamilton's summing up — "an address," says Mr. Seitz, "that solidified the foundation for liberty of press and free speech on this continent and was a worthy preface to the Declaration of Independence" — he reviewed the Penn trial:

"For (said the Court) the Meeting . . . is confessed, and we tell you it is unlawful . . . and the Meeting being unlawful, it follows of course that it was tumultuous, and to the Disturbance of the peace. But the jury did not think fit to take the Court's word for it, for they could find neither Riot nor Tumult. . . . Mr. Bushel, who valued the Right of a Juryman and the Liberty of his Country more than his own, refused to pay the Fine, and was resolved (tho' at great Expense and trouble too) to bring, and did bring, his Habeas Corpus, to be relieved from his Fine and Imprisonment, and he was released accordingly, and this being the Judgment in his Case, it is established for Law, That Judges how great soever they be, have no Right to Fine, imprison or punish a Jury, for not finding a verdict according to the Direction of the Court."

Bloody and costly battles are fought for results far less significant than the outcome of the conflict which Penn and his jury waged against authority on that far-off September day.

Friend Penn was now established as a full-fledged undesirable, for he was rocking the pet order of society in his day, and societies in any day regard their pet order with tenderness. Up to this time the Quakers had steadily adhered to the policy of boring from within, in their effort to undermine the autocratic power of the Church. While the persecuted Pilgrims found safety in flight to Holland, the Quakers stood by in the fight to make England safe for free speech and religious liberty. Meantime imponderable forces were pushing on Penn's "Holy Experiment."

Penn had made an exhaustive study of the theory and practice of government. Travel had familiarized him with the idiosyncrasies of continental governments, and conflict had given him a considerable experience of his own. He had become an interested adviser of the Quaker-owned territories in New Jersey, and insistent ideas of the true nature and end of government began to take shape in his active mind, ideas at that time rather startling. As he surveyed the situation, it hardly seemed credible that as governments went he could do much worse; he was haunted by the idea that he could do very much better, and was willing to try.

It was probably a visit from George Fox that brought Penn's ideas to a focus, and made his intermittent vision of a Christian Commonwealth dazzling and permanent. Fox was the general-in-chief of the Quaker fight, and its organizing genius. He visited Penn fresh from a tour of the American colonies, impressed by the potentialities of the red man, deeply concerned for the lot of the black man and thrilled by the possibility of establishing a sanctuary in the vast new world for the persecuted white man. To think, with Fox, was to act, and he had already gone so far as to inquire into the feasibility of purchasing a tract of land from the Susquehannock Indians. His fervor probably crystallized Penn's thoughts and turned them toward an inherited bad debt of the Crown.

Admiral Penn meanwhile had fought his last fight. As he approached his engagement with the conqueror, the world was much less with him; he had swung in the direction of his son. Loud and long were his bitter jeremiads for his doomed and infatuated country, blind to her true interests and happiness. One alluring gleam lightened the darkness: "Son William, if you and your Friends keep to your plain way of preaching, and keep to your plain way of living, you will make an end of the priests till the end of the world." With this pious prediction, he went out as he came into the world, taking nothing with him. William his son fell heir to all impedimenta, including a very bad debt.

Admiral Penn, as we have seen, stood in solidly with the King; to be precise, he stood in to the tune of sixteen thousand pounds. In the good old days before grasping governments appropriated the loot of war under the legal sanction of reparations, to the victor more immediately belonged the spoil. A naval commander, fortunate enough to intercept a rich Dutch merchantman or a Spanish galleon, could put by a tidy insurance against a rainy day. The Quaker chronicle does not concern itself with the source of the good Admiral's wealth, nor need we; the point of the story is that, however he got it, his sovereign Lord the King got it away from him, a pivotal point in the history of Pennsylvania.

The wilds of America meant little to Charles Stuart, the Quakers still less; money meant everything in the maintenance of his very extensive ménage. Repudiation of a debt to the Admiral who had extended the English dominion was not to be thought of. The opportunity to cancel the debt, and at the same time lose his least manageable subjects, by merely affixing his signature to a deed for unimproved real estate, to which his title was questionable, presented a brilliant solution of two disquieting problems. In lieu of the sixteen thousand pounds, King Charles made over to Penn a territory larger than the Kingdom of England, and in his elation he himself named it Pennsylvania, not in honor of Penn the pacifist, as is commonly supposed, but in honor of Penn the fighter, who made the West Indies a far-flung outpost of the British Empire.

So it happened that the seditious street preacher, before he was forty, became the feudal lord of a vast territory, which was, after a fashion, his personal property — but with one important qualification: Penn with all he possessed was subject to the pleasure of his overlord, the

King, who in turn was subject to the influence of powerful interests.

One powerful interest had no intention of leaving the Quakers footloose, with the power to do unto churchmen as churchmen had done unto them. The Bishop of London stepped in to scrutinize the royal charter, and insisted on a proviso that, whenever twenty planters should demand an established church, the Province of Pennsylvania must provide it.

Nevertheless, in working out a constitution for the New Province, Penn had no reason to be downhearted. He had no design of retaliating on the Church of England; it was his intention to give his colony a charter as free as possible from the cruelties of English law. The protest against the taking of human life was a fundamental Quaker "testimony," and in his constitution Penn was able to reduce the two hundred capital offenses recognized by the laws of England to two: treason and willful murder. On these two the English Crown stood firm.

Penn was indifferent to the form of his government. "Any government," he said, "is free to the people under it, whatever be the frame, where the laws rule, and the people are a party to those laws, and more than this is tyranny, oligarchy or confusion." Monarchies, aristocracies, republics, he discovered, had worked equally well under good men, and equally badly wanting them. The Jewish and Roman governments, which he considered triumphs of human wisdom, became sorry failures under unscrupulous rulers, while very inferior forms of government had jogged along satisfactorily under honest and capable direction.

Good men then he must have, and to secure them he advertised, directing his splendidly organized publicity campaign to the northern European countries, appealing to those groups whose dogged determination toward liberty had brought on them the heavy hand of persecution. He was to learn later that men willing to die for liberty sometimes find it difficult to live in peace with their fellows. To some of these good people government and tyranny had long been interchangeable terms, resistance to tyranny obedience to God, and resistance had become a fixed habit.

In the advertisements of his "free colony for all mankind" Penn made no attempt to minimize the dangers and drawbacks; Pennsylvania was no adventure for the timid. He was unwilling that "any should go out of a curious and unsettled mind, and act or hurry away beyond the wisdom and counsel of the Lord, . . . and not upon good and weighty grounds." He was not looking for drifters or adventurers, but desired "to raise up noble resolutions in all the freeholders in these new colonies not to give away anything of Liberty and Property that at present they do (or of right as loyal subjects ought to) enjoy, but take up the good example of our ancestors, and understand that it is easy to part with great privileges, but hard to be gained if once lost."

In spite of all the perils and hardships, the oppressed of Europe were eager to have a part in the "Holy Experiment," and the fall of 1682 saw the first band of emigrants start off in high hope on the *Welcome*, to a jubilant chorus of good riddance. They were free to brave the dangers of ocean travel, to face the hardships of an untamed land, to hack homes out of the wild woods, and to try their absurd religious notions on the heathen. But their freedom had a stout string attached to it, which could be drawn taut whenever it became necessary to release the tension on financial and political interests at home.

It might be imagined that, having ousted Penn and his undesirable Quakers to the uttermost parts of the earth, where it was supposed they had an excellent prospect of being finished off by the savages, their adversaries could now enjoy a breathing spell. Instead, their animosity increased, for in the remotest corner of the world the religious ideas of the Quakers were a menace to good business, and a cause of strife.

When the "Holy Experiment" was soaking up Penn's private fortune, he turned down a tempting offer of six thousand pounds for the monopoly of Indian trade in his territory, knowing that trade between the whites and the tinted skins was a cloak of verbal respectability for a legal hold-up. He could not, he said, yield to the temptation and defile that "which had come to him clean."

The Quaker attitude toward Indian trade caused much

concern in the New York province, so much, in fact, that the governor of that province made a crooked deal with the powerful Five Nations, and secured a deed to some of Penn's territory, to which the northern Indians laid claim by virtue of having licked the Susquehannocks. This chicanery made it necessary for Penn to repurchase some of his land for the third time. After years of struggle the New York governor was forced to sign over to Penn his ill-gotten deed; vexatious years they must have been for the Quaker.

Besides the menace to trade in Penn's Indian policy, his charter proposed that after fourteen years all black "servants" should go free, a stab in the back of slavery. His colony was only six years old when the German Quakers fired the first broadside against slavery. Of nine million slaves kidnaped from Africa, English traders handled six millions, and constituted a powerful business interest which the English government was not disposed to treat lightly. In drafting the great Declaration Thomas Jefferson, the Southerner, burned with a desire to inform all mankind that the perfidious home government which was inciting the slaves to insurrection against the long-suffering colonists, had, by nullifying all their abolition laws, forced these slaves upon them. By counsel of John Adams the information was withheld from mankind at that time. In the fullness of time this practical interest led to a cruel and costly war not yet entirely paid for. No inspired statistician has risen to figure out the cost in life and property of the overpowering political influence of the practical man.

To the list of Penn's handicaps must be added the hostility of neighboring colonists. New York was wroth with Pennsylvania for "spoiling" Indian trade. New England was incensed by the advent of heretics in the holy land, and had already manifested her warmth of feeling for Quakers by the whip and the gibbet. There is in print a letter of doubtful authenticity, which if not written by the eminent Puritan divine whose name is signed to it, is a very clever forgery of his style. It reads:

To the Aged and Beloved John Higginson.

There be at sea a shippe called Ye Welcome, R. Greenway, Master, which has on board a hundred or more of ye malignants called Quakers, with W. Penn, ye chief scampe at the head of them. Ye General Court has accordingly given secret orders to Master Malichi Huxett of ye brig Porpasse to walaye sed Welcome as near ye coast of Codde as may be, and make captive ye said Penn and his ungodly crew, so that ye Lord may be glorified and not mocked on ye soil of this new country with ye heathen worship of these people.

Much spoyle may be made by selling ye whole lot to Barbadoes, where slaves fetch good prices in rumme and sugar, and shall not only do ye Lord service in punishing ye wicked, but we shall make great good for His ministers and people. Master Huxett feels hopeful and I will set down ye news when his ship comes back.

Yours in ye bowels of Christ,

Cotton Mather.

Authentic or not, the sentiments of this letter would unquestionably have met with the warm approval of the

New England hierarchy. If such a peril really existed, the *Welcome* sailed up the Delaware in happy ignorance. From well prepared plans the City of Brotherly Love began to shape; the Province of Pennsylvania to be organized as a Christian Commonwealth. The Holy Experimenters were human and imperfect notwithstanding their belief in human perfectibility. Nevertheless, judged by the conditions of the times, and by the achievements of neighboring colonies, their venture was a great landmark in the trek of the race.

So profound a student of history as Lord Acton, a Roman Catholic, pays tribute to William Penn as the framer and founder of the freest government known in the world, at a time when the clamor for liberty excited as much horror as Bolshevism does today: "By the principles of the Society to which he belonged, it was necessary that the new State should be founded on liberty and equality. But Penn was further noted among the Quakers as a follower of the new doctrine of Toleration. Thus it came to pass that Pennsylvania enjoyed the most democratic constitution in the world, and held up to the admiration of the eighteenth century an almost solitary example of freedom."

To the disappointment of the horrified the heavens remained stationary. Twenty years after the *Welcome* sailed up the river through an untamed wilderness, the customs on Pennsylvania goods arriving in England amounted to eight thousand pounds, or twice as much as on goods from the older province of New York. This band of impractical idealists, whose absurdities drove practical men distracted, made of Pennsylvania the most secure and the most prosperous of all the American colonies. Not only from Europe, but from all the other colonies, settlers came flocking in, so that the Quaker colony by leaps and bounds outdistanced the populations of older settlements.

Eventually the invaders outnumbered the Quakers, and the extraordinary spectacle is presented of the political scepter passing from their hands, not by reason of the failure of their principles, but because of their phenomenal success. Greedy adventurers came for the golden eggs, and roasted the bird that laid them.

William Penn — *Continued*

Liberty, Equality and Fraternity have been preached through all time, but it was left for William Penn the Quaker, to come nearer establishing the ideal of this Trinity than any other being called Human before or since his day.

— Don C. Seitz.

While the persecuted were mustering for the "Holy Experiment" from all over the British Islands, Holland, and Germany, William Penn was enjoying the life of a well-born English gentleman, heir to a well-feathered nest. His personality was pleasing, his amiable vanities wholly free from arrogance. Admiral Penn before his death had bespoken for his son the good offices of the Duke of York, later James II; he enjoyed royal favor both at home and on the Continent.

Family ties, which included a revered father- and mother-in-law fully satisfied his affectionate nature. He was the devoted and admiring husband of Gulielma, the beautiful, charming, and fragile daughter of Sir William Springett; the overindulgent father of a young family, for whose welfare here and hereafter he was deeply concerned. Neither necessity nor personal ambition pushed him out into the wilderness. "Had I sought greatness, I had stayed at home."

In the son the personal ambition of the admiral was transmuted into an ambition to lead the oppressed out of the lands of bondage; with no abatement of the paternal energy, he followed the gleam that lured him, the ever-recurring vision of "a free colony for all mankind," a Holy Experiment. "Because I have been somewhat exercised at times about the nature and end of government among men, it is reasonable to expect that I should establish a just and righteous one in this Province, that others may take example by it, truly this my heart desires. For the Nations want a precedent." Through loss and bitter disappointment Penn was to discover his fallacy; the nations certainly wanted no such precedent as he proposed to establish. With fewer illusions about his fellow men, Thomas Jefferson knew that what they chiefly wanted was to be let alone.

In the reaction from a blind hero-worship, it is the passing fashion to analyze the great to their lowest common complex; a lap dog may bark at an elephant. The safest course is the middle of the road between unsophisticated sentimentalism and oversophisticated analysis. Again Lord Acton: "Great men are something different from an enlarged repetition of average and familiar types . . . living to avoid contingencies of danger and pain and sacrifice, and the weariness of constant thinking and far-seeing precaution. . . . We cannot understand Cromwell or Shaftesbury, Sunderland or Penn by studies made in the Parish."

Penn never pretended to complete detachment from self-interest; the anticipation of a modest profit on his investments afforded him satisfaction, the prospect of providing adequately for a large family even more, for his love of all mankind included even his family. He did claim — and the claim is borne out by facts and figures — that he had subordinated self interest to the general good, and that his " public spiritedness " had cost him both peace and profit.

Of the daring and magnitude of his undertaking he was quite sensible, and nothing loath to receive the recognition due to his achievement. " I must think," he writes the colonists during a time of turbulence, " there is a regard due me that has not of late been paid; pray consider it soberly what you have to desire of me, on the one hand, and ought to perform on the other."

Penn dreamed a great dream, of a state founded on justice and mercy, where " power is in reverence with the people, and the people secure from the abuse of power, free by just obedience, for liberty without obedience is confusion, and obedience without liberty is slavery." In his pleasant dream he saw successive generations of Penns, useful and honored, rendering service to the state, for among the many fairy gifts that cluttered his cradle, the gift of prophecy was wanting. In his seed neither he himself nor the generations of Pennsylvania were to be blessed.

Quitting England for the new land, with no certainty

of return, William Penn drew up a memorandum for the guidance of his beloved family. His dear wife, "the love of my youth, and much the joy of my life," was urged "to live sparingly till my debts are paid, and then to enlarge as thou seest convenient." In the education of the children, however, she was to "Spare no cost; for by such parsimony all is lost that is saved. Be sure to observe their genius and do not cross it as to learning." Such occupations were to be encouraged as promote usefulness, honesty and industry, as navigation, the building of ships and of houses, but "agriculture is especially in my eye. Let my children be husbandmen and housewives."

To promote family affection, "Allow them to send and give each other small things, to endear one another."

They were to be homely rather than finely bred, "yet I love sweetness mixed with gravity, and cheerfulness tempered with sobriety. Religion in the heart leads to this true civility — an accomplishment worthy indeed of praise."

The children were counseled: "Let your parsimony go no further than a sufficiency for life, and to make provision for your children, and that in moderation. Love not money nor the world, use them only and they will serve you, but if you love them you serve them, which will debase your spirits."

A frugal diet was recommended as "physic by prevention," promoting bodily and spiritual health.

"Speak no evil of any — no not of the meanest.

"Keep on the square, and be sure you see with your own eyes, and hear with your own ears.

"Liberal to the poor, pitiful to the miserable, humble and kind to all, but ruin not yourselves by kindness to others, for that exceeds the true bonds of friendship, neither will a true friend expect it."

Within the laws of consanguinity, Penn considered it desirable that his children choose mates among kinsfolk, but "marry such as you can love above all this world, and that may make your habitations desirable to you." Precept, example, and solemn injunction were all unavailing; the mantle of William Penn was neither to fit nor to fall upon his posterity.

Having put his household in order, Penn was ready to lead his band to the great experiment. Profiting by the experience of earlier pioneers, they went out well prepared to begin work on the City of Philadelphia. It was planned that the houses in the city should be built "with grounds on each side for gardens and orchards, so that it may be a green country town, which will never be burnt, and always be wholesome."

To the framing of a constitution for his colony, Penn applied himself with infinite pains, taking counsel of the wisest men of his time, and warning from sinister examples aplenty of bad government. "For matters of liberty and privilege, I propose that which is extraordinary, and to leave myself and successors no power of doing mischief, that the will of one man may not hinder the good of an whole country."

It was a wide space to clear at one jump, and Penn was proud of the leap. He had a comfortable sense of magnanimity, for, although the Province of Pennsylvania was his personal property, he proposed to establish in it a government of pure democracy. It is doubtful if he would have subscribed to Thomas Jefferson's declaration that all men are born free and equal, but as far as lay in his power, he was determined that all who were born in Pennsylvania should have an equal chance. "To provide the means of a good education for every child, and to see that all are taught some good trade or profession, would do more for the promotion of peace and happiness, than all the machinery of courts and prisons."

A most experienced prisoner himself, he longed to get his hand on that penal machinery, that he might put it to work on reformation instead of revenge. More than fifteen thousand contemporary Quakers had shared his prison experiences, without doubt the most intelligent flock of jail birds ever thrown back into society, to whose intelligence and zeal we owe the beginnings of prison reform. Thomas Ellwood, secretary to John Milton, and tutor to Penn's wife, Gulielma, improved his sojourn in Newgate; by pretending to be so absorbed in his reading that he could not hear conversation addressed to him, he overheard all that was going on among the convicts, and discovered that prisons were educational institutions for crime. If society had been willing to heed Quakers instead of trying to exterminate them, prison reform would have had a start of two hundred years.

Many were the innovations, regarded as dangerous, introduced into the Pennsylvania charter; the keystone of the whole structure was liberty of conscience and religious toleration, for, said Penn, "whether the grounds of a man's religious dissent be rational or not, severity is unjustifiable; whoever is wrong, the persecutor cannot be right. . . . We can never be the better for our religion if our neighbor is the worse for it. . . . It is a great presumption to send our passions upon God's errands, as it is to palliate them with God's name. We are too apt to retaliate, rather than to forgive, or to gain by love and information." Penn's toleration extended even to the Catholics, who were persecuted as much from political fear as from religious bigotry. It was customary to punish Quakers under laws made to suppress Catholics, against which they vigorously protested, but said Penn, "I am far from thinking it fit, because I exclaim against the injustice of whipping Quakers for Papists, that Papists should be whipped for their conscience."

And then, when all that diligence, discretion and wisdom could do had been done, and the constitution was finally launched, no claim of sanctity was made for it; the achievement of human wisdom, it was hoped that human wisdom might better it. The most perfect theories develop flaws in practice, Penn told the colonists. "I do not find a model in the world, that time, place and some singular emergencies have not altered." This constitution, too, would need amendment; the power is in your hands, said he, amend it. With this warning to the impetuous, "We cannot go too slowly to make laws, nor too fast to execute them when made, and that with diligence and discretion."

Next to the constitution, the problem of greatest moment was the laying of a firm foundation for Indian friendship. Pennsylvania was the only colony that welcomed the Indians as neighbors. Penn wrote:

TO THE EMPEROR OF CANADA:

The great God that made thee and me and all the world, incline our hearts to love peace and justice, that we may live friendly together and become the workmanship of the great God. The King of England who is a great prince, hath, for divers reasons, granted me a large country in America, which, however, *I am willing to enjoy upon friendly terms with thee*, and this I will say, that the people who come with me are a just, plain and honest people, that neither make war upon others, nor fear war from others, because they will be just.

Penn's Indian treaty has become a world legend; the secret of his success is less well known. The territory purchased from the King of England, to whom it did not of right belong, was repurchased from the natives in actual possession. This just and exemplary behavior was by no means singular to the Quakers; other settlers had been as fair — *fair, but always fearful.* In their fear they rattled the sword and made ominous noises with their marvelous shooting irons, noises which excited and exhilarated the Indians, exhilaration increasing with their grievances. Other settlers came asserting that they were a peaceable people, but God help those who disturbed their peace, a warning emphasized by the display of murderous weapons, always an irritating and irresistible dare to the savage.

Penn came to the wild men saying, it is our intention to deal justly, that we may live in peace and security with all men, therefore we make no preparations for trouble. This was a novel and extremely entertaining idea to the red man, and above all convincing. In the seventy-five years of Quaker ascendancy, no one of that persuasion was killed by an Indian. Even in the days of the Scotch-Irish influence, when life in Pennsylvania had become so precarious that a Presbyterian clergyman entered the pulpit with a Bible in one hand and a rifle in the other, Quakers traveled through the country and held their meetings as usual, without fear of molestation. "They harm no one," the savages explained, "and none shall hurt them."

Cotton Mather accounted for the presence of the natives as a farsighted craftiness of the Evil One, with intent to outwit the Deity and thwart his chosen people; a belief which justified the Puritans in pushing back the heathen when it seemed prudent, and possessing his best land. Unfortunately, it frequently proved less prudent than it seemed. The heathen raged vainly until such time as, inspired and ably assisted by the Devil, they fell upon the saints and well-nigh made an end of them.

Penn surmised that the natives were a people of Hebraic origin; but whether or no, he was confident that God alone was responsible for their creation, therefore, however dim and flickering, the divine spark glowed in them. Penn's settlers were peculiarly adapted for association with their new neighbors; the profound silences of the long drawn out powwows, which made other white men nervous and restless, refreshed the Quakers. They could sit and say nothing longer than the least garrulous of Indians. Shrewd bargainers themselves, they did not attribute Indian shrewdness to original sin. "He will deserve the name of wise," says Penn approvingly of his red friends, "who outwits them in any treaty they understand." Indians and Quakers reacted quickly to injustice; both were intense individualists, with an unusual toleration for the individualism of others.

To facilitate understanding, Penn acquired the language, "that I might not want an interpreter; I must say I know not a language in Europe that hath words of more sweetness or greatness." The intense love of the Indians for their children delighted the Governor; he praised their unbounded hospitality to strangers, generosity to friends, their gaiety and sports, in which he sometimes joined and acquitted himself creditably, to the astonishment of more sedate Friends. "The most merry creatures that live," he writes. "We sweat and toil to live.

. . . Their pleasure feeds them; I mean their hunting, fishing and fowling, and this table is spread everywhere."

In his contacts with men whose names history has preserved, it is doubtful if any gave him more unalloyed pleasure than his association with Indian chiefs. "They have some great men among them, I mean for wisdom, truth and justice."

"It is rare," he wrote home, "that they fall out if sober, and if drunk they forgive it, saying that it was the drink and not the man that abused them. The worst is that they are the worse for Christians, who have propagated their vices and yielded them tradition for ill and not for good things. But as low an ebb as these people are at, the Christians have not outlived their sight, with all their pretensions to a higher manifestation. . . . It were miserable indeed for us to fall under the just censure of the poor Indian conscience, while we make a profession of things so far transcending."

The assumption of a conscience in the savage, and the hint that example would be more profitable to him than theology, put Penn outside the pale of Christianity in his day.

Certain honest historians, unsympathetic to fantastic Quaker notions, have attempted to explain away Penn's success with the Indians; his Indians, they say, were tame Indians, too cowardly to attack anything more formidable than domesticated animals. The Massachusetts Indians had also been cowed by war and terrible pestilence before the arrival of the Pilgrims, yet they revived sufficiently to devastate New England with fire and tomahawk. Moreover, the complaints of Penn's neighbors lend no color to this explanation.

Less than a decade before his arrival, at the very gate of his territory, occurred one of the most disgraceful passages between the whites and the reds, the leading rôle played by no less a personage than the great-grandfather of our country, Colonel John Washington. The Maryland colony, living in perpetual conflict with their aggrieved neighbors, the Susquehannocks, resorted to the devious policy of alliances, flirting first with one then another of the tribes, favoring always the most powerful.

A hostile alien race in possession of the land where his fathers died, was a disheartening sight to the Indian; when the usurpers gave aid and comfort to his most relentless foes, his reactions were identical with those of the white man under similar provocation; his protest was spirited, his wrath fell upon the just and the unjust. Christian and savage were equally devout adherents of the reprisal system, the most self-perpetuating ever devised by human kind, the original endless chain. Reprisal demanded an eye for an eye, whose eye was relatively unimportant, so that each side soon piled up reliable statistics proving the treachery and duplicity of the other.

The feud came to such a pass that Maryland appealed to Virginia to lend a hand in putting a quietus on the Susquehannocks. This tribe had always been friendly to the Virginians, and they were puzzled to know why their old friends came out against them. They sent a scout to find out, and to protest that they had no quarrel with Virginia, and desired peace. The colonials agreed to a peace parley on condition that the five greatest "kings" should be sent to treat.

Under the usual guarantee of safe conduct, the five Indian leaders came into the white camp, only to be seized and securely bound, in defiance of all the usage of war. The less temperate colonials were for speedily dispatching the captive envoys to the peace of the happy hunting grounds; the more prudent Marylanders demurred, not on a point of honor, but as nearer neighbors of these Indians, they were for reprisal tempered with discretion.

"Why delay longer?" queried Colonel Washington. "Let us knock them on the head. We shall take the fort to-day." The impetuous Virginian carried the day, overruling wiser counsel; the five helpless captives were tapped on the head, and for them trouble was over; their executioners fell heir to it. Their outraged followers retreated to the stockade, where they were surrounded by the overconfident colonials, who, however, failed to capture the fort that day. Under cover of darkness, those wily warriors crept through the line, taking all their women and children with them, tapping as they went the heads of ten besiegers. Furthermore, they put in a claim for reparations, demanding the scalps of ten common whites for the head of each murdered chief, a claim they promptly collected.

When the Virginia Assembly convened, Colonel Washington in his seat, Governor Berkeley declared that if the Indians had killed his last relative, if they came to treat for peace, they should have gone in peace. Other than this mild reproof, it is not recorded that the gallant colonel suffered any inconvenience; the price of his exploit was paid by sixty innocent white men whose scalps adorned the belts of the Susquehannocks, for the reprisal system is short-sighted and impersonal.

With this triumphant revenge the remnant of the tribe made an exit from the stage, dispersing among other groups and eloquently inciting their hosts to hostility against the whites. It was an Indian boast that historical data was as reliably preserved in their memories as in the white man's books; it might, therefore, be interesting to trace the relation, if any, between this episode and the terrible mutilation of Braddock's army half a century later, among those present being the illustrious descendant of the choleric Virginia colonel.

The bad blood resulting from this neighborly interchange was still festering, when Penn appeared, preaching his fanatical doctrines which he proposed to practice regardless of color line. The Indian listened with enthusiasm; the Christian with disgust and consternation. The white man's burden has often been lightened by trading with the unsophisticated heathen; Indian trade was extremely remunerative, the percentage of profit often reckoned in the thousands. A bit of lurid calico, worthless trinkets, a hatchet, firearms, and, above all, the firewater of the bootlegger, could be exchanged for valuable furs.

The public exhibition of all goods intended for Indian trade was compulsory in Pennsylvania, that honest citizens might judge their value, and no worthless rubbish be foisted on the natives. Without fear of the law, they were privileged to stave in any liquor found on their land. Under Quaker tutelage the Indians soon developed a sense of values; traders became alarmed and protested that the Quakers were ruining trade. The bootleggers were less disturbed; they moved further out near the hunting grounds to intercept returning braves, treated them to a round of drinks, and when they came out of the ensuing slumber, it was to discover that the pelts of a whole season's hunt had been taken by their hosts as the price of liquid refreshment. Greedy entertainers were known to take not only the skins, but the blankets and guns of their victims as well. Against such behavior the only effective argument the Indian could advance was the tomahawk. Incidentally he became the first and most earnest prohibitionist on this Continent.

Penn's treaty, a high light of American history, was the simplest contract ever made between two peoples, and the most effective. "The only treaty," exulted Voltaire, "between these people and the Christians not ratified by an oath, and that never was broken." Nor, it may be added, were lawyers ever called in to interpret it, that profession being unpopular in Pennsylvania.

The natives were not summoned into the presence of the superior race, nor were the usual tricks employed for impressing them with the white man's supremacy. Under a giant elm at Shackamaxon, their own immemorial treaty place, the tribes assembled; there the anti-ceremonial Quakers staged the most impressive pageant ever seen on this continent.

Creatures of great natural dignity, with a flair for pageantry, the Indians turned out in full regalia for the great occasion, "an innumerable host stretching as far as the eye could see, painted, armed and frightful to behold." With a few soberly clad, unarmed Quakers, Penn rowed down the River in a barge, his blue silk sash giving the one touch of color to his party. As the Quakers stepped out into the weird and awe-inspiring assembly, the convention opened Indian fashion; a wreath from which protruded a horn was placed upon the head of the great chief. With this symbol of power properly adjusted, the place became sacred, the persons of all assembled inviolate, in token of which the painted warriors dramatically cast away their weapons; they were ready to hear the words of the white chief.

His words were few and simple. They were met, he said, in sincerity and good faith, the children of one Great Father, each desiring peace and security by just dealings one with the other. On both sides were good men, and unprincipled ones as well. Discord among peoples was promoted by the greedy and unscrupulous, who to serve their own ends, by false rumors engendered fear and hatred even in the hearts of the well disposed. Let us agree, said Penn, to deprive the foolish and wrong-headed of this power for mischief. Wrongs will be done, disconcerting rumors will be started; let us not leave panic and revenge to take their sinister course; let us send our wisest men on both sides to make a just settlement.

That we may know and understand each other, let the dwellings of each be always hospitably open to the other.

And neither party to this treaty shall take advantage of the other, but by mutual fair play live always in good neighborhood.

It was so simple that a child could grasp it, and to Penn the Indians were sagacious children. Half a century later, when the Founder rested in the quiet of an English churchyard, a governor of Pennsylvania assured the Indians that they had been faithful to their covenant, that their hearts were clean, that they had preserved the sacred chain of friendship without spot or rust. For few treaties contrived with diplomatic subtlety can as much be said.

The treaty signed, the Quakers settled down in perfect security, enjoying a neighborly kindness among the savages, to which they had been strangers in Christian lands, though the reprisal system was in full swing all about them. The stock excuse for attacking the natives, the cruelty of the savage, left them cold, these men and women whose property had been confiscated, their ears lopped off, their tongues pierced with hot pokers, their naked bodies shamefully scourged, by their fellow Christians.

In the will of one old Quaker, his heirs were charged to faithfully return to the Indians the kindness shown to his people in time of need. And among the early records there is a tale of a frontier family setting off on a long journey to Yearly Meeting, leaving their young brood entrusted to the watchful eye of Indian neighbors camped near by. The Quakers were quite as keen as the Puritans for the Christianizing of the red man, but differed in the method. As co-workers with God, to whom a thousand years are as yesterday, they were in no haste, and thought it no part of wisdom "to crowd them faster than they can bear." Time and good example were their allies.

One real Indian scare disturbed the quiet and calm of the Quaker City, and was promptly met in terms of the treaty. The rumor blew in to Philadelphia that fifteen hundred braves were on the warpath, mowing down the whites and bent on their complete destruction. Details speedily followed, giving the names and number of the victims. In the Council then in session sat Penn's trusted friend Caleb Pusey, and imagination had not yet invented the rumor that could ripple the surface of the abysmal deep of Caleb Pusey's calm. The treaty provided that in case of trouble six wise men on each side should meet.

Pusey rose in the council and asked that five wholly unarmed men volunteer to accompany him to the scene of carnage.

As the six Quakers cantered into the Indian village, they found the children playing, the women going about their occasions, the old chief peacefully dozing on his skins. Roused from slumber, as he listened to their story, he became irritated and expressed an ardent desire to see the author of the rumor burned at the stake. "As God has given you corn," he advised, "go home and get it in. We intend you no harm." In every other settlement such rumors invariably resulted in hectic preparations for defense, preparations which excited Indian suspicion and attack, and war was on.

Witchcraft, the fashionable excitement in New England, was stillborn in Pennsylvania, lacking necessary nourishment. Penn himself sat on the bench and heard the evidence against a poor Swedish woman. It was the usual variety, the wretched woman had once looked upon a cow, and the animal had not lived to die an unnatural death. "Guilty of the common fame of a witch," was the curious verdict, "but not guilty in manner and form as charged in the indictment," and the frightened old woman went home, the first and last case of witchcraft in the colony.

The story of Penn and the Indians has a happy ending; the long and pleasant relationship was maintained in the spirit of the treaty. The story of Penn and his good colonists ended much less happily. On the whole, the Pennsylvanians were above the average in their sense of justice and social obligation; the majority were as cool and reasonable as the minority were intractable. To all liberty was a new and exciting possession; they never haggled about the high price paid for it, but delivery of the goods they would have. Some there were in whom gratitude for the enjoyment of it proved a more transitory emotion than the lively fear of losing it, by no means a baseless fear. Experience had not stimulated their faith in government; they sniffed oppression in every demand of the English Crown, and came to alert resistance at the drop of the handkerchief. Unfortunately dropping the handkerchief was a favorite game of the home government.

So long as Penn kept his hand on the steering gear, the ship of state seems to have run a fairly smooth course. Though prone to a patriarchal attitude, he was the least overbearing of men, acting always on the advice he gave to the colonists to "yield in circumstantials to preserve essentials." It was his pride and pastime to make his colonists a happy people, a recreation with which his enemies interfered. Their machinations made his presence in England necessary when he was needed in his Province. Under the deputies he was obliged to appoint, the ship began to rock.

It is idle to speculate on what might have happened if Penn had possessed George Fox's insight into character, a faculty which was no part of his genius. It is obvious that omniscience itself, unsupported by omnipotence, could not have carried the Holy Experiment to final victory against the hostility which it aroused; only fanatical faith could have kept it so long afloat.

Penn's experiment was made at a time when English imperialism was in the stage of growing pains; war was continuous, the demands of the home government for aid incessant. The pro-Indian, antislavery pacifists of Pennsylvania were far from favorite sons of that government. As for the colonists who had crossed the seas because they had completely lost their taste for the government under which they lived and suffered, they chose rather to keep a watchful eye on the old menace, than excite themselves about a new danger abroad. Short of extermination, what further oppression could a foreign government put upon them than they had already experienced under their own? England's enemies were not their enemies; they would give no assistance in killing them.

Between these two irreconcilables Penn was buffeted; if he failed to make concessions to the government, the string to his grant would be drawn in, the Holy Experiment would topple. The least suspicion of a movement toward yielding unto Caesar the things which they believed belonged unto God, and the Quakers made ready to fight, and if need be, die. They claimed quite reasonably, that when they were allowed to withdraw into the wilderness, their principles were well known, and liberty of conscience was granted to them; that the taking of life was one of the gravest concerns of their consciences. Therefore, they would not fight, neither would they raise supplies for war. As matters went from bad to worse, they hit upon a subterranean way of rendering to Caesar what he was determined to have; they would raise a sum of money "for the King's use" and no questions asked. The use to which the King put the gift would be a matter for his own conscience, not theirs. This subterfuge was not popular, and the royal gift was seldom munificent.

Penn, on his part, endeavored to appoint deputies more or less pleasing to the Crown, who invariably proved far from pleasing to the colony. The situation was one which the most expert political juggler of all time could not have juggled successfully, and Penn's deputies were conspicuously unskillful.

When Evans was sent out from England as deputy governor, Penn thought so highly of him that William Jr., was committed to his care, in the hope that Pennsylvania would exert a quieting influence on that dissipated young blackguard. Both young men instead proved highly disquieting to the Pennsylvanians, the least likely of all people in the world to stand for the airs of a prospective ruler. Painting the town a pale red one night, the two cronies were sharply pulled up at a tavern by a watchman. Young Penn grew bellicose, even pulled a gun, so the legend goes, whereupon some one turned out the lights, and in the darkness a pair of lusty pioneers unhampered by scruples about the use of force, vigorously belabored the new governor and the heir apparent.

Both sides were given an opportunity to tell the court how it happened, the current of public opinion running strongly against the young bloods. The watchman was judged to have done no more than his duty and was discharged; as for his robust volunteer aides, how could they in the dark distinguish the governor and the proprietor's son? They, too, were freed. Thoroughly disgusted, young Penn sold his Pennsylvania estate, and shook the dust of the province and Quakerism forever from his feet. The proprietor was a bit peeved by the miscarriage of his plan, and complained that his son had been more hurt by bad Quakers, than benefited by good ones.

Governor Evans stuck it out to test the resistance of a stone wall by butting his head against it. France was at that time execrated as the barbarous foe of civilization and of England; for the rescue of civilization and itself, the home government must have money and men. The atmosphere became noticeably chilly when Governor Evans presented this noble cause for aid. To warm things up a bit, the governor hit upon a strange spectacular device. A letter from himself to himself gave warning that the French were coming up the Bay, and when the messenger delivered it, he seized his sword, mounted his steed, and rode frantically through the City of Brotherly Love, shouting the news and a call to arms.

In the rôle of Paul Revere he met with a blighting

frost; a few timid souls hastily buried their treasures and fled in fear, but as it happened to be Meeting day, a stream of unperturbed Quakers calmly wended their way to worship, leaving the field to the governor and the French. "Not a Friend of any note," wrote Isaac Norris with quiet satisfaction, "but behaved as becomes our profession."

The governor's hoax brought things to a worse pass than before, and both sides dug themselves in. Unabashed, the governor renewed his demands on the Assembly, and they countered with a demand for "condign punishment" of the author of the false rumor. Still Governor Evans refused to admit he was licked; he advertised that he would collect a tax of half a pound of powder on every ton of freight brought up the river, although by royal charter navigation was free.

Outward-bound for Barbados, the Quaker skipper Richard Hill begged to inform the governor that he was sailing, and that nobody would collect anything from him. The fort was ordered to intercept Captain Hill, but by skillful navigation he slid by with only one shot in his sail. Pursued by the commandant in a small boat, Hill obligingly threw him a rope to come aboard; directly he stepped on deck the rope was cut, and the Quaker sailed on, the commandant a prisoner. Governor Evans himself took up the chase, and the whole party ended up in the office of the vice admiral, Lord Cornbury. The admiral sustained the Quaker and rebuked the governor.

Evans's extraordinary talent for getting in wrong had now got on the nerves of the populace; he had smoothed the path for the agitator, who promptly appeared in the person of David Lloyd, a wild Welsh lawyer who was frank to admit that Penn had incurred his implacable enmity by removing him from office. The hot-headed Celt drew a following from the non-Quaker influx, and from the Quaker irreconcilables, who were not hard to persuade that wide open-eyed vigilance was the price of liberty, of which the English government had the disposal.

Penn was too much a man of the world to imagine that he or any man could face it about suddenly; he knew too well that even the King could not have things all his own way. And temperamentally he was too conciliatory to expect his opponents to do all the yielding, he was at all times ready to go the limit in compromise. "We must not pretend to see all that we see if we would be easy. . . . It were endless to dispute upon everything that is disputable." So, on the one hand, he tried to coax enough money out of the Province to keep the Crown quiet; on the other hand, making out a good case for the loyalty of the suspected colonists, and defending their right to refuse military aid, since their charter granted them liberty of conscience.

While he was performing this acrobatic trick, David Lloyd was amusing himself in Pennsylvania by hurling insults at the King in the presence of the monarch's emissaries, by his indiscretions supplying weapons to the numerous enemies of Penn and Pennsylvania. Lloyd himself had a generous allotment of enemies, and Penn in extreme exasperation threatened "to take them by the hand." In the heat of the controversy his serenity melted away. He would sink in sorrow, he writes, "if not supported by a superior hand," and complains to Logan, "I cannot but think it hard measure, that while that has proved a land of freedom and flourishing, it should become to me by whose hand it was principally made a country, the cause of grief, trouble and poverty."

Twenty years of political responsibility had brought the Quakers to the point where they started, the belief that politics and the Christian life could not be run tandem. A letter to Penn tells him: "Friends here, at least the generality of the best informed, think government at this time so ill fitted to their principles, that it renders them indifferent in that point, further than that they earnestly desire thy success in vindicating the country's reputation, and that they may not fall a spoil to such base hands as now seek their ruin."

As for Penn's stanch Scotch friend, James Logan, who next to the proprietor shouldered the heaviest load of the Holy Experiment, the success of Lloyd's Celtic eloquence made him very weary, and the spectacle of democracy in the saddle gave no lift to his spirit. He writes Penn: "I cannot but pity the poor misled people, who really design honestly, but know not whom to trust for their directors; they are so often told that things want to be mended, that at length they are persuaded it is the case, and not knowing how to set about it themselves, believe that those who can discover the disease are the most capable to direct the remedies. . . . We might be happy if this promoter of discord went from among us."

Between the English cry of disloyalty and the Pennsylvania cry of oppression, Penn's suavity and patience began to show thin spots. In one of his patriarchal letters he writes: "It is a certain sign you are strangers to oppression, and know nothing but the name, when you so highly bestow it on matters so inconsiderable."

Some of the matters on which it was bestowed were not only inconsiderable but ludicrous. One droll complaint of persecution might have been laughed down, but for the furore created in England when the hue and cry was raised that the Quakers were persecuting churchmen. Penn was much upset by the embarrassment which this report caused him, and instructed Logan to go in haste and secure from those of the established church a statement that the rumor was pure invention. To Logan's astonishment the Episcopalian brethren were quite unprepared to deny the story; they were deprived of the special privileges they enjoyed in England, and such deprivation they accounted persecution. A cherished privilege was the right to rid the world of Quakers, but Logan's Scotch humor could not rise to the occasion. "I can see no hope," he sadly replied, "of getting any material subscription from those of the church against the report of persecution, they having consulted together on that head, and concluded that not allowing their clergy here what they of right claim in England, and not suffering them to be superior, may justly bear that name."

While Penn was still in the colony, he was importuned personally by one of the oppressed, and referred the matter to his secretary in Philadelphia: "I here inclose this honest but weak man's paper. I think I have convinced him that I am one of the poorest men in the government, and that my sin has been neglect of myself and not selfishness, and therefore ought and must make the best of everything. It seems he has much stony and mountainous land, and thinks two bushels of apples per acre (rent) an oppression. I referred him to thee, and told him I did believe thou wouldst be just and reasonable. He tells me of the hard circumstances of one James Davis. Hear it."

While Penn was being racked between the Crown and the colony, his family chipped in their bit toward a martyr's crown. Penn's first wife, the brave but delicate Gulielma, had found life as companion to a public-spirited benefactor of the race too strenuous; her gentle spirit had given up the harrowing struggle. On her son, William, Jr., at the time of his marriage, Penn settled her dowry, as well as his Irish estates. This worthless spendthrift retired to the Continent to squander his fortune in riotous living, quartering his family on his long-suffering father.

Daughter Letitia had married a grasping gentleman, one Aubrey, of whom Penn writes very confidentially to Logan, "A scraping fellow, who would count interest for a guinea." Letitia brought as part of her dowry property in Pennsylvania; the Province was slow pay, and by "mad and tempestuous bullyings" son-in-law Aubrey insisted on extorting from his distracted, debt-ridden father-in-law, the money he was unable to collect in the colony.

The friendship formed by Penn in his impressionable youth for James II, by a shift in the political world, suddenly became a relationship of great danger. For years Penn had been the mediator between the persecuted of all shades of belief and the King, and he seems to have fancied himself as purveyor of the royal clemency. His London residence became a bureau of relief from persecution; not only the Quakers, but their late and bitter foes the Episcopalians, whose turn under the harrow had come, benefited by his good will, for in the matter of persecution he played no favorites.

Now at last the Stuarts had come to the end of a long rope. King James was an aggressive and bigoted Catholic ruling a Protestant country, an unwise and headstrong king. Apprehension of French interference by connivance of the King and the dread of a return to Papal supremacy stirred an easily inflamed Protestant bigotry, and the King slipped across the Channel to his French friend for safety. Deserted by his own children, an exile from his own country, he found the friendship of the Penns steadfast; their personal relations were not affected by their political sympathies, which must undoubtedly have been with the opposite party. Gulielma Penn made trips across the channel to carry to the Queen presents from her English friends. An acutely suspicious public scented treason, and Penn's enemies made the most of it; he was undoubtedly a Jesuit, conspiring to restore the Stuarts. They took up with one Fuller, a highly imaginative and inventive gentleman, who produced documents to support their worst suspicions. Things took a serious turn for the Proprietor of Pennsylvania; he was charged with high treason.

The tolerant Dutchman, William of Orange, personally conducted the examination, and seems to have been impressed by the Quaker's frankness. Fuller's papers Penn declared to be pure fabrication. The deposed King he frankly admitted had been his father's friend, and his own, "and in gratitude he was the King's, and did ever, as much as in him lay, influence him to his true interest." As he had loved him in the day of his power, he would not turn on him now that he was down and out, but still loved him, and would render him any personal kindness within his power. "That he had never had the wickedness even to think of endeavoring to restore him that crown which had fallen from his head."

Since King William, the object of the supposed conspiracy, was satisfied to accept these statements at their face value, there was nothing more to be done by Penn's disappointed enemies. Fuller, his accuser, was subsequently recommended by the House of Commons for permanent sequestration as "a notorious cheat, rogue and false accuser."

Penn was not yet an old man, but he was ageing; even with the "support of a superior hand," his load was beginning to drag heavily. The strain of debts, domestic sorrows, never-ending calumnies, the indiscretions of deputies, the fractiousness of provincial malcontents, were rasping his amiability. And then the blow fell which moved William Penn into the class of the Patriarch Job.

"Queens as well as kings," so Penn once wrote disapprovingly, "never read what they sign. They are signed upon the credit of secretaries." That so wise, shrewd, and unpretentious a man as Penn should have slipped into this royal habit is strange; yet his unbounded confidence in his steward, Philip Ford, led him repeatedly to place his name to papers presented him without a glance at their contents. Ford succeeded in impressing his employer as a man utterly indifferent to his own interests, and Penn begs his American agent to have a special care for his steward's affairs, "for he deserves of the whole country to be preferred that for the good of it neglected the advancement of his own."

Mr. Ford, however, made considerable progress in looking out for himself, and faced his amazed employer with a demand for ten thousand pounds, well secured by a lien on the Province. In his simplicity, believing that Ford was misled rather than crooked, Penn proposed to lay all the evidence before disinterested arbitrators, which Ford promptly declined to do. He had been at a deal of trouble to provide a strong legal foundation for his villainy, and was convinced he had a better chance in law than in equity; the courts justified the wisdom of his choice.

The Quakers went thoroughly into the whole matter, and finding Ford's claim to be preposterous and fraudulent, disowned the unrepentent family, a sore which was no doubt easily healed by a poultice of pounds sterling. On the victim of the fraud the Quaker judgment fell more heavily; rather than pay an unjust debt and condone a fraud, it was Penn's duty to go to jail, and to a debtor's jail he went. For nine months an old man was deprived of his liberty whose whole life had been a fight to win it for others. In his youth he had the consolation of suffering for a great cause; in his age the bitterness of betrayal by a trusted friend.

Ford never lived to enjoy the reward of his cunning, and for nearly a year his stiff-necked widow and the Quakers wrestled. Not only Penn, but his province as well, suffered by his imprisonment. Even the Quakers were obliged to compromise at last, and when they had succeeded in reducing the claim to seven thousand six hundred pounds they settled and took over the mortgage on Pennsylvania. "God darkens this world to us," was Penn's solace, "that our eyes may behold the greater brightness of His kingdom."

Many less solacing thoughts intruded; debts were staggering, enemies active; the Penn family was producing no timber of statesman size; Pennsylvania was pulling at the bit; the Crown was eager to tighten the rein over the neck of the headstrong colonials. The threat of transferring his interest back to the Crown had usually called a halt to colonial turbulence; even the persecuted Episcopalians protested against the change; this course was now urged on Penn by his well wishers. There was prolonged wrangling before the Crown would agree to guarantee to Pennsylvania the liberties enjoyed under Penn's charter.

"Fear not my bargain with the Crown," he writes to Logan, "for it shall never be made without a security to the inhabitants according to the constitution and laws of the country," adding in peevish reproach, the key in which his later correspondence with the Province was written, "though my supplies to defend them come so slowly and costly to my support."

Pennsylvania had come to Penn a desolate wilderness in exchange for sixteen thousand pounds, taking no account of the money spent in purchases from the Indians. It was turned back a thriving colony for the sum of twelve thousand pounds, not a particularly brilliant piece of profiteering.

And then came the last lap of the journey, when there was quiet; a tiny clot on the brain, and the clamor of friends, the calumny of foes disturbed him no more. Only the voice which he had heard in his youth was audible and comforting. In his pleasant country estate among the green and growing things which delighted him, the kindly, courteous old gentleman wandered serenely. He often got to Meeting, and occasionally spoke a few stammering sentences, "clear as to truth" the Friends pronounced, and therefore the paralysis was thought to be a dispensation of mercy rather than of judgment, a well-deserved rest at the end of a long and difficult journey.

"I have continued in this large house and expense," writes Hannah Callowhill, Penn's capable second wife, "only to keep him as comfortable as I can, for he has all along delighted in walking and taking the air here, when the weather allows, and at other times diverts himself from room to room, and the satisfaction he takes therein is the greatest pleasure I have in enjoying so large a house, which I have (with the necessary expenses and loads I bear) long found too much for me and our shrunk income."

The call came in his seventy-fourth year, on the fifth of July, just forty-eight years before the Declaration of Independence was signed in the city he built and dedicated to liberty, and the bell on which the Quakers had inscribed "Proclaim liberty throughout the land to all the inhabitants thereof," rang out the news to a new nation.

Penn's faithful friends, the "sagacious" Indians, sent a message of condolence to the widow of the beloved white chief, accompanied by a present of furs, "materials to form a garment of skins, suitable for travelling in a thorny wilderness." Mrs. Penn appreciated the understanding of the givers; as the wife of a philanthropist she was experienced in travel of the sort.

Penn's ideals, fanatical in their time, have become in part our American heritage, though much of his program remains to be caught up with. They have colored, if not deeply dyed, our institutions. The life of a great man too often reminds us that he who aspires to lead his race further out of the wilderness of ignorance and prejudice would do well to take a hint from the sagacious savage, and provide a garment suitable for traveling a thorny trail, made of the substance of things hoped for, the evidence of things not seen.

Edward Burrough—The Avenging Quaker

Nothing is so contagious as enthusiasm; it moves stones, it charms brutes. Enthusiasm is the genius of sincerity, and truth accomplishes no victories without it. —LYTTON.

ADJOINING the Friends Meeting House in London is an old graveyard, which has been leveled with the exception of one gravestone. Within the Meeting House a tablet perpetuates the memory of the dead who lie in the unmarked graves, Edward Burrough and seventy others, all of whom "died in the prisons of London." On the remaining gravestone is chiseled the name of George Fox; fate has given the Quaker leader a distinction in death, which in life he would have scorned.

Of all the young spirits fired by Fox's preaching, and now quietly resting beside him, none of the Valiant Sixty was more exuberant than Edward Burrough, known as the Son of Thunder and Consolation. Fox was an expert in handling enthusiasm, the moral dynamite without which he could make no progress in blasting those "Mountains of Encumbrance." His own conduct was as decorous as his task would permit, and by private admonition he took all necessary precautions for the safeguarding of his explosives; publicly he never deserted his left wing.

Burrough was a mettlesome youth, gifted by nature with other attributes than the meek and quiet spirit which is considered the proper adornment of the Christian. It was an age of serious children, and at twelve Burrough was a seeker after the Light. He found neither Light nor life in the state religion in which he had been reared. For a time he browsed in the Presbyterian pastures where he was made much of; as the son of respectable parents he had received a good education, and the Presbyterians venerated knowledge. It was not until he had listened to George Fox that he found rest for his soul, and for the pearl of great price he gladly gave in exchange all that he possessed. For when he became a Quaker, his highly respectable parents turned their boy out of doors, bag and baggage, refusing his entreaty to be allowed to remain as a servant. Presbyterianism they tolerated, for it was respectable, and at the moment in the ascendant; Quakerism they refused to stand for.

On the meager pickings of an itinerant preacher among a generous but poor and harried people, Burrough lived and delivered his trenchant message. His pacifism we must assume to have been a matter of "convincement" rather than of temperament. When his wanderings led him across the Channel to fight the Jesuits on their own ground, he found an English garrison at Dunkirk, and his vehement outburst to the soldiers went far beyond orthodox Quaker doctrine. As they had chosen a soldier's life, why not, he urged, fight for something worth while, why not march on to Rome and capture the torture houses of the Inquisition? "What do you know but the Lord may have some good work for you to do, if you be faithful to him? The Lord once armed them (the English) with the spirit of courage and zeal, and gave them victory and dominion over much injustice and oppression and cruel laws." Why not continue the good fight all the way to Rome, "till you have inquired after and sought out the innocent blood buried there, and avenged the guiltless through all the dominions of the Pope. The blood of the just, it cries through Italy and Spain."

Sewel explains this lapse from the pure pacifist doctrine by Burrough's desire "not to give them too rough a brush, but to meet them somewhat in their own way." Without dampening their passionate ardor for justice, Fox had a way of leading his overzealous disciples back into the straight and thorny path of principle, of suffering without reprisal. In his ten years of strenuous ministry, fighting for dominion over injustice and oppression in his own land, Burrough bore his share of suffering with all the meekness he could muster.

He was but twenty years old when he invaded the town of Bristol with his inseparable companion, Francis Howgill, who had been trained for ministry in the established church. The populace found the oratory of the youths so extremely entertaining that no building could be found to hold their audiences. They were forced to preach in the open fields, where in the most inclement weather as many as four thousand people would stand listening patiently. This great following roused the clergy who preached to empty pews, and they in turn inflamed the mob "to the highest pitch of fury." The mob was in a lynching mood, and knocked the young preachers about, to cries of "Knock them down. Hang them." More law-abiding counsel prevailed and they were taken instead before the magistrates.

In the warrant for their arrest, they were described as "of the Franciscan order of Rome," a description which must have stirred the mirth of even so serious a youth as Burrough, he who incited the English garrison to move on Rome and clean it up of innocent blood. Papist was the term of popular opprobrium, equivalent to Red in our day, and a convenient label to pin on the holder of any new and unpalatable opinion.

Besse tells us that "the innocent Men were as Lambs dumb before their shearers," a dumbness not apparent to the magistrates who ordered their deportation. "We came not in the Will of Man," they said, "nor stand in the Will of Man, but when He moves us to depart, who moved us hither, we shall obey; but your Wills we cannot obey, for your Will is no Law; if we are guilty of the Transgression of any Law, let us suffer by it, but rather than we will Transgress the righteous Law of God, written in our hearts, by subjecting to your Wills and Lusts, we shall chuse to walk in the Law of God, and to suffer under your Wills what you can lay upon us. We are freeborn Englishmen, and have served the Commonwealth in Faithfulness, being free in the presence of God from the Transgression of any Law. To your commands we cannot be obedient, but if by Violence you put us out of the City, and have Power to do it, we cannot resist."

Whether this peculiar exhibition of dumbness was the reason for their release, we are not told, but released they were. Braving the hostility of the magistrates and of the mob which was backed by the respectable business men of the town, they resumed their meetings. Burrough was no stranger in practice to the brand of courage he preached to the English soldiers at Dunkirk, nor was he more tolerant of English than of Romish injustice.

It was no uncommon experience for the Quakers to discover that the unregenerate were more charitable than the congregations of the self-righteous. Leaving the righteous of Bristol, Burrough moved on to London, where he got a more cordial reception from the sinners. "At London there is a custom in summer time, when tradesmen leave off working, that many lusty fellows meet in the fields, to try their skill and strength in wrestling, where a multitude of people stands gazing in a round. Now it fell out that E. Burrough passed by the place where they were wrestling, and standing still among the spectators, saw how a strong and dexterous fellow had already thrown three others, and was waiting for a fourth champion, if any durst venture into the lists."

E. Burrough durst venture into anything; to the astonishment of the victorious pugilist, the slender youth leaped into the ring. "All stood amazed at the sight, eagerly expecting what would be the issue of this combat. But it was quite another fight E. Burrough aimed at. He began very seriously to speak to the standers by, with such heart piercing power, that he was heard by this mixed multitude with no less attention than admiration; for his speech tended to turn them from darkness to light. He labored with convincing power, showing how God had not left himself without a witness, but had given to man a measure of His grace. Though many might look upon this as a novelty, yet it was of such effect that some were convinced of the truth; for he was a breaker of stony hearts, not unjustly called a Son of Thunder."

It may have flattered the sinners of the wicked metropolis to be told that they, too, were the children of light and grace; at any rate, they did not combine pugilism with piety, after the manner of the stony-hearted churchmen of Bristol.

A round of preaching, persecution, and prisons was the order of young Burrough's life. Imprisoned, he developed talent as a letter writer, and still carried on. Parliament was warned that the same abuse of power which had cost Charles I his head would prove equally disastrous to his beheaders. When Charles II came into his own again, he was favored with an equally frank admonition. "Charles Stuart must either be converted to God, and ruled by Him, or he cannot rightly rule for God in this Nation." It was conceded by the writer, however, that the power which moves in a mysterious way, might make use of the King as a rod to smite the oppressors "that once smote him."

Admonishing his Majesty was a favorite pastime of young Quakers under the irksome restraint of prison discipline. The King's irregular and extensive domesticity was rebuked. "The Lord is grieved with the pride and wickedness that is lived in, both in thy family and dominions, and thou thyself hast not been such a pattern and example as thou oughtest to have been," wrote one who expressed at the same time a love for the King's soul. Kings in those days apparently gave personal attention to their mail, and as Charles merrily read aloud this good advice to brother James, the Duke of York, whose own conduct was open to like criticism, Prince James angrily insisted on severe punishment for the impudent letter writer. The King "who never said a foolish thing, nor ever did a wise one" laughed good-naturedly. "It were better for us to amend our lives," was his sensible comment.

It is not surprising that Burrough, described by Ellwood as "a brisk young man with a ready tongue," should have captured the roving fancy of the Merry Monarch. The tepid interest of a King proved to be of less value to the Quaker, however, than the timely assistance of a poor Quaker when that same King was running for his life. Nevertheless, the King's favor enabled Burrough to puncture the overweening pride of the New England theocracy, humble the haughty spirit of Governor Endicott, and save the lives of many Quakers from Puritan ferocity. Edward Burrough was the author of a drama never surpassed on the stage for the melodramatic downfall of the villain in the presence of innocence triumphant. Endicott, the ruthless Governor of Massachusetts, was cast for the rôle of villain, a poor Quaker shoemaker for the part of hero.

For the beginning of this story we must leave Edward Burrough to the mercies of English mobs and magistrates, and shift the scene to the Puritan colony. A Boston shoemaker, Samuel Shattock, had become restive under the heavy yoke of the Massachusetts State Church, where the sermons, so a compulsory listener testified, were "meat for digestion, but only for the heart and stomach of an ostrich." Samuel's digestion was weak, and "being found on the First Day of the week at Home in time of Public Worship, he was sent to the House of Correction, and there cruelly whipt." In addition to corporeal punishment, this poor workman, with a young family to support, was fined beyond his ability to pay. And further to make a good job of the business, the authorities terrified his wife with the threat of perpetual imprisonment for her husband, and amiably insinuated that his conduct was prompted by a desire to be rid of her. Failing to break Samuel's spirit, they were determined to break up his home. All things considered, Samuel, when set at liberty, thought it wise "to depart that Jurisdiction" and submitted to expulsion from the colony. He removed to Salem, but found little advantage in this change of residence; all New England settlements being under the sway of Boston.

Settling in Salem, Samuel attached himself to the unorthodox worshipers, and he with others was taken in the net, on a charge of blasphemy. The Friends submitted to the officials of Salem that "they would do well to send some one to their Meetings, that they might hear and give an Account of what was done and spoken there, and not conclude any Thing they knew not." Major General Denison considered such evidence altogether unnecessary, for said he, "If ye meet together and say any Thing, we may conclude that ye speak Blasphemy," a pronouncement which the Quaker historian considers "An inference altogether weak and Irrational."

Herded with "felons and murderers," the blasphemous heretics were passed on to Boston. By the most eminent Calvinist divines, a murderer was considered a much less dangerous citizen than a heretic. At the Quaker trials Governor Endicott contributed a dogmatic decision: "The Quakers have nothing to prove their Commission but the Spirit within them, and that is the devil." They in rebuttal: "We have seen some of your Laws that have many Scriptures in the Margin, but what example have you for cutting off ears?" They further submitted,

" that they counted not their lives dear unto themselves, for the Sake of Him who called them." To which Endicott grimly retorted: " And we shall be as ready to take away your lives as ye shall be to lay them down; " which proved to be no exaggeration.

To that worthy forefather and founder, Major General Denison, we are indebted for the simplest and most concise statement in history of the right of might. " He should not go about," he said, " to speak much concerning their Errors of Judgment. But you and we are not well able to live together, and at Present the Power is in our hand, therefore the Stronger must send off." On this principle, Samuel Shattock was separated from his frightened wife and small children and deported to Barbados. But a dose of his own logic was being prepared for General Denison.

Samuel Shattock was the merest atom in the social body, an atom vibrating with the eternal energy, however. It never occurred to this humble shoemaker to settle down in Barbados with the plaintive inquiry: " What is there to do about it? " He took the first available boat for England, to inform the Friends there, that, in violation of English law, members of their Society in New England were being put to death for saying their prayers in an irregular manner. George Fox in his journal declares that, when the Quakers were hanged in Boston, " I was in prison at Lancaster, and had a perfect sense of their sufferings as though it had been myself, and as though the halter had been put about my own neck, though we had not at that time heard of it." The Massachusetts worthies were known among the English Friends as "The New England Inquisition," and Inquisitions whether Papal or Puritan had a singularly inflaming effect on the mind of young Burrough.

On hearing Shattock's story, he rushed off to inform King Charles himself, "that a vein of innocent blood was opened in his dominions, which if not stopped would overrun all." By a happy coincidence, the King was just then perusing, with more astonishment than satisfaction, a book recording the flippant and unfavorable comment on the English government, of the heady General Denison, who expressed hopeful doubts as to the permanency of the kingly rule.

Calling his Lords to hear it, he said: "Lo these are my good subjects of New England." There was no love lost between the King and the Puritans who had so roughly consigned his father to the discard. Moreover, those regicides who had escaped to New England could never be discovered, though the approach of a Quaker was scented afar off. Therefore, when Burrough came with his tale of the vein of innocent blood opened in New England, the King was in the best of all possible moods to listen.

"But I will stop that vein," said he emphatically.

"Do it speedily," Burrough insisted, "for we know not how many may soon be put to death."

"As speedily as you will," said the King. "Call the secretary, and I will do it presently."

With the King's mandamus in his possession, Burrough's problem was to get it delivered without delay. Within a day or two he was back again to the King, who told him it would be impossible to dispatch a ship at once. Burrough in the two days' interim had collected three hundred pounds among the Friends, and had hunted out a Quaker captain, "Ralph Goldsmith, an honest Friend who was master of a good ship," and who agreed to sail within ten days "goods or no goods." More than all this, Burrough had worked up his dramatic plot, which he now broached to his Majesty, "would it please him to grant his deputation to one called a Quaker, to carry his mandamus to New England?"

"Yes, to whom you will," returned the King, who had a relish for a practical joke, more especially one on his trusty and well-beloved New England subjects. "Whereupon E. Burrough named one Samuel Shattock, who being an inhabitant of New England was banished on pain of death, if ever he returned thither." King Charles accordingly "granted the deputation to him, with full power to carry the mandamus, which was as followeth:"

CHARLES R.

Trusty and well-beloved, we greet you well. — Having been informed that several of our subjects amongst you called Quakers have been, and are imprisoned by you, whereof some have been executed and others (as hath been represented unto us) are in danger to undergo the like: we have thought fit to signify our pleasure in this behalf for the future; and do hereby require that if there be any of those people called Quakers amongst you, now already condemned to suffer death, or other corporeal punishment, or that are imprisoned and obnoxious to like condemnation, you are to forbear to proceed any further therein; but that forthwith you send the said persons, (whether condemned or imprisoned) over to this our Kingdom of England together with the respective crimes or offenses laid to their charge; to the end that such course may be taken with them, as shall be agreeable to our laws, and their demerits.

And for so doing these letters shall be your sufficient warrant and discharge.

Given at our court at Whitehall, the 9th day of September, 1661, in the 13th year of our reign.

By His Majesty's command,

WILLIAM MORRIS.

To our trusty and well-beloved John Endicott, Esq., and to all and every other governor, or governors of our plantations of New England, and of all other colonies thereunto belonging, that are now, or hereafter shall be; and to all and every the ministers and officers of our said plantations and colonies whatsoever, within the continent of New England.

There was no sugar coating on this bitter pill prescribed for poor Endicott, he who had shouted "No appeal to England," whose feeling for his country's flag was so intense, that he had cut out all but the border of the Union Jack, claiming that the cross was offensive to him. Quakers had died in English prisons, but none had been legally condemned to death as in New England, nor had they suffered under the home government such savagery as had befallen them in the colony. His Majesty was serving notice on the Puritan Fathers, that for the future when any hanging was to be done, his own officers would relieve them of the responsibility.

The Quaker captain, Ralph Goldsmith, was off as soon as he could get his ship under way, carrying Samuel Shattock, who carried the King's mandamus. With favoring winds he made the New England coast in six weeks, and dropped into Boston harbor on a Sabbath morning. Captain Goldsmith had been informed of the situation, and had an eye for the dramatic; his sailors were not allowed ashore, and the townspeople who came aboard inquiring for mail were told, yes, he had mail, but none would be delivered that day. He meant to keep the lid on till Endicott's meal of crow could be served in good style. The townspeople flew back with the exciting news that Goldsmith carried an unlawful cargo of Quakers, among them the deported Samuel Shattock, under sentence of death.

New England magistrates and clergy were extremely jealous of their dignity and authority, none more so than Governor Endicott. He had severely thrashed a citizen with his own hands, and justified his conduct by saying, "If you had seen the manner of his carriage, with such daring of me with his arms on kembow, it would have provoked a very patient man." And the Governor was not patient. One Ratcliff was whipped, fined and had his ears removed, to be made an example of, said Endicott, "for all carnal men, to presume to speak the least word that might tend to the dishonor of the Church of Salem; yea, the mother Church of all that Holy Land."

Captain Goldsmith's carriage was propriety itself; early Monday morning he escorted King's Deputy Shattock to Endicott's door. "He sending a man to know their business, they sent him word that their business was from the King of England, and that they would deliver their message to none but the Governor himself. Thereupon they were admitted to go in."

The Governor's ungovernable rage was stirred by the sight of shoemaker Shattock standing covered in his presence; he commanded an attendant to pull the hat off. Perusal of the King's politely menacing letter reduced Endicott's temperature somewhat, and removing his own head covering in the presence of King's Deputy Shattock, as by etiquette required, he ordered, "Give *Mr.* Shattock his hat." Before committing himself further, Endicott retired to confer with his deputy governor, and returning in a humbled state of mind, curtly announced: "We shall obey the King's orders." The stronger was sending off, for New England was still too weak to clash with the Crown.

It was a day of unspeakable humiliation for the violent old autocrat. Rumors of trouble brewing in England had already forced him into some sober reflection. Burrough and the English Friends had been moved to such prompt and energetic action by the news of the hanging of several

Quakers, and of twenty-seven under death sentence in the Boston prison, among them Wenlock Christison, condemned by Endicott himself against the protests of his colleagues, and in violation of the laws of the government under which the colony held its charter. Endicott failed to get a majority vote for Christison's death sentence. With the disapprobation of the home government on the one hand, and the disaffection of their own people on the other, the moderates felt that it was time to call a halt. Endicott refused to halt, and flew into a rage: "'I could find it in my heart to go home,' being in such a rage that he flung something furiously on the table. 'You that will not consent to record it (the vote): I thank God that I am not afraid to give judgment. Wenlock Christison, harken to your sentence: You must return unto the place from whence you came, and from thence to the place of execution, and there you must be hang'd until you are dead, dead, *dead.*'"

To which the condemned answered prophetically: "Known be it unto you all, that if you have the power to take my life from me, my soul shall enter into everlasting rest and peace with God, where you yourselves shall never come. And if ye have the power to take my life from me, *which I do question*, I do believe ye shall never more take Quakers lives from them: *note my words.*"

And this day was that prophecy fulfilled; not only were the prison doors thrown open by order of the hated English government, but a fresh shipload of the "accursed heretics" was discharged on the holy soil of New England. A great Quaker reunion was the grand finale of the drama staged by young Burrough.

Burrough had saved others, himself he could not save. Hatred of the Puritans was a stronger motive with King Charles than an enduring love for Quakers, or a passion for abstract justice. Grievous persecution was now the lot of the London Quakers, and Burrough was again working the stony ground of Bristol, when tales of their sufferings reached him. With a premonition of his fate, he took leave of the Faithful in Bristol to go where the battle was hottest. "I am now going up to the City of London to lay down my life for the gospel, and suffer amongst Friends in that place."

Arch-persecutor Alderman Richard Brown was waiting to greet him; in Newgate, where so many had died of suffocation, he caged the thundering young lion. Burrough had survived much rough usage, but this airless captivity was his undoing, and Friends petitioned the King, representing that his life was in danger. Charles was indebted to the audacious young man with the ready tongue, who had so dramatically taken a fall out of his trusty New Englanders, and readily signed the warrant for his release. The prisoner was already so far gone that Alderman Brown took the liberty of suppressing the King's warrant, and had the satisfaction of forever silencing the ready tongue of the young preacher.

Conscious that his end was near, Burrough sent a dying message to Friends, " To live in love and peace, and love one another." A good Christian must go further, and forgive his enemies, and for them Burrough prayed earnestly. He stumbled at Alderman Brown, and a flame of the old fire shot up. If any of His creatures could get beyond the pale of the Divine Mercy, Alderman Richard Brown was that man, cringing to the powerful, brutal to the humble and helpless. He put a heavy strain on the principles of the dying Quaker, who prayed, " Lord, forgive Richard Brown, if he may be forgiven."

Quaker biographies come in pairs; Burrough's devoted and inseparable companion Francis Howgill mourned his friend, but not as one without hope. " Shall days or months or years wear out thy name, as though thou hadst no being? Oh, nay: Shall not thy noble and valiant acts, and mighty works which thou hast wrought . . . live in generations to come? Oh, yes! The children that are yet unborn shall have thee in their mouths, and thy works shall testify of thee in the generations who yet have no being."

Howgill carried on the work vigorously after Burrough's death, and with such success that he was soon overtaken by a like fate. As there was nothing against him but his preaching, he was caught in the snare of the oath. His trial affords some tragic humor.

JUDGES: What do you tell us of conscience? We

meddle not with conscience, but you contemn the laws, and keep up great meetings, and go not to church.

HOWGILL: We are fallen on a sad age; if meeting together peaceably without force or arms, or intention to hurt any man, only to worship God in spirit, and exhort one another to righteousness, as the primitive Christians of old, that this should be reckoned breach of peace or misbehavior.

JUDGE TWISDEN: Do you compare these times with those? They were heathens that persecuted, but we are Christian magistrates.

HOWGILL: It is a doctrine always held by us, that Christ's Kingdom could not be set up with carnal weapons; nor the gospel propagated by force of arms, nor the church of God built with violence, but the Prince of Peace was manifested amongst us, and we could learn war no more, but could love enemies and forgive them that did evil to us.

JUDGE FLEMING: My Lord, he is a great speaker, it may be the Quakers cannot do without him.

PHILIP MUSGRAVE: My Lord, we have been remiss toward these people, and have striven with them, and put them in prison, again and again, and as soon as they are out they meet again.

JUDGE LOWTHER: My Lord, they grow insolent, notwithstanding all laws, and execution of them, yet they grow upon us, and their meetings are dangerous.

My Lord: I have spent much time with you, I will discourse no more.

Howgill: I acknowledge your moderation toward me, allowing me liberty to speak.

The judges were moderate even in their moderation; Howgill's personal property was confiscated forever for the King; his real estate seized during his life, himself imprisoned for life. During the five years he lay in prison, many distinguished citizens visited him, among them the Mayor of the town. As his life was slowly squeezed out by prison suffering, the Mayor prayed with him that God would speak peace to his soul.

"He hath done it," said Howgill, and, without rancor in his heart, another of the Valiant Sixty went out, a hero of the war for the liberation of humanity, a humanity powerfully resistant to liberation.

Mary Dyer—The Bloody Town of Boston

I am in earnest — I will not equivocate — I will not excuse — I will not yield a single inch, *and I will be heard.*

— WILLIAM LLOYD GARRISON.

"THE hard condition of the historian is," says the Venerable Bede, "that if he speak the truth he provokes the anger of men; but if he commits falsehoods to writing he will be unacceptable to God, who will distinguish in his judgments between truth and adulation." The Quaker campaign against Puritan despotism, which for the purpose of this story culminates in the hanging of Mary Dyer "as a flag" on Boston Common, can only be properly understood by brushing away the dust and cobweb of hokum and buncombe which lie thick on history. Charles Francis Adams and his brother Brooks Adams, whose family played a conspicuous part in our history, have dusted it off a bit, deploring that apologists for Puritan brutality condone in the Founding Fathers the same conduct they scathingly condemn in their enemies.

The Puritan superiority complex, which the adulation of historians soon crystallized into legend, got an early start. In a family letter written from Cambridge, Massachusetts, in 1775, General Washington registers surprise: "The People of this Government [Massachusetts] have obtained a character which they by no means deserved. . . . I have already broke one Colonel and five Captains for Cowardice, or for drawing more Pay and Provisions than they had Men in their Companies. . . . They are by no means such Troops, in any respect, as you are led to believe of them from the accounts which are published, but I need not make myself enemies among them by this declaration, although it is consistent with truth. I dare say the men would fight very well (if properly officered) although they are exceeding dirty nasty people." Again to General Reed he complains of the "dearth of public spirit, and such want of virtue, such stock jobbing and fertility in all low arts to obtain advantage of one kind or another, that I never before saw, and pray God's mercy that I may never be witness to again. Such a mercenary spirit pervades the whole, that I should not at all be surprised at any disaster that may happen. Could I have foreseen what I have experienced . . . no consideration upon earth should have induced me to accept this command. . . . It grieves me to see so little of that patriotic spirit which I was taught to believe was characteristic of this people."

Though a pinch of salt must be added to the prejudices of the Virginia aristocrat, his soreness was excusable. Washington had less to gain and more to lose by the Revolution which New England had precipitated than others. He could have named his own price to the English government for a return to "loyalty," while in the event of failure, whoever escaped, the rebel-in-chief was a doomed man.

The Quaker histories, published long before Washington's disillusionment, if they had been popular reading in their day, would have interrupted the Puritan legend. Certainly the stirring song, which has so long rejoiced the patriot heart, would have been lost to the world:

> What sought they thus roaming
> Far, far away?
> Oh, they sought and found
> Where the soul unbound
> To the God of the free might pray.

These Quaker histories furnish ample proof that the soul unbound encountered as rough travel in the Puritan settlements as in any other part of the world; in them the Cradle of Liberty is constantly referred to as "The Bloody Town of Boston," the hierarchy as the New England Inquisition. The Puritan Fathers were a plucky band of pioneers, with all the nerve their hazardous adventure required, but the God of the free was not a Deity that appealed to them; they were devout worshipers at the shrine of the Great Jehovah, God of Vengeance. Among Governor Dudley's cherished papers these lines were salvaged:

> Let men of God in Courts and Churches watch
> O'er such as do a toleration hatch,
> Lest that Ill Egg bring forth a Cockatrice
> To poison all with heresies and vice.

The flattering myth that the Fathers divided their spare time between the honest ballot box and the Mercy Seat must also go down before the facts. The ballot box was not stuffed, for they had a simpler and more effective method of bringing the vote out right; only church members could vote, and any who were suspected of hatching the ill egg of toleration were promptly excommunicated.

It is true they continually besieged the Mercy Seat, but the quality of their mercy was so well strained that the savages looked on aghast at the ferocity of the Puritans to the enemies of Jehovah. It is evident from their own records that the ruling caste of the Puritan settlements lived in a busy little world of hate, springing from fear. They feared the power of the English government and hated it; they feared and hated the Indians; in their lust for absolute power they hated "all and every" who questioned their power. God-fearing is the traditional characterization of the Puritans, yet that fear was a much less powerful emotional stimulant than their fear of their enemies, of which there were not a few. Their apologists not unreasonably claim that the Puritans had good grounds for fear; and so by the same token had those who excited it. Of these, the Indians nearest at hand fared the worst.

As our story covers the first forty years of the Puritan journey in the wilderness, we may as well begin at the beginning, and take in the whole picture. A few years before the historic landing at Plymouth Rock, and within sight of that symbol of freedom, Captain Thomas Hunt, an enterprising Englishman, had enticed aboard his vessel a number of natives, to be profitably disposed of as slaves in Spain, for the English were the most successful slavers. All white men looked alike to the natives, and a French vessel soon after entering the harbor they made their inning, "treacherously" thrusting their knives "in the French men's Bellys," treachery being the word dedicated to descriptions of Indian behavior. One of the first exploring expeditions made by the redoubtable Miles Standish encountered a very old Indian woman, who burst into passionate weeping at sight of the white men; her three sons had been among those captured for slaves, and were never heard from again.

About the time the Pilgrims took possession of Plymouth, another vessel, less known to fame, unloaded a band of London scalawags, who settled close by at Wessagusset, causing much anxiety to the Mayflower group, and something more than anxiety to the Indians, whom they robbed and harried, rather than otherwise exert themselves. "Under these circumstances," says C. F. Adams, "the Indians showed in their conduct a self-restraint and respect for persons which, had the position been reversed, would assuredly have been looked for in vain among Europeans."

These coast Indians had been all but exterminated by a terrible pestilence, the bleaching bones of their tribe covered the earth. Suffering themselves from a scarcity of food, they had been generous to the strangers. When even their hidden seed corn was stolen by the shiftless band of whites at Wessagusset, instead of administering summary justice, they turned the culprits over to their own people at Plymouth for punishment. Beyond admonishing their countrymen of the danger of rousing Indian animosity, the colonists paid little heed to the repeated appeals of the natives for redress and relief; they either could not or would not have it out with the Wessagusset settlers. Not to carry self-restraint beyond reasonable limits, the "silly savages" finally decided to prune the earth of these rotten branches. If this useful service had been proposed by white men, the Pilgrims would have rejoiced and given glory to God's providence.

The intention of the Indians was revealed to the Plymouth people by Chief Massasoit, in gratitude for their good offices in curing him of a serious illness. The "conspiracy" of the Indians to make an end of the London toughs who had so long tormented them, quite naturally disturbed the colony. The logic of the situation as they saw it was that, if the Indians once tasted the blood of an Englishman, they might thirst for more, and descend upon Plymouth. This fear seems to have been carefully fostered by Captain Standish, in whose heart rankled a fierce personal enmity to Chief Wituwamut, and Mr. Adams tells us that with Standish, "it was not a word and a blow, it was a glance and a blow."

Standish had honestly endeavored to impress upon the

natives that the Plymouth colonists were fair and square, but he was unable to refrain from a nasty threat as to what would happen to Indians who failed to walk circumspectly, although up to that time their conduct had been conspicuously more circumspect than that of the white men. Chief Wituwamut carried himself with disrespectful bravado in the presence of the white chief of Plymouth.

So far as their portraits can be discerned in the dim light of history, in all but physical perfection wherein the Indian had the advantage, Wituwamut was an Indian replica of Standish himself. He made it clear that the white man, too, had better mind his P's and Q's, that any one treading on the heel of his moccasin would have ample cause for regret. There was no interpreter to decode his eloquence, but his opinions were rendered in pantomime which was lucidity itself — an unpardonable insult to Nordic superiority in general, and to the vanity of the little Napoleon of Plymouth in particular, to be wiped out by blood.

Captain Standish got authority from the colony to go out and put the Indians in their proper place — under the sod. With the public safety on his tongue, and wounded vanity in his heart demanding a showdown with the insolent sachem, Standish set off with only a few men (for he was not lacking in courage), each instructed in the part he was to play. Treachery is a word rarely used in connection with the conduct of the whites; Standish sent out word that he had come as usual to trade. "His hope had been to get a larger number of savages together before he fell on them," but it was "against Wituwamut in particular he was meditating dire vengeance," and as that chief was among those who came in with furs, he decided to proceed with his plan. Had the public safety been uppermost in his mind, rather than his personal feud with Wituwamut, he would probably have waited.

When the unsuspecting Indians had been quietly locked in the blockhouse, at a signal from the captain, the Pilgrims fell upon them, "with a stealth which exceeded that of the savages." Standish stabbed one of the braves with his own knife, and in less time than it takes to tell, all the Indians were butchered. "Though wholly taken by surprise and at a fearful disadvantage, the savages neither cried out, nor tried to fly, nor asked for quarter. Catching at their weapons and vainly resisting they struggled to the last." White superiority was vindicated, the insult to Captain Standish's *amour propre* avenged; he cut off the head of Wituwamut, and took it back in his boat to the settlement, to mount it on a pole, which must have made Plymouth seem more homelike to the exiled Englishman.

The exploit of the strong man of Plymouth Mr. Adams calls "a massacre, and a cold blooded one," yet he claims Standish instinctively knew what the Jesuits learned by experience, that the way to deal with Indians was to treat them rough from the start, that "he never made a mistake." This, of course, is a matter of opinion. What would have happened if the Pilgrims had trusted to the arm of Jehovah, as they professed, is a matter of conjecture; what actually followed this high-handed murder is a matter of history. The whites began existence in the new world by incurring a blood debt with the Indians, a debt of honor which by tribal code they were bound to collect though payment were deferred to the third or fourth generation. For offenses much less serious than those the Indians had patiently suffered, the Puritans themselves mutilated and killed the offenders.

So, in addition to the Old World fear which they brought with them, they now lived in fear of reaping as they had sown in the New World — a very abundant harvest it proved. As they grew in strength and power they developed a jealous fear of "opinionists" who might question their power; all who differed from them were opinionists, and differences soon appeared. That the contest they waged under cover of religion was the age-long struggle for power, we have the testimony of William Coddington, himself a Founding Father, a governor of Rhode Island, and lately treasurer of the Massachusetts colony, replying to a letter from the Governor of New England:

"That persecution hath been in New England is apparent, and must not and cannot be denied, and it is the Shame and Reproach of New England, that those that were persecuted in England, and bore their testimonies against Bishops and Ceremonies, should in New England put to death four of the servants of the everliving God, banish upon pain of death, cut off ears, fine, whip and imprison, *for keeping their consciences pure to God;* the like all things considered is hardly parallelled, which hath been in the former Governor's Days; and not only those of *my Way* as thou callst it.

"After seven years the New England Ministers, so-called, began to persecute about the testimony of the Spirit, the Light within. . . . Now was the Time the Magistrates were priest ridden, and now others and myself did draw up Remonstrances as Members of the Court against persecution for succeeding Times; for now it was that the priests would have Accommodations for Lands, with the Best Houses built for them; now were they grown warm in their Accommodations: Now was the iron bed, like that of the Tyrant made use of, to cut all according to it shorter or longer. . . . If Men in Reference to Soul and Body, things appertaining both to this and the other World, shall be subject to their fellow Creatures, what follows, but that Caesar, however he got it, has all God's share and his own too."

This is an account of the Puritan struggle by a participant, who had already gone through the same struggle in Europe. Waxing fat, the clergy became greedy for power. Roger Williams, Coddington, and their followers, a courageous minority who resisted, were driven out of the colony. In the Jewish legends we read that a wrathful Deity promised the pleading Abraham to spare the wicked Sodomites if even ten righteous men could be found among them. When all has been said against the Puritans, they never lacked their necessary quota to insure salvation, and it was to the aid of the courageous saving minority that the Quakers came.

Determined perpetuators of the Puritan myth have put up some curious apologies for the Fathers. Thus Dr. Ellis, a Lowell lecturer: "It might appear as if good manners, and generosity and magnanimity of spirit, would have kept the Quakers away. Certainly by every rule of right and reason, they ought to have kept away. Those magistrates never intended them harm. . . . It is frankly and positively affirmed that their Quaker tormentors were the aggressive party; that they wantonly initiated the strife, and with a dogged pertinacity persisted in outrages which drove the authorities to a frenzy." Aside from its inaccuracy, this argument entirely misses the point of the Quaker activity, as we shall see.

On the other hand, those wearied by such apologies for the Puritans go so far as to assert that the victims of their intolerance looked for redress to the calm impartial justice of England. Factions on both sides of the water aimed at wholesale extermination of their opponents; between Old and New England it was a case of "kettle call the pot black," as exemplified in the gruesome execution of Hugh Peters, the most vindicative of all the New England divines who come into our story.

A man of untempered violence, Mr. Peters had vociferously urged the execution of King Charles. The impartial justice meted out to such enthusiasts by the son of that shifty monarch included disemboweling, that before being dispatched the doomed might view the burning of his own entrails. There was no immunity for the cloth, and Mr. Peters, cheered on his way to the scaffold by the company of a newly severed head, was compelled by the hangman to witness the execution of his companion, and the beheading and quartering of the body. His hands dripping with blood, that facetious functionary chuckled to the shivering wretch awaiting a like fate, "Come, Mr. Peters, how do you like this work?" These were the people who continually invoked the aid of the Almighty in punishing the cruelty of the savage.

To return to the unctuous Massachusetts "oligarchy of theocrats," as Adams calls them, of which Mr. Peters was one. As they settled down to enjoy the fat of the land of Canaan, just eighteen years before the Quakers had had the bad manners to intrude, a fly was discovered in the ointment in the person of Mistress Anne Hutchinson, a lively lady, extremely opinionated, and without any sense of concealment. This well-born, cultivated Englishwoman with her family had followed the Puritan preacher, John Cotton, over the sea, for the delight of sitting under his ministry. Too temperamental and too energetic to sit long idle, Mistress Anne sublimated her repressions by organizing the first American Woman's

Club, the object being to rehash to the women
the dreary Sabbath sermons. Aside from these
of unbelievable length, Boston was short on e
ment, there were very few books, and no public
any sort, not even a news sheet. Mrs. Hutchinson was an excellent nurse, a most sympathetic neighbor, unfailingly helpful to the women in their times of trouble. Taken from her friendly hand the Pilgrim Mothers seem to have found the Puritan dose more palatable.

As her popularity grew, she became emboldened and took the liberty of embroidering the pure doctrine of the preachers with ideas of her own. The clerical caste monopolized the field of ideas; the people, if permitted to entertain ideas of their own, would soon get out of hand. The hierarchy were much alarmed by Mrs. Hutchinson's audacity, and the fight was on.

Doctrine was an obsession with the Puritans; said an eminent Calvinist leader, better that a hundred parricides should escape punishment than that one doctrinally unsound person should go at large. The behavior of these Massachusetts contestants, and the religious jargon in which the controversy was carried on, suggests the psychopathic ward; vehement debates as to whether sanctification was an evidence of justification, passionate arguments as to which preceded the other. When Mistress Anne opined that St. Peter leaned toward a covenant of works, while St. Paul inclined toward a covenant of grace, the clergy threw up their hands at the blasphemy of comparing two Apostles.

Mr. Adams suggests that the voluble gentlemen themselves had no idea what they were talking about; Governor Winthrop declared that he was muddled. The clerical caste in New England were a canny lot, and in all probability knew perfectly well what they were driving at. One guess is as good as another, and it is not unlikely that instinctively, and perhaps unconsciously, they protected their authority by the tricks of the soothsayer. To the hard working unsophisticated colonial, with no mental relaxation outside his religion, the Niagara of words seemed to float a holy mystery; the theological jargon like a baby's pacifier, gave their minds something on which to work endlessly, what they could not understand they dare not refute. The Puritan rank and file were doubtless awed and mystified by the abracadabra, mumbo jumbo of the clericals, as the Indians were awed and mystified by the weird incantations of their medicine men.

Mistress Anne herself was expert in the use of theological patter, which with her good offices and personal magnetism made her an oracle to the tired Pilgrim Mothers. Wilson, the pastor of the Boston church, seems to have been as unlovely a character as can well be imagined; Mistress Anne distinctly disliked him, and so did they all of them, rather too conspicuously. An assault on authority by the laity, especially at the hest of a feminine agitator, Pastor Wilson could not take lying down, and his united brother clericals came solidly to his support; an injury to one was an injury to all.

The congregation, on the other hand, stood as solidly behind Mrs. Hutchinson, who riding her popularity let loose the reins of discretion and came a cropper. Her brother-in-law Wheelright and her friend John Cotton, so she informed her club, were the exponents of the covenant of grace, all other preachers held by the inferior covenant of works.

They certainly worked to some purpose; Mrs. Hutchinson was pulled up short and brought to trial before the clergy and the " priest ridden " magistrates. The records expressly state that she was " convented for traducing the ministers and their ministry in this country." There were other serious charges against her; Hugh Peters, for whom as we have just seen predestination had in store a tragic end, made the accusation, " You have been a husband rather than a wife; a preacher than a hearer; and a magistrate than a subject." In addition to the serious crime of *lèse-majesté*, Mistress Anne had stepped out of her place in all the walks of life.

The most cruel of all the blows showered on the unfortunate woman was laid on by her beloved teacher, John Cotton, whom she called as a witness for the defense. In the course of her examination, Mrs. Hutchinson admitted that a question had risen in her mind as to whether the very same body consigned to the grave would be the one to rise again at the sound of the last trumpet. John Cotton had long enjoyed Mrs. Hutchinson's friendship and hospitality; he had stood with his disciples on the covenant of grace till the ground began to get slippery, when he cautiously edged toward a firmer footing; accommodations of lands and the best houses are not to be abandoned lightly. He now turned on his hunted friend with the solemn assurance that looseness of thought regarding the resurrection inevitably led to the practice of community of women (there is nothing new under the sun it seems, not even the nationalizing of women). If the accused, said Cotton, admitted grave error in the matter of the resurrection, "then you cannot evade the argument pressed on you by our brother Buckle and others, that filthy sin of community of women, and all other promiscuous coming together of men and women without distinction or relation of marriage."

If chivalry moved Cotton to soften the blow, it was an extremely cautious chivalry: "Though I have not heard, neither do I think, you have been unfaithful to your husband in his marriage covenant, yet that will follow upon it." Praise could hardly be fainter, but Mrs. Hutchinson was already damned; if her cherished friend could do no more than this for her, there was little to hope from the venom of her enemies.

One lone hero, insufficiently known to fame, faced that assembly of bigots — William Coddington, treasurer of the colony, already quoted: "I beseech you do not speak so to force things along, for I do not for my own part see any equity in the court in all your proceedings. Here is no law of God that she hath broken, nor any law of the country that she hath broke, and therefore deserves no censure; and if she say that the elders preach as the apostles did, why they preached a covenant of grace, and what wrong is that to them. . . . Therefore I pray consider what you do, for here is no law of God or man broken." Coddington and Colburn only voted against the verdict of the court, after which they were no longer able to dwell within the congregation of the righteous, and withdrew to settle among the Rhode Island heretics.

The sentence of damnation was pronounced on Mrs. Hutchinson as follows:

"In the name of the Lord Jesus Christ, and in the name of the church, I do not only pronounce you worthy to be cast out, but I do cast you out! and in the name of Christ I do deliver you up to Satan *that you may learn no more to blaspheme*, and to seduce and to lie; And I do account you from this time forth to be a Heathen and a Publican, and so to be held of all the Brethren and Sisters of this congregation and of others; therefore I command you in the name of Jesus Christ and of his church, as a Leper to withdraw yourself out of this congregation."

Excommunicated from the church and banished from the colony, Mrs. Hutchinson withdrew to invite her unbound soul and endure the pains of childbirth in the wilderness among the wild beasts and the "savages." She did not leave the court alone, one recalcitrant intrepid sister, also an expectant mother, under the disapproving eyes of the hierarchy rose and lent support to the moral leper. The young woman was Mary Dyer, later a Quaker convert, whose rebellious spirit brought her at last to a scaffold on Boston Common, and for whose picture the story so far makes a frame. Following the strain of the trial, both women miscarried, a proof to the clergy that the Almighty had sustained their judgment.

Without palliating the brutal facts, Mr. C. F. Adams believes that Mrs. Hutchinson shielded herself behind her womanhood, that she played her sex. If so, she played a very poor hand. If thrusting a pregnant woman out into the wilds in that bleak climate may be considered lenient, as it may well be in the light of Mary Dyer's sentence later on, there is a more plausible explanation than Mistress Anne's sex or condition; she was "qualitie" and the founders of our democracy had great respect for social distinctions.

For there were times when the stern sense of righteousness, so often used as a cloak for the conduct of the Puritans, was modified by less exalted principles. A few years before Mrs. Hutchinson tripped over that sense of righteousness, Sir Christopher Gardiner breezed into the colony with a "comly" young woman whom he introduced as his cousin. Governor Winthrop, one of Mrs. Hutchinson's judges, got a line on this gentleman's character by the simple device of opening his private mail. Two angry deserted wives gladly furnished him with further details, all unsavory, one Lady Gardiner accusing the knight of having robbed her. It was further submitted that the comely cousin was a "known harlot." Sir Christopher then was not only a fornicator (and adultery was a capital offense in the colony), but by standards much less rigorous than the Puritan he was an absconder, a thief and a bigamist.

Legally, however, he was a true gentleman, and by the Massachusetts Body of the Liberties, though a common person might be tortured in the stocks and lashed up to forty strokes, it was provided: "nor shall any true gentleman, nor any man equall to a gentleman, be punished with whipping, *unless his crime be very shameful.*" Neither by whipping nor otherwise was Sir Christopher punished; indeed, Governor Winthrop of Boston assures Governor Bradford of Plymouth that he never even "intended any hard measure to him, but to respect and use him *according to his qualitie.*" This incident throws some light on the leniency of Mrs. Hutchinson's sentence, and more on the Quaker protest against "the honor of man," and their habit of invariably qualifying the use of lady and gentleman by "so-called."

Mrs. Hutchinson's trial is evidence that the snake had crawled into the Puritan paradise in advance of the Quakers; it proves conclusively that the trouble started by disaffection within, not by agitation from without.

The causes of the disaffection attracted the Quaker agitators, for the decorum of whose behavior it is unnecessary to put up an argument; they showed as little respect for the ecclesiastical despots of Massachusetts as the Puritans had shown for the ecclesiastical despots of England, though they pressed their non-violent offensive with infinitely more courage.

The pith of the Quaker heresy was, that God expects every man to do his own thinking. Wherever in any corner of the world this divine right was denied, the powers of darkness had usurped authority and by command of God, His soldiers at whatever hazard, were to sally forth to rout the usurpers. Naturally the places where they were least welcome were the points to which duty called them. As Roger Williams shrewdly pointed out, where they were unmolested they gave no trouble and became exemplary citizens.

Before a single Quaker had bobbed up to dispute the power of the Puritan clericals, Roger Williams and his group had been forced out of New England; after the Hutchinson trial, another group followed William Coddington, a man of perfectly good manners and any amount of good sense, to the more congenial spiritual climate of Rhode Island. It was then that the Quakers took up the work of cleaning up that dark spot from which the most enlightened inhabitants fled.

Eighteen years after the landing of the *Mayflower*, Mrs. Hutchinson led the Puritan Mothers in the way of disaffection; her judges were another eighteen years older, but no wiser, when Mary Fisher and Anne Austin came from England preaching repentance to the New England inquisitors. The indwelling light preached by Mrs. Hutchinson seems to have been rather misty moonshine; the Quakers came, declaring that for them the inner light illuminated the Divine command to Christians, that under all circumstances they were to do unto others as they would that men should do unto them. The authorities took precautions against any ray of irregular illumination penetrating that Holy Land; they boarded up the prison windows of the Quakers, yet somehow a flame was kindled in the rebellious heart of Mary Dyer. Mary Fisher could make no breach in the walls of bigotry, but undiscouraged by loss of ears and scourgings, the siege was kept up; within the week after her deportation, nine others of her sect landed.

Governor Endicott gave the Quakers fair warning: "Take heed that ye break not our ecclesiastical laws, for then ye are sure to stretch by a halter," a challenge which was certain to bring the Quakers down like wolves on the fold. In spite of the Governor's most careful attention to possible leaks, and the confiscatory fines levied on ship captains who carried them, Quakers began to seep through; by landing in Virginia, where captains had no fear of fines, they could tramp up the coast to Massachusetts, and defy Endicott to do his worst, which he was not slow to do.

"Many sober people declared their Aversion to such cruelty: but John Norton and other priests were so forward in promoting such a Purpose, that they petitioned the Magistrates to cause the Court to make some Law to banish Quakers upon pain of Death. The Magistrates thus excited by the Priests, made the less Scruple in this Bloody Business."

Just twenty years after Mrs. Hutchinson's light had been snuffed out, Endicott's death threat, at the instigation of the clergy, passed into a legal enactment: "Whereas there is a pernicious sect (commonly called Quakers) lately risen, who by word and writing have published and maintained many dangerous and horrid tenets and do take upon themselves to change and alter the received and laudable customs of our nation in giving civil respect to equals, *or reverence to superiors*, whose actions tend to undermine the civil government, and also to destroy the order of the churches . . . by withdrawing from orderly church fellowship, allowed and approved by all orthodox professors of Truth, meeting by themselves, insinuating themselves into the minds of the simple, *or such as are least affected to the order and government of church and commonwealth*, whereby divers of our inhabitants have been infected. Notwithstanding all former laws made upon the experience of their arrogant and bold intrusions . . . they have not been deterred from their impetuous attempts to undermine our peace and hazard our ruin."

By this comprehensive act, not only the outside agitators, but "every inhabitant of this jurisdiction" merely for "taking up, publishing or defending the horrid opinions of the Quakers," or for even "approving of any known Quaker, or the tenets and practices of the Quakers, that are opposite to the orthodox received opinions of the godly," could make his stand and take his choice of banishment or death. The framers of this law were of that party, which, with the aid of the executioner, had destroyed the civil and church government of their native land, altered its received and laudable customs, and removed the head of their sovereign. They themselves, when overtaken by persecution had been driven underground, and they looked for a similar exhibition of prudence in the Quakers.

Governor Endicott and the chief priests of New England imagined a vain thing; death and burial were the only possible means of getting their disturbers underground, and for every one so disposed of a dozen more appeared to torment the killers. Most alarming of all, a steadily increasing number of the simple, those "least affected to the order of government in church and commonwealth" murmured at the atrocities committed in the name of law and order. No wonder Endicott complained to England that they were not persecuting the Quakers, that the Quakers were persecuting them.

Among the first to feel the teeth of the new law was an old settler, the irrepressible Nicholas Upshall, he who by bribing the jailer had prevented the starving of the Quaker women in prison. On publication of the drastic law, Upshall boldly warned the Governor to take heed himself, "lest he be not found fighting against God." This suggestion was "taken so ill, that though he was a member of their church, and of good repute, and a man of unblamable conversation yet he was fined twenty pounds, and imprisoned also for not coming to church," and as he refused to be convinced that it was the duty of the authorities to decide what religious opinions he might hold, was finally banished, under the death penalty.

Endicott was importuned to remit his heavy fines; Upshall was an old and infirm man; if the public safety required his deportation from the colony he had helped to build up, and where his life had been spent, it assuredly did not require that he be sent out empty handed to start anew in a strange place. The Puritans were thrifty, and heterodoxy was an unfailing source of revenue; "I will not bait him one groat," said the Governor. The "old ancient man" was allowed "but one month's space for his removal, so that he was forced to depart in the winter."

Filched of a considerable sum of money, the sturdy old fellow set out for the Rhode Island refuge for heretics. Trudging through the snow, he had the good fortune to fall in with a savage, an "Indian Prince," who took compassion on his hoary head and infirmities, and entertained him royally, offering to build him a warm house if he would stay. The untutored savage mind was unable to grasp the subtleties of Puritan theology; in his simple code cruelty was practiced only on enemies: "What a God have the English," he commented, "who deal so cruelly one with another about their God."

Notwithstanding the strict official quarantine, the infection spread, Mrs. Hutchinson's friend and defender being the most notable victim. Mary's self-appointed mission seems to have been defense of the under dog. It has been said and sung that God moves in a mysterious way his wonders to perform; the tightening of a rope on Mary Dyer's neck started the work of unbinding the soul of New England.

Two worthy and respectable Englishmen, William Robinson and Marmaduke Stevenson, appeared in the colony, to inquire into the matter of freedom to worship God. Mary's fiery spirit was still as much aflame as on that day twenty years before when she had defiantly left the ecclesiastical court with her excommunicated friend: she was ready and eager to assist in their researches. As peaceable and loyal subjects of England, these men claimed the right to travel unmolested throughout her dominion. As we have noted elsewhere, the authority of England was a sensitive point with Endicott, who flouted it as far as he dared. He banished the two strangers who came to scatter the seeds of religious toleration and free speech, and along with them Mary Dyer, who had volunteered to water the seed. The three retreated in good order to Salem, but soon returned to test the law which placed them under sentence of death. As Governor Endicott had said, " neither imprisonment, nor whipping, nor cutting off of ears " had proved an effectual deterrent to the missionaries; killing them was the only way to be rid of them.

On their return to Boston, Mary made straight for the prison to console Christopher Holder and his Friends, who had lost their ears in a skirmish with Endicott. Holder had insisted that the surgical operation be publicly performed; it was contrary to English law to do it privately, but was told, " We do it in private to keep you from Tatling." Mary's visit to the prison resulted, of course, in her detention; for many years she had been a thorn in the side of authority, now with the two English Friends she had deliberately incurred the death penalty. All three were sentenced, and as they marched to the scaffold on Boston Common, a military band played before and behind them to drown out any heresy they might utter. Before her eyes Mary's two companions were " turned off," their bodies mangled and thrown uncoffined into the Common; their friends were denied the privilege of giving them decent burial. " Priest Wilson " was now an old man, but time had made no dent on that flinty spirit. He jeered at the dying men, " Shall such jacks as you come in before authority with your hats on? "

" Mind you, mind you," one of the condemned called

back, " it is for not putting off our hats we are put to death."

" Then Mary seeing her companions hanging dead before her, also stepped upon the ladder; but after her coats were tied about her; and the halter put about her neck, and her face covered with a handkerchief, which Priest Wilson lent the hangman, just as she was about to be turned off, a cry was heard, ' Stop for she is reprieved.' " This excitement gave Mary an opportunity at last to get in a few words, and standing on the gallows she declared to the multitude that she was willing to go the way of her two companions, " unless they would annul their wicked laws." The taunt of the Reverend Mr. Wilson to the two men and Mary's speech puts the whole case of New England versus the Quakers in a nutshell.

In an autocratic commonwealth, Mary was certainly an undesirable citizen. It is improbable that the authorities intended to hang her, for she had many friends among those " least affected " to the sacerdotal order, and hanging might be going a step too far. This was an occasion when Puritan piety walked in the light of political prudence. The ordeal preceding the spectacular reprieve was designed to scare Mary out of any further attempt to enlighten New England.

Unfortunately, the Quakers refused to be scared into submission. The two who were hanged left behind a very disrespectful letter addressed " To the Rulers, Chief Priests and Inhabitants of Boston," in part:

"Oh ye Hypocrites! How can ye sing and keep up such a Noise concerning Religion, when your Hands are full of Blood, and your Hearts full of iniquity? . . . Clense your Hearts you sinners, and your Hands, you Hypocrites; for your prayers are an Abomination to me, saith the Lord of Hosts: Your singing is as the Howling of a Dog in the Streets. . . . Wo! Wo! to thee, thou Bloody Town of Boston, and the rest that are Confederate with thee."

The results of the hanging scare were disappointing; Michael Shafflin was arrested for nonappearance at church service, who on "being demanded by the Court, How long he had absented from their worship? answered, Ever since you put the servants of the Lord to Death." Priest-ridden New England shied at these atrocities, and evinced a disposition to throw the rider.

As for Mary, she recuperated on Long Island from the ordeal of the gallows, where she spent the winter months preaching. With the coming of spring there were no signs that the seeds of toleration were germinating in her old home, and back she came to apply a stimulant. This was more than Endicott could be expected to stand; the pestilent woman must be silenced. When the death sentence was read to her a second time, Mary pertly remarked, "This is no more than what thou saidst before."

"But now it is to be executed," was the Governor's grim retort; "therefore prepare yourself to-morrow morning at nine o'clock."

THE PILGRIMS READY TO SAIL

(From a Print in the New York Public Library)

"I came in obedience to the will of God to last General Court," said Mary, "desiring you to repeal your unrighteous laws of banishment on pain of death; and that same is my work now, and earnest request; although I told you that if you refused to repeal them, the Lord would send others of His servants to witness against them."

"Are you a prophetess?" Endicott sneered.

She answered that "she spoke the words that the Lord spoke in her, and would have said more," but Endicott shouted "Away with her; away with her," a cry that had been heard more than sixteen hundred years before at a famous heresy-sedition trial.

The Reverend Mr. Wilson, who appears to have been a regular attendant at executions, was on hand to urge Mary to repentance.

"Nay, man, I am not now to repent."

Asked whether she would have any of the people to pray for her she answered that she desired the prayers of "all the people of God." "A wag thereupon scoffingly said, 'It may be she thinks there is none here.' She looking about said, 'I know but few here.' Then they spoke again that one of the elders might pray for her."

"Nay," the obdurate woman returned, "first a child, then a young man, then a strong man, before an elder in Jesus Christ." And, unrepentant, she was turned off.

"Thus," says Sewel, "this honest valiant woman finished her days, but so hardened were these persecutors, that one of the Court said scoffingly, 'She did hang as a flag for others to take example by.'" They overlooked the sequel to the familiar story of one lifted up in like manner.

Mary's execution flagged into the front trenches William Leddra. No better illustration can be given of the momentum of the force against which Endicott and the pundits vainly struggled, than the story of William Leddra, the force characterized by Dr. Ellis as "a dogged pertinacity which drove the authorities to a frenzy." The heavy fines exacted in New England from captains who brought in Quakers made them extremely careful about the religion of prospective passengers. Just about the time measures were taken to check the missionary rovings of the Quakers, divine commands began to relate to vessels. Robert Fowler of Bridlington got a message from the Lord to build a ship "in the cause of truth." It was a preposterous little cockle shell, so utterly unfit for ocean travel that no insurance company would have ventured a shilling on it. Eleven Friends, some of whom had been banished from Massachusetts, were quite willing to venture their lives in it; the performance of the impossible was an everyday occurrence with these people, and the tiny tub set sail. The shipbuilder wrote an account of the exploit: "A true relation of the voyage undertaken by me, Robert Fowler, with my small vessel called the *Woodhouse* but performed by the Lord, like as He did Noah's Ark, wherein He shut up a few righteous persons and landed them safe even at the Hill Ararat . . . the Lord leading our vessel as it were a man leading a horse by the head; we regarding neither latitude nor longitude." For two months the tiny craft rode the storms, eluded men of war, and actually landed the missionary band safe and sound. Against such invaders, the Puritan hope of a short and decisive campaign was a forlorn one; William Leddra, one of the passengers on the *Woodhouse*, came to reënforce the siege of New England. He was imprisoned, badly beaten from time to time, and finally banished under penalty of the law. He soon reappeared to visit imprisoned Friends, was again taken up and "kept Night and Day *in an open prison*, chained to a Log of Wood, during an extream hard Winter. . . . During that confinement of Body, he enjoyed a Christian Freedom and Liberty of Spirit."

That freedom was of short duration; when the death sentence was pronounced: "He asked them, What evil he had done? The Court answered, He owned those that were put to death, and said they were innocent." In addition to thus traducing those in power, he had refused to put off his hat in Court, and he would say thee and thou.

"Will you put me to death for speaking English, and for not putting off my clothes?"

"A Man may speak Treason in English," replied the ever ready General Denison.

"Will you put me to death for breathing in the Air

of your Jurisdiction?" Leddra asked again, and appealed to the laws of England. "The Court would not accept his Appeal, but attempted to persuade him to Recantation and Compliance with their Will: To which he answered with a remarkable Magnanimity, What! to join with such murderers as you are: then let every Man that meets me say, Lo, this is the Man that hath forsaken the God of his Salvation." It is to be noted that the mildest criticism of the theocracy was treason; petitions for redress resulted in fines, imprisonment, flogging and banishment. New England had been repeatedly warned by the English government, from which they held their charter, that they were acting in violation of English law. Their own party in England had begged them to go slow, lest the Puritans in England should suffer from reprisals. No remonstrance availed to check Endicott in his headlong course.

Leddra on the scaffold commended his righteous cause to God. "A comely Man," commented the executioner as he stripped the body, adding that "Mary Dyer was a comely woman." The cause which Leddra commended to God was zealously defended, its champions kept Endicott busy whipping and sentencing them to death. Twenty-seven were under the death sentence when Wenlock Christison prophesied that the end had come. It came, as we have seen, when the adventurous Shoemaker Shattock, instead of coming back to swing after his deportation, took passage for England and roused that human dynamo, Edward Burrough. The warrant Burrough got from the King put a snuffer on the New England murders, and thoroughly frightened Endicott and the hierarchy, but it would have been easier to convert a tiger to vegetarianism than to change those stubborn natures.

"Now," says our chronicler, "the Persecution of this people to Death was put a stop to, and a Liberty granted them for the present, yet it continued not long, the Inclination of the Magistrates being still the same, and the Cessation of their Cruelties being not voluntary, but constrained, they returned again to their wonted Oppression of this People, by reviving the Execution of their laws for whipping Quakers out of their Jurisdiction; which they did with an almost unparallelled Barbarity."

Commanded by the King to abrogate the death penalty, they skirted it as closely as they dared in the floggings. The cords of the whips were the thickness of a man's finger, and were often tarred; each of the several cords had three knots. Hanging would have been more merciful than the punishment meted out to old William Brend. He was put in irons, "Neck and Heels so close together, that there was no more Room left between each than the Lock that fastened them." After five days of fasting, and sixteen hours of this torture the old Quaker preacher was ordered to work, and refused. The infuriated jailer then gave him ninety lashes with a tarred whip, leaving him unconscious, his body a black and blue pulp, the blood "hanging in bags."

With an eye to England, Endicott sent his own doctor to the jail. "The Surgeon found the Body of Brend in such a deplorable Condition, that as one without Hope, he said, His Flesh would rot from His Bones e'er the bruised parts would be brought to digest. This so exasperated the People, that the Magistrates to prevent a Tumult, set up a Paper at their Meeting-house Door, as it were to show their Dislike of this most abominable and barbarous Cruelty. . . . But this Paper was soon taken down again by the Instigation of their chief Priest John Norton, who having been from the Beginning a fierce Promotor of Persecution, now did not stick to say, W. Brend endeavored to beat our Gospel-ordinances black and blue; if he then be beaten black and blue, it is but just upon him; and I will appear in his Behalf that did so." John Norton was the chief promoter of the act which provided capital punishment for such as were lacking in respect to their superiors.

The strain of Pilgrim life bore harder on the women than on the men; the unorthodox found relief from the emotional pressure by worrying the Governor and the clergy. Hysteria, which in the Puritans took the form of accusing their neighbors of witchcraft, manifested in the Quaker women in strange symbolism. Mary Dyer hanging as a flag on Boston Common, the procession of women tied to cart tails and flogged from town to town, blood streaming down their bare backs, were sights to release any latent hysteria. When Wenlock Christison was being railroaded through to the gallows, one woman went insane and wandered the streets naked. It was admitted by the Court that this unfortunate creature was "distempered in her head," and she got off with a moderate flogging.

Lydia Wardell was another casualty of the Christison trial. Lydia was sorely pressed, close to, if not over the border line of sanity. Christison was a friend of her young husband, Eliakim, who got into trouble with his lawful spiritual guide, Seaborn Cotton, by sheltering the heretic. Seaborn Cotton was the worthy son of Anne Hutchinson's valiant friend, John Cotton; he fined Eliakim for the sin of harboring his hunted friend and "took away a pretty beast for the saddle, worth fourteen pounds." This extraordinary fine failed to satisfy his cupidity; "the said Eliakim being rated to the said priest Seaborn Cotton, the said Seaborn having a mind to a pied Heiffer Eliakim had, as Ahab had to Naboth's vineyard, sent his servant nigh two miles to fetch her; who having robbed Eliakim of her brought her to his master." Eliakim's marsh lands and meadow-ground soon followed his personal property, and the young couple were in desperately straightened circumstances. In this anxiety, Lydia was subjected to repeated visits from the indefatigable Seaborn to insist on her attendance at the sanctuary. Reduced almost to starvation, harried on all sides, the young woman's reason tottered; as a protest against the flogging of naked women, she startled the congregation of the self-righteous one Sabbath morning, by appearing in the style of undress which went out of fashion with the downfall of our first parents. She was fastened to a rough board, the splinters of which penetrated her breasts. Eliakim, her husband, was a knight of dames; he could not prevent the floggings, but made a point of being on hand to protest against the brutality, which in addition to his many losses, cost him much loss of blood. Incensed by derogatory comments of the bystanders on his young wife's character, he stoutly defended her innocence and maintained her exemplary behavior.

Insubordination had already cleaned him out of anything on which the authorities could levy, and his defense of his wife's character let him in for a lashing. With unquenchable humor as he was released from the whipping post, he turned to the man of God: "Among the spectators of his Sufferings was Seaborn Cotton, a Priest, who had a little before taken away an Heiffer of Eliakim's by Distress. Eliakim being loosed from the tree, and perceiving the Priest there, said to him before the People, Seaborn, has my pied Heiffer calved yet? At which the Priest was Sore Abashed, and slunk away."

And now Elizabeth Hooton came forward to uphold the cause for which Anne Hutchinson suffered and Mary Dyer and her Friends died; although well on the way toward seventy, Elizabeth's extraordinary natural vigor was unabated. She was roughly handled on her first appearance, and then driven a two days' journey into "the vast and howling wilderness," where she was left without food or shelter. She managed to make her way to England, and pestered the King till she got what she wanted. When the monarch rode abroad, the persistent old lady was standing by his coach; she was waiting for him at the tennis court: "I wait for justice of thee O king. The cry of the innocent regard." And, waiting, she cried till she was regarded, more for being a nuisance perhaps than for her innocence; lese majesty, a death-inviting crime in New England, never ruffled the temper of the easily accessible Charles Stuart. No doubt the fun-loving monarch was delighted with the opportunity to wish such pertinacity on his trusty, well-beloved, stiff-necked oversea subjects; at any rate, Elizabeth got a warrant over the King's own signature, permitting her to buy land in Massachusetts, and to build a house on it in which to harbor Friends, for it must be remembered that there were ridiculously heavy fines exacted in the colony for so much as giving a Quaker a cup of milk. Fortified with the royal grant, Elizabeth took passage for America, and landed in Virginia, no captain daring to book a passenger of her religious faith for any New England port. Elizabeth worked her way up the coast to Massachusetts, but her clever ruse did not work; the Massachusetts worthies refused to honor the King's requisition. That the Founding Fathers have become models of law-abiding loyalty to government, is one of the little jokers of history; as

Mr. Adams points out, they had the immense advantage of having the only law which they respected safely locked up in their own breasts, and could interpret it as they chose. With the King's warrant in her pocket, Elizabeth was imprisoned, flogged, and starved; a good Samaritan who gave her a little milk was unmercifully beaten and unmercifully fined. With a companion, the venerable woman was tied to a cart tail, and ordered beaten through eleven towns. Fearing interference from the home government, the colony had abandoned the public executions of Quakers, but a journey of eighty miles through winter snow, half naked, with one hundred and ten lashes may be considered a pretty good substitute for the death sentence. Terribly bruised from the beatings, the old woman was driven beyond the colony boundary, and once more left without food or shelter in the forest primeval.

Three of her Friends came under a similar sentence. They had expressed opinions regarding the trinity, and the authority of the clergy, which the Reverend Mr. Raynor found extremely irritating, so much so, that an order was given:

> To the Constables of Dover, Hampton, Salisbury, Rowley, Ipswich, Wenham, Linn, Boston, Dedham, and until these Vagabond Quakers are carried out of our Jurisdiction.
>
> You and every one of you are required, *in the King's Majesty's name*, to take these Vagabond Quakers, Anne Coleman, Mary Tomkins, and Alice Ambrose, and make them fast to the Cart's tail, and driving the Cart through your several Towns, to whip them on their Backs, not exceeding ten stripes

a-piece on each of them in each Town, and so to convey them from Constable to Constable, till they come out of our Jurisdiction, as you will answer at your Peril: and this shall be your Warrant.

RICHARD WALDEN.

DOVER, DECEMBER 22ND.
1662

"This order was cruelly executed at Dover, while the Priest (the Reverend Raynor) stood by, lookt on, and laught at it: for which Levity" our good friend Eliakim Wardell was on hand to reprove him and take the consequences. December was a chilly month to make a long journey through snow "half way the leg deep"; the blood as it ran down their backs froze to their clothes.

The Parade was halted at Salisbury by one of those obstacles which redeem early New England history, celebrated by Whittier in verse, "How the Women Went from Dover."

With shame in his eye and wrath on his lip
The Salisbury constable dropped his whip.
"This warrant means murder foul and red;
Cursed is he who serves it," he said.

He read the warrant, *These convey*
From our precincts; at every town on the way
Give each ten lashes. "God judge the brute!
I tread his order under my foot!

"Cut loose these poor ones and let them go;
Come what will of it, all men shall know
No warrant is good though backed by the Crown
For whipping women in Salisbury town!"

Set at liberty, these three inflexible women headed straight back to Dover, from which town they had been banished, and insolently met openly for worship on "First Day." While she was praying, Alice Ambrose was seized, and dragged through the snow face downward with the avowed purpose of making an end of her this time; she was thrown into the water, and her clothing froze on her body as "hard as boards."

Anne Coleman finished the sentence interrupted at Salisbury a year later in Boston Town, where the authority of the pundits was more respected. Deputy Governor Bellingham himself inspected the warrant for whipping her, and finding it "firm" bade the executioner lay on, "who, thus encouraged, laid on so severely" that it was "thought she would have died through the extreme Torture she was put to by the Knots of the Whip splitting one of the Nipples of her Breast." "And she who was a little weakly woman, thinking this would have been her lot, said once, that if she should happen to die thus, she was willing her body should be laid at Bellingham's door, with a charge from her mouth that he was guilty of her blood." Her Friends, hazarding the same fate, would readily have carried out her last will and testament.

The last of the acts of the Fathers which we cull from those chronicled in "The Collection of Sufferings" is the attempt to sell children into slavery to satisfy a fine.

"Let us now go back to Boston where we left in prison those godly aged Confessors, Laurence and Cassandra

Southick, with their son Josiah. They had left at home their son Daniel and their daughter Provided: these Children seeing how unchristianly their Parents and Brother were dealt with, were so far from being deterred thereby, that they rather felt themselves encouraged to follow their Steps, and to relinquish the Assemblies of such a Persecuting Generation, for which absence they were fined ten pounds, though it was well known that they had no Estate, their Parents being already brought to poverty by their Rapacious Persecutors. To get this Money the following order was made in the General Court at Boston, viz.:

" Whereas Daniel Southick and Provided Southick, Son and Daughter of Laurence Southick, absenting themselves from the public Ordinances, have been fined in the Courts of Salem and Ipswich, pretending they have no Estates, and resolving not to work: The Court, upon Perusal of a Law, *which was made upon account of debts*, in Answer to what should be done for the Satisfaction of the Fines; resolves, That the Treasurers of the several Counties, are and shall be fully empowered to sell the said Persons to any of the English Nation, at Virginia or Barbados, to answer the said Fines, &c."

This Herodian scheme to obtain " booty " by visiting the iniquities of the father on the children, met with obstruction; the masters of vessels balked, all of them. Unregenerate sailors seem to have met such situations with an unvarying formula, they feared mutiny. " And a certain Master of a Ship, to put the Thing off, pretended that, They would spoil the Ship's Company." The colonial official, Edward Batter, assured him, "No, you need not fear that, for they are poor harmless Creatures, and will not hurt any Body." The captain dropped his mask: "Will they not so? And will you offer to make slaves of such harmless Creatures?' Thus was Batter disappointed of his wicked Intentions, and could get no Opportunity to send them away, wherefore, Winter coming on, he sent them Home again, to shift for themselves." Under the Puritan regime the family life of unbound souls must have been rather hectic.

Besse ends his harrowing tale of New England atrocities by adroitly introducing an unexpurgated and lengthy pastoral letter of the Reverend Cotton Mather, enumerating the list of calamities which had fallen upon the Massachusetts saints, "one strange Casualty after another." Pestilence had swept the land, few had escaped its ravages to tend upon the sick. "The blasting Strokes of Heaven upon the secular Affairs of this Country have been such, as rather to abate than enlarge the Growth of it." The young men had been cut off by war, every house was a house of mourning. "The constant Frown of Heaven upon our Husbandry," worms, drought, etc., had ruined the crops. "Inordinate Passions, sinful Heats and Hatreds" among the faithful, "a long series of Afflictions and Calamities, whereby we have suffered successively in all our precious and Pleasant Things." Captives taken by the Indians "Tygers, whose tender Mercies are cruel," had been whipped "after a cruel and bloody Manner . . . and so with exquisite, leisurely, horrible Torments, roasted out of the World."

It is a long list, with the recurring refrain, "Our God hath humbled us," a statement which the Quakers accepted with reservation. Besse would "not in this Case make any positive Determination," far be it from a good Quaker to gloat over the misfortunes of his enemies. He implies, nevertheless, in all "Lowliness and Humility of Mind," that the judgments of the Lord are just and righteous altogether.

Always the milder of the two Quaker Historians, Sewel brings his New England narration to an end: "I could relate many more severities of the New England persecutors; but I long to come to an end, and shall therefore make a long step, and outrun some space of time."

Following his good example, we quote from the Quaker journal of Thomas Chalkley, who toured New England some thirty years later, when Quaker obstinacy had worn down the resistance of the stubborn New England conscience. "I being a stranger and Traveller, could not but observe the barbarous and unchristian-like Welcome I had in Boston, the Metropolis of New England. Oh! what a pity, said one, it was, that all your Society were not hanged with the other four! This shows that the Spirit of Persecution was alive in some of that People, long after the power of exercising it was restrained."

The Martyred Children

And they built the high places of Baal, which are in the valley of the son of Hinnom, to cause their sons and their daughters to pass through the fire unto Moloch which I commanded them not, neither came it into my mind that they should do this abomination, to cause Judah to sin. — JEREMIAH.

THE gruesome tale of the martyrdom of little Elizabeth Fletcher and little James Parnell, and other Quaker youth and children, is evidence that the devotees of Moloch, under constantly changing subterfuges, have from age to age appeased the thirst of their God for the blood of the young.

The peculiar garb which so long distinguished the Quakers was the ordinary everyday fashion of the early Quaker period; when fashion moved on, it moved without them, they remained faithful to the old forms in speech and dress. The present generation have abandoned the distinctive uniform dress of earlier Friends; therefore the term Quaker usually calls up a picture of a saintly old gentleman of the preceding generation, in a wide hat, or a serene old lady in ample gray skirt and a severe bonnet. In the beginning the Society was characterized neither by hoary heads nor by tranquillity; it was distinctly a youth movement, and consequently noted for intense enthusiasm rather than the caution and discretion that comes with years.

Fox was twenty years old when he quit the absorbing task of making a living to follow his vocation through poverty and danger. At thirty his most inveterate enemies acknowledged him to be a forceful though dangerous leader. Around him gathered a group of devoted young crusaders who faced privation unshrinkingly, and laughed at death, known among their own people as the Valiant Sixty. They might well have been called the Battalion of Death; society fell upon them with murderous rage, and many valorous young lives were snuffed out in dank and stinking prisons, of which we have realistic pictures. "They were most inhumanly used, being put into a Dismal Dungeon called Doomesdale, a place where the excrements of the prisoners had lain for many years, so that it was like mire, and in some parts of it up to the shoes in Ordure and Urine. Nor would the jailer suffer them to have any straw to lie on."

Under the law there was no closed season for Quaker hunting, a very profitable occupation for those who fancied that sort of sport. Outside the religion recognized by law, any gathering for religious worship, above the number of five persons, constituted an unlawful conventicle; the worshipers were subject to heavy fines, a considerable portion of which went to the informer. As there was no risk involved, this opened up a lucrative field for the most cowardly and predatory characters. Houses of sick and dying Friends were closely watched; when two or three neighbors came in to pray with the sick, or to console the bereaved, these with the unhappy family made up the required number for unlawful assembly, and the ghoulish informers had them all haled into court on that charge. In many instances the clergy were the informers, and the least merciful.

If it were not for the proof furnished by the court records, it would be difficult to believe that a minister of Christ would seize the sheepskins provided by a poor laboring man for the winter clothing of his children. An orthodox neighbor, looking on a Quaker horse or cow with covetous eye, had only to make a charge and get the owner into court; if the original charge proved to be trumped up, an obliging magistrate would proffer one of the many oaths of allegiance, abjuration, or supremacy, and the Quakers refusing to make oath, the coveted property would be divided between the court and the informer. Whatever the charge, the seizure of Quaker property was a foregone conclusion; banditry and piracy, but recently frowned down by society, enjoyed a respectable existence under the form of law. We read in the "History of Sufferings" of a sheriff, appealed to by kindly neighbors to take the live stock of a poor Quaker family in satisfaction for his fines, and spare them their household goods. He made no bones about stating that he could not acquiesce, as he was setting up housekeeping for himself and needed the household equipment for his own use.

The Church had the legal right not only to tax citizens

for its support, but also to inquire minutely into their beliefs, drag them from non-conformist meeting houses, batter down the buildings, confiscate the property of the unorthodox and throw them into jail. Young enthusiasts with a passion for justice and liberty naturally fought back, not always with perfect decorum. Physical violence was prohibited by their religious code; there was no prohibition against the use of the tongue, "the tongue can no man tame." The mild and truthful Sewel is constrained to admit of those whose exploits he records that they sometimes felt free to use the "language of Elijah to the prophets of Baal." They would repair to the "steeple-house," as they dubbed the church building, listen to an abuse of their cult, with a restraint on which they prided themselves, and when the sermon ended rise and exhort pastor and people to repentance, in the classical exuberance of Old Testament scripture. Becoming a public nuisance was their one chance for a hearing, and they usually managed to release an admonition or two before an enraged congregation, cheered on by the clergyman, beat them up and had them thrown into jail.

Before they were twenty, Elizabeth Fletcher and James Parnell were both done to death by highly respectable and pious upholders of the established system. An eloquent and persuasive preacher at sixteen, Elizabeth was fired with an ambition to civilize and Christianize the institutions of higher learning where the clergy were trained; her idea was to catch them young. Her first offensive was directed against Oxford, where the red-blooded, he-man model was in vogue. The high-born, high-spirited youth in that aristocratic University, many of whom were to take holy orders, had formed a habit of breaking in on Quaker meetings and throwing the worshipers to the floor, after demolishing the architecture. They would ride upon the backs of men and women, strangle them with beer when they declined to drink, saturate their clothing with it, use obscene language, behave most indecently to the women, fire off gunpowder and bullets, and otherwise assert themselves as jolly English gentlemen. Enumerating the activities of these young cavaliers, our chronicler shows some heat: "I am weary of transcribing their Abominations, and shall cease with the Remark, which however severe it may seem, is natural and just, Viz. Had these Scholars been professedly educated for Ministers of the Devil, they could not have given more certain proofs of their Proficiency."

Stirred by the reports of the atrocities committed by these young savages, Elizabeth with another earnest north-country woman moved on Oxford, "under a Religious Concern, to exhort the Inhabitants of that Place, and the Scholars in the Colleges, to Repentence and Amendment of Life." The call to repentance was most unfavorably received by the vivacious students, who carried the two girls to the college pump, forced water down their throats until they were partially strangled; then roped them together and dragged them through a muddy ditch to the cemetery. Here, after a battering against gravestones they were thrown into an open grave.

Mangled in body, but of the same opinion still regarding the desirability of amendment of life in the students, they rose from the grave to recommend it again, and were arrested and taken before the court. The vice chancellor of the University was the most severe of their judges; for the merry pranks of the students he had no condemnation — boys will be boys — and Quakers were undoubtedly a nuisance. The conduct of the Quaker girls, however, horrified him; in a lengthy discourse on the duty of obedience to magistrates, he declared that the spirit of God and the grace of Christ had been dishonored by their unseemly and riotous behavior, and commanded that they be whipped out of town.

For the execution of the drastic sentence, an order from the Mayor was necessary, and here the chancellor encountered a snag. Not only did that independent official refuse to affix his name to the chancellor's order, he went further, and offered to replace the clothing of the women, which the students had torn to tatters, and to provide them with food, and such other necessaries as they might be in need of.

Apparently the duty of obedience to magistrates, on which the vice chancellor had so eloquently enlarged was not binding on the college faculty; he absolved himself of that duty and signed the order for flogging over the Mayor's veto. Still suffering from the man-handling of the students, the women were whipped out of town by a very reluctant executioner, more compassionate than his superior. Little Elizabeth's frail body was not constructed to withstand the water treatment, followed by scourgings and violent contact with gravestones. The wounds she received in the battle of Oxford proved mortal, though she lingered on for some time in great pain, fighting valiantly to the end.

The most curious and interesting feature of the Quaker fight is the part played by very young children ten to twelve years old: "Our little children kept the meetings up when we were all in prison, notwithstanding their wicked justice, when he came and found them there, with a staff that he had, with a spear in it, would pull them out of the meeting, and punch them in the back, till some of them have been black in the face. I cannot much enlarge; his fellow, I believe, is not to be found in England a Justice of the Peace."

To violate the Conventicle Act, it was only necessary to meet for silent worship and meditation, a violation of the law which the little folk could and did accomplish. The meeting houses in Bristol were raided and battered down, the adults imprisoned; but the meetings were continued by the children:

"On the 7th of July they dispersed the meeting, which then consisted chiefly of children, for the men and women being generally in prison, the children kept up their meetings regularly, and with a remarkable gravity and composure. It was surprising to see the manly courage and constancy with which some of the boys behaved on this occasion, keeping close to meetings in the absence of their parents, and undergoing on that account many abuses with patience.

"On the 16th Tilly caused five of the boys to be set in the stocks for three quarters of an hour. On the 23rd eight of the boys were put in stocks for two hours and a half. On the 30th about fifty-five children were at the meeting, when Helliar, with a twisted whalebone stick, beat many of them unmercifully, striking them violent blows on their heads, necks and faces, few of them escaping without some marks of his fury.

"On the 3rd of the month called August, Tilly with a small fagot stick, beat many of the children, but they bore it patiently and cheerfully. On the 6th he beat some of them with a whalebone stick, and sent four boys to Bridewell, who were released in the evening, with threats of whipping if they met together again. He also sent eleven boys and four girls to Bridewell, till a Friend engaged for their appearance next day before the Deputy-Mayor, who endeavored both by persuasions and threats to make them promise to come at no more meetings; but the children in that respect were unmovable. Wherefore, they were sent to Bridewell again, Helliar to terrify them, charging the keeper to provide a new cat-o'-nine-tails against next morning."

The stability of a government rests on the consent of the governed; the people called Quakers, in this signal manner, refused their consent to the Conventicle Act, and the government was obliged to give way.

The tragic fate of the lad known as little James Parnell furnishes a perfect companion piece to the story of little Elizabeth Fletcher. At the age of fourteen, this child began a quest for the peace which the world cannot give. He was quite wicked, he gravely assures us, no doubt preferring other diversions to the entertainment offered in the sanctuary. One George Fox, he was told, wandering on the same quest, had at last found what he sought, and the boy set off afoot to Carlisle where Fox was imprisoned. His search was over; in that miry dungeon he found the young Quaker leader, joyful and triumphant, and immediately joined the ranks. The peace he sought and found was certainly not of this world, for his brief Quaker life ended as it began, in prison.

The records tell us that Parnell was "raised in the schools of literature." His family had not raised their boy to be a Quaker; they had given him educational advantages with more ambitious views, and his conversion to that despised sect resulted in his being turned out of doors. The notorious behavior of the young gentlemen in the universities decided young Parnell to embark on the dangerous life of Christian missionary to the divinity students of Cambridge, youths of the same robust type as their fellows at Oxford. These received him "with rude and bad entertainment."

He was imprisoned and finally expelled as a vagabond; wholly undissuaded in the matter of "convincing" the students, he continued his mission in the outskirts of the town, delivering his message with such fervor and eloquence that many of the plainer people were won over. The die-hards were of the better class, who encouraged the mob, and the young preacher was very ungently handled.

Coming out of church one pleasant Sabbath morning, a zealous worshiper struck him a cruel blow with a staff, saying, "For Christ's sake take that." The little fellow replied, "Friend, I do receive it for Jesus Christ's sake." Outside the ranks of the more highly cultivated, the little preacher met with marked success, so marked indeed, that the startled clergy proclaimed a day of fasting and prayer against Quaker errors. James attended church on the day appointed, listened quietly to invective from the pulpit denouncing Quakers as deceivers, their doctrines built on sandy foundations. The sermon ended, he rose and said, "I will prove our foundations not to be sandy, and thee to be a false prophet."

He got no opportunity to prove anything; it was unlawful to speak lightly of or to the clergy, and James was seized and escorted to jail, charged with contempt of magistracy, of creating a riot, and of otherwise indecently behaving himself.

James conducted his own defense; he did not think it indecent to call an unjust judge unjust, a persecutor a persecutor, or a deceiver a deceiver; his superiors ruled otherwise. He was manacled night and day to felons and murderers, and forced to walk eighteen miles to his trial — unnecessary severity which caused murmuring among the populace, murmuring with that unpleasant, menacing note which English authority had learned to respect — and on the second hearing, it was deemed prudent to omit the most objectionable features of his discipline.

Four magistrates and seven clergymen sat on the bench to try the dangerous criminal. After the naïve manner of the time, the jury was warned that if they failed to bring in a verdict of guilty, the sin would rest upon their own heads. Hard-headed, and equal to the burden of sin, the jury refused to convict the prisoner. Not to be balked by an obstacle so inconsiderable as the verdict of the jury, the judges had one last shot which never failed to bring down their game: they tendered him the oath which his religion prohibited him from taking, fined him forty pounds for refusal, which his principles would not permit him to pay, and in spite of the good will of the jury, he went to prison.

Crimes against authority are always more harshly punished than crimes against humanity. Chief priests and scribes may relent toward Barabbas, never toward Jesus, who " stirreth up the people." For the same crime little James was to pay the same penalty. His jailer was a brutal man, with a vigorous and venomous wife who outdid him in cruelty, beating the lad continually and swearing to have his blood. The jail was a relic of the old Roman occupation; strictly speaking, the boy was confined not in a cell but in a sarcophagus, a mere shelf in a thick stone wall, twelve feet from the ground, approached by a ladder reaching only halfway up; the remainder of the ascent was a scramble effected by means of a rope. Prisoners in days gone by were obliged to furnish their own food and bedding; the Friends who cared for the boy begged leave to supply him with a rope with which to draw up his victuals; the jailers would hear of no such indulgence.

What with the beatings of the jailer's gentle spouse, and the chill damp of the unheated stone inclosure, the fragile body which housed James's indomitable spirit was soon wrecked. Making the perilous climb on a bitter winter day, numb with cold, the stiff hands missed the rope, and he plunged to the stone floor below, shattered. It was necessary now to assign him a shelf nearer the floor, but a breath of pure air, or any other alleviation of his misery, the malice of his jailors denied him.

For some months he lingered on the stones, gradually fading out of a hostile world, tenderly cared for by Thomas Shortland and Ann Langley. The Quakers believed they restored their sick to health by prayer; this very tired boy with a mangled body felt unequal to prolonged martyrdom, he pleaded earnestly with his good Friends.

"Thomas," he begged, "I have seen great things, don't hold me, but let me go." And not satisfied, he questioned again: "Will you hold me?"

"No, dear heart," Ann soothed, "we will not hold thee." Comforted, he went peacefully to sleep, never again to be disturbed.

The story of another youthful victim might lead to the inference, that in the onward march of toleration the laity took the lead, the clergy lagging far behind. Roger Hudson having proved delinquent "in a certain matter of Tithes and other Ecclesiastical Rights, the right worshipful Richard Lloyd, Knight and Dr. of Laws, vicar general and Official of the right Reverend Father in God, Nathaniel, by Divine Providence Lord Bishop of Durham," so the warrant reads, attached the body of the said Roger Hudson. A dark and airless dungeon, it was hoped, would bring Roger round to the ecclesiastical stand in the matter of tithes, and unloosen his purse strings. The tithe in question was a matter of only a few shillings; the principle involved was important to both sides.

For many months Roger lay in close confinement, to the great detriment of his health. He pleaded with the warden for a breath of fresh air, but the right worshipful vicar general had warned the jailer against any indulgence to a foe of the established order, and incidentally to his own perquisites. As the prisoner became desperately weak, compassion overcame fear; the jailer placed him where he could inhale a whiff of uncontaminated air. For this unauthorized benevolence the watchful vicar had the jailer summoned before a magistrate, who severely reprimanded him, and fined him twenty pounds, a sum of sufficient magnitude to discourage any further effort to temper clerical austerity.

Robert Selby, a physician of Durham, now had the hardihood to enter the lists for a tilt with the vicar. In a curt letter he pointed out that Roger Hudson was not a criminal, that he had committed no offense that could be called a crime, and that his life would surely be forfeited unless he was removed from his dark cell. The vicar was a man of principle, as his reply to the meddlesome doctor shows:

"I hope I am, and desire to continue a tender hearted Man. Yet I would not have you or others judge me a soft fool, and one easily to be wheedled out of his right Reason and Senses by little Phanatick Bugbears. If Roger Hudson were not able to pay (though a Turk) I know what I have to say, but if either he or you pretend Conscience for non-payment of just Debts or dues, you must pardon me if I have as little Credit for, and give as little respect to that Coynage and Cozenage, as one that picks a Purse or cuts a Throat by the same Pretense."

Smothered to death for picking the vicar's purse of a few shillings tax, which he held to be unjust, Roger Hudson died in the dungeon. Even when he had reached the place where the wicked are said to cease from troubling, the ire of the tender-hearted man of God pursued him. As required by law, his body was wrapped in woollen; his bereaved sister was a day late in making the affidavit that the law had been properly observed. Like a hawk the Argus-eyed vicar swooped down upon her with a warrant. The fine for failure to comply with the law was five pounds, and although the law had been complied with, this fine was exacted from her, half of it going into the pocket of the good man, as informer. Certainly none but the most unreasonably censorious would judge the vicar to be a soft fool.

The Peregrinations of the Callow Family

One may boldly say that no man has a right perception of any truth who has not been reacted on by it so as to be ready to be its martyr. — EMERSON.

"THE end of government is protection, and should be its aim, but too often people need protection from their protectors." So said the patriot Franklin, and so long before his time the Romans discovered. Under the usurpations of the army they created for their protection, the liberties of Roman citizens so gradually disappeared, that, before they realized their loss, they had become helpless; it was then that assassination, the redress of slaves, became a national institution; only one of nineteen successive emperors died a natural death.

The long stretch of power enjoyed by the English ruling class, with a minimum of internal violence, is due in no small measure to the obscure, inglorious heroes who offered immediate and determined resistance to any invasion of their liberty; humble champions of the Goddess of Liberty who hastened to the aid of their deity before the good dame was completely overpowered. The English rattle before they strike, and with a lively sense of self-preservation, their rulers have usually heard the noise and heeded it.

Privilege wielded a power in the seventeenth century on which we now look back with wonder. The wages of a maidservant of that time would not keep a modern domestic in ice-cream sodas, yet she could be hanged for stealing a shilling from her master; while hungry men, for the theft of a sheep, or even a wild rabbit, went to the scaffold. Even the Quakers, whose religious beliefs emphasized the sacredness of human life, were more shocked by the fact that a clergyman had stolen a horse than by his being hanged for it. So general was the acquiescence in the sacredness of property that there was little outcry against these drastic sentences; and it is worth noting, in passing, that property is much safer in England today under milder laws.

When the courageous few called a halt to power, however, it was done with a marvelous audacity. In this story we find the sailors in the lead; men who constantly faced the rage of the sea were not easily terrified by the rage of man. It is a very significant fact that, when the English government began to deport Quakers, and to sell them into slavery, it was found necessary to pass a law withholding clearance papers from any ship refusing to carry them.

When the Church of England came back to power with the restoration of the Stuarts, neither the ecclesiastics nor the monarch were a whit the wiser for the lessons of the revolution. Within two years of the return from exile, an act was in force making it a penal offense for more than five persons to assemble for worship other than that of the established church. This act the Quakers held to be contrary to the laws of God and the just liberties of freeborn Englishmen; open violation of the law became a religious and patriotic duty. The lawbreakers were gathered in, in such numbers that the prisons could not accommodate them.

We take up the story of seven who were arraigned before the Grand Jury. "Witnesses deposed that they found those persons at certain times and places assembled above five together, but added that they neither heard any of them speak, nor saw them do anything." The jury was unable to interpret silent meditation as a crime against the State, but "expected a proof of something said or done"; therefore after prolonged debate, they returned a "bill of Ignoramus." In a trial for sedition, Judge Orlando Bridgman was not disposed to show any flabby sentimentality, nor indisposed to stretch the law a trifle. He flew into a rage with the jury: "My Masters, What do you mean? Will you make a nose of wax of the law? Those that think to deceive the law, the law will deceive them. . . . 'Tis not your business to enter into the meaning of the law, but singly to determine the fact of meeting." It would seem an unnecessary waste of the gray matter of twelve good men and true to determine a fact which the prisoners frankly admitted. As was customary at that time, the Judge gave the jury an idea of what the verdict should be, punctiliously insisting, however, on the ceremony of withdrawal to find that verdict. "With this reproof, and fresh instructions he sent them out again, who then found the bill, at which the court seemed well pleased."

These seven men had been taken in the act of silent prayer for the third time; the penalty for a third offense was transportation beyond the seas, and casting about for a vessel to carry them out of the country, the authorities discovered that a very insignificant obstacle dropped into the machinery of power may arrest motion. In this case the obstacle was Thomas May, master of the good ship *Anne* of London, and incidentally of his own fate as well. Judge Bridgman might browbeat the twelve jurors; Thomas May was good for a struggle.

When the jailer approached the captain to negotiate passage for the seven prisoners, Thomas required the assurance that they were freemen, and sailed with their own consent. Not fully satisfied with the jailer's assurance, Thomas went to the trouble of a personal call at the Bull's Inn, where the seven men were locked up, to ascertain if they were willing to sail with him. "They answered that they were compelled to go against their wills by the Act. He replied, I agreed to carry freemen, and will carry no others, and so went away, and after him the gaoler, leaving the prisoners locked up with an under keeper that night."

Next morning the jailer attempted to steal a march on the captain, and smuggle the prisoners aboard in his absence, but the sailors, who shared their master's prejudices, were only too willing to carry out his orders, which were, to refuse to receive any passengers in his absence. Hurrying off to the Secretary of State, the jailer made oath that he had contracted with Thomas May for passages for seven men to Barbados, who now refused to fulfill his contract. Thomas was summoned, and appeared accompanied by witnesses to prove his case. The extreme plasticity of the law manipulated by those who fashion it was something of an eye-opener to Captain May; he learned that as oath had already been made for the King, his oath could not be taken, that he must carry the prisoners. This legal chicanery had no soothing effect on the Master's temper, nor any appreciable effect on his determination; matters settled down to a test of endurance between the skipper and sailors of the *Anne* of London on the one hand, and of law and order on the other.

With the exception of the mate, every man of the crew of the *Anne* was on the side of the captain. Directly the Quakers came aboard the vessel the ship became unmanageable, so that it was necessary to set them ashore with instructions to meet farther down the line. Six times those weary prisoners were taken on, and each time trouble started. While the rest of the merchant fleet got safely off to sea, the limping *Anne* stumbled on her course for seven long weeks, always, however, creeping nearer the open sea. Within sprinting distance of the boundless ocean and the law of the sea, Thomas shot his broadside;

for the last time he sent the Quakers ashore, and with them a document to serve on the King, the law, the English nation, or whoever it might concern, a document entirely free from ambiguity.

"Whereas there were seven Men called Quakers, brought on board my ship, called the *Anne* of London, by William Edmonds, gaoler of Hartford, to wit, Nicholas Lucas, Henry Feast, Henry Marshall, Francis Pryor, John Blendall, Jeremiah Herne and Samuel Traberne, all of which have continued waiting on my ship from London to Deal from the 14th day of September till this Day: And I feeling that Providence hath much crossed me hitherto, whereby I perceive that the Hand of the Lord is against me, that I dare not proceed on my Voyage to carry them, *they being innocent persons*, and no crime signified against them worthy of banishment; and that there is a law in force that no Englishman shall be carried out of his native country against his will, and also my Men refuse to go the Voyage if I carry them which will be much to my hindrance, Men being very scarce by reason of the long press. For these reasons therefore and many more, *I will not carry them.* These therefore are to certify to any Person or Persons that shall question them, that they did not make an escape, but I put them on shore again, to go whither they please. All this is certified under my own Hand, this tenth day of November, 1664."

The lawless philanthropy of the skipper found no favor

with the mate. The sale of Quakers was profitable, and under such circumstances the mate was law-abiding. Deal was the last point at which the ship could touch; if the prisoners could be got aboard again, aboard they must stay until the ship reached Barbados, where Quakers fetched real money. The mate secretly notified the deputy at Deal to apprehend seven escaped convicts. That official acted promptly, but a perusal of Thomas's defiant letter decided him against any interference. While the captain was ashore the mate himself rounded up the seven men, intending to get them back to the ship. For this enterprise he required a boat and some assistance, and in all the town of Deal, not a man could be found who would lend a hand or a boat for such a purpose.

When Thomas returned, and ordered full speed ahead, the *Anne* which for seven long weeks had been hardly able to crawl, suddenly became manageable and fleet; suddenly the heavy hand of Providence was lifted, and the ship bounded nimbly into the ocean, showing a clean pair of heels, leaving the released Quakers to convey to the custodians of law and order the respects of Skipper Thomas May.. And we can take it from that able seaman as his legacy to posterity, that no injustice can long have dominion over men with convictions and the backbone to suffer inconvenience to make them effective.

Thomas introduced an epistolary style for sailors. Common seamen took the liberty of setting ashore Quakers sentenced to transportation, thus doing their bit toward the cause of bloodless revolution. The seamen of the *Mary Fortune* of Bristol discharged three deported Quakers with an epistle almost identical with Thomas May's, and some interesting additions. They wrote:

"But now going to depart, their Cry, and the Cry of their Family and Friends, are entered into the ears of the Lord, and He hath smitten us to the very Heart, saying, Cursed is he that parteth Man and Wife.

"And moreover they that Oppress his People, his Plagues shall follow them wheresoever they go, and assuredly we do in part partake of them already, for our conscience will in no wise let us rest. . . . And moreover we do wholly believe that our most gracious Sovereign doth not intend in the least to destroy his Subjects, because he hath not made void the Law of the Nation, which saith that no Englishman shall be carried out of his country against his will. *We also know that they are innocent persons.*"

In this wise the mariners of England overruled the decisions of the courts, and delicately conveyed a threat to their most gracious Sovereign. No tablet commemorates their valor; their fame lies buried in the Quaker "Collection of Sufferings." Peace to the souls of the tars who sailed the seas in the *Anne* of London and the *Mary Fortune* of Bristol.

Although the sailors reversed the verdict of the courts, the released prisoners could not go where they would. They went to their homes, and dropped a note to the

King, informing him that "the Ship being sailed and gone, and left us behind, we came back in order to go Home to our Wives and Families: And thus we thought it expedient to inform the King thereof. . . . And if it be the King's Pleasure to be farther informed in this Matter . . . we may be found or heard of at our respective Dwellings." Nevertheless the warrant issued for their rearrest in the name of the King's Most Excellent Majesty, in a flight of fancy not uncommon in legal documents, declares that their escape was "a Matter of Contrivance and Design between the said Master (Captain May) and Persons before mentioned."

These seven men never reached Barbados; they were remanded to prison, till means of transportation could be found, and there they lay for seven years until released by the proclamation of a general amnesty; no means of transportation were ever found, too many English seamen were making the rattling noise which discouraged the powerful from taking enough rope to hang themselves. Sir John Lowther sadly complains that for "the want of the executive part, transportation, our good intentions stand us in little stead."

The tug of war between the sailors and the better classes now shifts to the little Isle of Man; from port to port the seafaring men carried sedition. The battle between the Quakers and the Bishop of Man involved even the royal family, as allies of the former. Royal aid, however, proved less effective than that of the able-bodied seamen; the conviction that they were defending innocent men of their own class from the oppression of overlords put a punch into their fight. Needless to say, the sailors were not all idealists, nor were the clergy invariably actuated by malice; occasionally we read of clergymen who were "moderate" and a few were even "loving," the latter usually of the poorer class. The Quakers were attacking an autocratic priesthood, and it was the clergy, therefore, from whom they got the hardest blows.

In Besse's "Collection of Sufferings of the People called Quakers," two huge volumes of twelve hundred pages, it must be admitted there is little to indicate that the clergy, by and large, had come under the influence of the teachings of Jesus. It is certainly a bit stiff for a minister of Christ to clinch an argument on His teachings by knocking his opponent down within the walls of the sanctuary, or to cane a sick woman, or to imprison neighbors for the crime of ministering to the victims of clerical malice, yet the chronicle bulges with incidents of the sort.

The Bishop of Soder and Man was a militant Christian, with the emphasis on the qualifying adjective. It was the proud boast of his church that not a single dissenter was numbered among the inhabitants of the tight little isle, and it was a fixed idea with the Bishop that this highly desirable state of affairs must continue. The sterilization was not quite so complete as the Bishop believed, for somehow William Callow had been exposed to the Quaker heresy and caught it, communicating it in turn to his wife, who passed it on to her sister and brother-in-law, the Christens.

Their defection threw the whole island into a state of turmoil "for the Magistrates of this place being early prepossessed with an Aversion to the Quakers and their Doctrines which the Preachers of Those times, whose interest it thwarted, had industriously misrepresented, made laws against them at their first coming hither, one of them was for banishing all of that Persuasion whether Natives or others." This the authorities regarded as a simple and effective quarantine measure.

Trouble started when the parish clergyman preached an abusive sermon against the Quakers, and William Callow was moved to correct his statements. As a member of the order privileged to do all the thinking on religious matters, the priest denied Callow's right to hold independent opinions, and had him taken into custody along with considerable of his worldly goods. The following Sunday morning announcement was made from the pulpit, that by order of the Governor, the Quaker's oats and corn would be distributed among the poor of the parish. The poor were good churchmen, but they were also good neighbors of the Callows, and with surprising insolence they refused to benefit at a neighbor's expense, declaring that if the Governor was bent on charity, he might better use his own goods, than give away the goods of others.

Rebellion was spreading, and must be quelled; the poor were commanded to appear at Callow's barn for the purpose of being done good to at his expense. They obeyed the orders of their superiors to the extent of appearing, but with a single exception, they all doggedly refused to take anything that was their neighbor's. Callow's produce rotted in the barn, and in time was thrown to the pigs.

Matters came to a head when the two families refused to pay the tax levied for the bread and wine of the Holy Sacrament; as anti-ritualists the Quakers did not partake of the sacrament, and therefore declined on principle to pay for it. The clergyman got out a warrant for their arrest and " one morning early as soon as they came on Shore, having been out all Night in the Wet and Cold at sea (for they were fishermen) they were hurried to prison in their wet clothes." The outcome of this controversy over a tax of twopence was an endless succession of confiscation, dungeons and deportations; reduced to pauperism the unfortunate families floated from port to port for several years, denied admission wherever the attempt was made to land them.

Marcus Aurelius somewhere expresses gratitude to the preceptor who taught him that the highborn are heartless. High prelates of the Church of England often exhibited this mark of breeding, the Bishop of Soder and Man to a noticeable degree. " At this time there came to the Island to be sworn in " the Bishop of Soder and Man, who immediately declared his policy: no Quaker should remain a resident of the island, if he had any influence with " My Lord."

Notwithstanding the Bishop's pronouncement, the Callows and Christens refused as Quakers to receive the sacrament or to pay the tax. The Bishop rounded up the two families, man, woman and child; the Bishop's curse, or excommunication, was formally pronounced against them. Without further process of law, they were sentenced to deportation. The Bishop undoubtedly had influence with My Lord, who supported his policy; with the sailors he had no influence, and they took it upon themselves to question the justice of his ruling.

The deportees were ordered aboard a ship "Whereof Thomas Brittain was the Master. As the prisoners entered on one side of the ship, the seamen went out on the other side of the boat, telling the Master that they were not hired to carry people out of their native country against their wills, neither would they go with him if he carried them. The Master seeing his men resolute, and himself unable to proceed on his Voyage without them, conferred with the soldiers, and set the prisoners on shore again, which being done, the seamen returned to the ship, and set Sail." This transport workers' strike spread; several other vessels came into the Roads after Brittain had sailed, and all refused to take on the prisoners.

The good Bishop then fell back on the bulwark of authority, the army, and "the soldiers would have forced them on board the ship of Anthony Nicholson, a Whitehaven Man, but he stoutly opposed it, saying, He would carry no prisoners, except they would send a guard of soldiers, and money to maintain both the prisoners and them, and also signify in writing the crime laid to their charge, adding, that if they were such dangerous Persons, as were unworthy to live in their own country, he would not trust them on Board, lest perhaps they should overpower him and take away his vessel. This he spoke ironically."

Cromwell's revolution had left a swell in its wake, but the resoluteness of the sailors, the stoutness and irony of the skipper, battered in vain against the wooden-headed obstinacy of the Bishop; the highborn could not be brought to bend to the low. At midnight soldiers dragged the two families from their beds, separated the parents from their little children, stole in on the sleeping skippers, and forcibly deposited one pair of undesirables on Nicholson's ship, the other on Crossthwaite's vessel, with orders to both to sail for Dublin.

For the unsatisfied debt of twopence the Bishop had confiscated " the ancient possessions " of both families; his scheme to domicile these people whom he had made paupers within the jurisdiction of the Irish Mayor ruffled the temper of that official, who promptly loaded all four deportees on Crossthwaite's ship, with a terse order to restore them to the place where they belonged, " of which you may not fail at your peril."

For Crossthwaite, however, there was peril ahead if he obeyed the order of the Irish Mayor. Before leaving the Island he had resisted the Bishop's deportation order so stoutly that command was given to dismantle his vessel, a punishment for insubordination which came near to causing a wreck. Rather than encounter the Bishop again, he decided to try his luck on the mainland, and accordingly turned his vessel toward Cumberland. There the Justice of the Peace was fearful that four Quakers might upset the tranquillity of a whole county, and Crossthwaite was greeted with an order to take his Quakers and move on.

Crossthwaite's motto seems to have been, any port but the Isle of Man; he therefore attempted another invasion of Ireland, with no better luck than before. Back he went to the mainland, and this time luck was on his side; he managed to slip the two men ashore, whereupon he mustered up courage to take the two women home, for they were in much distress about the fate of their children. Surely the Bishop would not insist on separating the mothers from their young families. Crossthwaite miscalculated the Bishop's intense devotion to his principles; immediately they set foot on the Island the two women were clapped into jail.

To shorten the lengthy and harrowing tale, the little coastwise boats played the game of battledore and shuttlecock for three years, in the endeavor to dump this unwelcome cargo of undesirables. Ports in England, Ireland and Scotland were tried, all without success. Magistrates, wherever a landing was attempted, served the masters of the vessels with papers, some of which are enlivened with the spice of personality, rather unusual in legal documents, for example the following, by his Majesty's guardians of the peace at Peel:

" Whereas complaint is made to us whose names are subscribed, two of his Majesty's Justices of the Peace for this county of Lancaster, that there hath lately been landed at Peel within the Parish of Dalton in this county, several Persons late Inhabitants within the Isle of Man, that is to say, William Callow and Anne his wife, and Jane Christen, who have all estates within the said Isle of Man wherein to subsist, but have none elsewhere, and are likely to become burdensome to His Majesty's subjects in these Parts, if they shall be permitted to settle, and have been banished out of the said Island, the Place of their Habitation, without any legal Proceedings, as is by them alleged, or doth any Way appear to us, and not sent or confined to any certain Place of Banishment, by any legal Authority, but turned out as Vagabonds to the wide World, to the Scandal of the Laws, and His Majesty's Government. These are therefore to require you in His Majesty's name, and every of you, that you put them on board the ship called the *Trinity* of Ramsay, which vessel brought them hither, . . . the Master whereof is hereby required to receive them, and to convey them over to the Island, which if he refuses to do, then you are to stay the Ship, and bring the said Master before us forthwith to answer his Contempt, and further to do and receive as Justice appertaineth. Fail not hereof at your peril."

There was no rejoicing among the magistrates over the return of the Bishops to power; one and all, they were prompt to let his Lordship of Soder and Man know that he was poaching on their preserves; that families could not be sentenced to perpetual migration at the whim of a bishop who found their presence objectionable. To the Quakers it was a matter of small concern whether they were despoiled of their property and imperiled of their lives by the order of the court or the prejudice of an ecclesiastic; to the magistrates it was highly important that clericals should not presume to ignore the authority of the civil officers.

Neither Church nor State gave a thought to the ship masters, who were heavily penalized by reason of the controversy between them; they had no choice but to support these unwilling travelers, or throw them into the sea. Thanks to the enduring patience of Captain Crossthwaite, the two wandering Manxmen finally effected an entrance on the mainland. They promptly sought out Lord Derby, absentee Lord of the Isle of Man, begging him to consider the justice of their case, and bring their travels to an end. Lord Derby was firm in his support of the Bishop; unless the men were willing to conform and yield to ecclesiastical authority, said his Lordship, they should not return "to poison his Island," for although these two families had labored on it for centuries back, it was Lord Derby's Island. The men refused to conform.

Patterning after the importunate widow, they patiently moved on to Windsor, the residence of the absentee Bishop. Their account of the interview does not exhibit that gentleman as a logician of parts; his real strength lay in tenacity. The mere mention of persecution annoyed the good man; persecution in fact was the very last idea that entered his mind. He had quite properly confiscated the property of the two families, and set them to riding the waves, "because you will not come to church." When the petitioners argued their right to liberty of conscience, the Bishop was aggrieved:

BISHOP: Let me have the Liberty of my conscience. My conscience tells me that I must punish you, and that I do well in punishing you.

QUAKERS: Then the scripture is fulfilled upon thee, which saith, He that killeth you shall think he doeth God good service.

BISHOP: But if you had your liberty, you would corrupt all your neighbors about you.

QUAKERS: Nay we would not corrupt them, they are corrupted enough: Swearers, Liars, Whoremongers are all corrupted.

BISHOP: But you would be bad examples for them to follow in your ways.

QUAKERS: They have seventeen priests among them to be Examples to them, if they be as good as they ought to be; what need have they to fear us who are but two Men, if we had been as thou said. The people are their

Hearers, and ought to follow the best Examples, whether it be us or them.

BISHOP: This is all your discourse both in the Island and here, but you will neither give reason nor take reason. I will have nothing to say to you, neither will I consent that you go to the Island again if I can help it.

The Quakers undoubtedly had the best of the debate, but the Bishop had the best of the situation; with sweet reasonableness he sat in the seat of power. "Thus the conference ended. So they went into Cumberland, and being determined at any risque to see their distressed families," they boarded the *Pickering* in an attempt to run the blockade of their home town. But the Bishop was thorough in his undertaking, soldiers were guarding the Island, protecting it from new ideas. On the appeal of the master of the *Pickering*, and his agreement to put up security for the men, they were allowed at large only till he could pull up anchor. Callow's weeping wife and his relations came to the boat to take leave of him as he went voyaging once more. "The Master of the vessel also wept, compassionating her Condition, and to William's wife said, 'Fear not, your Husband is an Honest Man: We will live and die together, and he shall want for nothing that I can do for him.' So he put to sea."

With the connivance of the friendly sailor, the indefatigable William landed again in Lancashire, and again appealed to the Lord of the Isle, and was again rebuffed. Even to these patient fishermen, it was now apparent that further angling in these waters was a waste of time; Lord Derby and his Bishop were immovable. Undismayed they determined to take their case up to royalty; on they trudged and at last got the ear of Prince Rupert, cousin to the King, and a brother of Princess Elizabeth of the Palatinate, who was a Quaker, a circumstance which may have made the Prince favorable to their appeal. At any rate, Prince Rupert wrote to Lord Derby on their behalf:

My Lord:

There is one William Callow, an ancient Tenant of your Lordship, in the Isle of Man, is now, it seems, turned Quaker, and for that reason Banisht the Country. I am desired by another of that Profession, whom I know to be a faithful and Loyal subject of his Majesty in the time of the late War, to intreat with you for the said Callow, he assuring me that he is a quiet and inoffensive Person in every Thing, save in the Matter of his Religion, and though I would not be an advocate of any dangerous unpeaceable Person, yet in such an Instance I am induced to give your Lordship this Trouble, the Man himself appearing to me not likely to be dangerous, and also expressing with as much Respect and Reverence toward your Lordship, as his Profession will give him leave. If there be no more in it than being a Quaker, I do presume your Lordship may be inclined to restore him and his Family to their ancient possessions, and that you may please to do so, is the reason I give your Lordship this Trouble, who am,

Your Lordship's faithful friend and servant,

Rupert.

His Lordship did not please to comply with the request of his Royal Highness, whose letter overlooked one important point. The Quakers were not dangerous persons so far as concerned the monarchy, the class to which his

Royal Highness belonged, for they never meddled with politics; they were dangerous to the clericals, the class to which the Bishop belonged, and Lord Derby was supporting the Bishop. Moreover, Lord Derby may have had enough sense of humor to be amused by the idea of Prince Rupert in the rôle of patron to peaceable persons. At any rate, he and the Bishop meant to sit immovably tight, and he intimated as much to his Royal Highness.

May it Please Your Highness:

I had the honor to receive a letter from your Highness, by the hand of a Manx Quaker, wherein your Highness is pleased to intimate your command to me, that he should be permitted to return to the Isle of Man, from whence he stands banished (with others because they are Quakers) by the Laws of that Place. I make bold to inform your Highness that there is now in the Island not one Quaker or dissenting Person of any Persuasion from the Church of England, and I humbly conceive your Highness, for that one Man's concern, would not have that place in danger to be infected with scism or Heresy, which it might be liable to, if Quakers should be permitted to reside there. Having given your Highness this Account I shall now detain your Highness no longer from your more serious Affairs. I shall only add that I am your Highness's most humble servant,

Derby.

Translated into our own familiar vernacular, his Highness's most humble servant, Derby, was calling the royal attention to the fact that it was his island, and nobody could tell him how to run his own island.

Defying public opinion, for the simple Manx fisherfolk sympathized with their unfortunate neighbors, defying with Lord Derby's aid the commands of royalty, with iron will and unremitting vigilance the Bishop maintained his hundred-per-cent policy. The Callows and Christens continued to toss about the English seas in uncomfortable little tubs, refused admittance at every port they attempted to enter in the United Kingdom. The monotony of the sea voyage was occasionally varied by a break into the Isle of Man, which invariably resulted in a sojourn in a dark dungeon, till the patient Bishop could find a ship to take them sailing again.

The Bishop's ecclesiastical Christianity admitted of a harshness in dealing with the two women, rather shocking to those who interpret the Gospels more literally. Between the two families they had a dozen small children, some of whom were born on the enforced sea trips. Anne Callow was near her confinement on one occasion when the soldiers were sent to oust her from her home, so near that even the rough men pitied her, taking it upon themselves to represent her condition to the Bishop. Where a great principle was involved, the Bishop was a stickler; he ordered the soldiers to go back, and if the woman was found in actual labor, she might have another day of grace, otherwise they were to get her on board a boat, if it was necessary to remove her in a cart.

A scrupulous Quaker, Anne could not say that her struggle had begun; she insisted that she was far from well, "and knew not her hour." Under the circumstances the soldiers were obliged to carry her off, and she spent the remainder of the night in an open boat. Three neighbors indignantly refused to assist in the work of removing her, and they were imprisoned by the Bishop who argued: "If they miscarry in their health or lives, it is through their own wilful disobedience, and they will be their own murderers." Anne fortunately escaped the sin of willful murder; she reached a bed on dry land in good time. She was left alone with her trouble, however, in a strange place; her companions were separated from her, and hustled off to continue the endless voyage.

Her sister Jane, with a newborn child in her arms, was dragged from her bed one night by soldiers, to be put aboard a boat. "What shall I do with my sucking child?" she demanded. "We care not if the Dogs eat him," the national protectors made reply.

The Quaker chronicle, having gathered the little band on the mainland of England, drops their story without a word as to their ultimate fate. It seems probable, therefore, that the tenacious patience of the Quakers triumphed finally over the tenacious violence of the Bishop; that the Callow-Christen contingent went over the top, and returned to their own homes, with the loss perhaps of the persistent William. Fifteen years later there is a record of one Anne Callow despoiled of a cow for refusal to pay a small clerical tax; apparently the fight was still on, though the voyaging was over. As William had so often braved the Bishop and the dungeon to speak a comforting word to his anxious wife, it is probable that he had fallen in the fray, and that his widow was still carrying on.

Elizabeth Haddon—The Girl Who Founded a Town

Love labor; for if thou dost not want it for food, thou mayst for physick. —WILLIAM PENN.

THROUGH cruel sufferings, into dungeons, to the scaffold, we have followed the pioneer Quakers; we leave them, after their long and victorious struggle, in green pastures, beside the still waters. Elizabeth Haddon's name does not help to swell the "Collection of Sufferings"; it was her good fortune to come on the scene just as the fight for freedom was won, and her life ended as it began, happily. The tremendous energy which the preceding generation put into their fight, Elizabeth turned to the activities of peace; the town of Haddonfield, New Jersey, probably the only one in America founded by a young girl, is a perpetual monument to her enterprise and ability.

Some had pioneering thrust upon them, Elizabeth was born to it; at the age of five the child was mother to the woman. In her long life she had many irons in the fire, and enough warmth of temperament to keep them all hot. She was born in London, the eldest of three daughters of John Haddon, who had acquired a tidy fortune in the ship supply business. The family enjoyed a comfortable London home, furnished in elegant simplicity, their domestic life was unusually peaceful and happy. The parents are described as "well educated and genteel"; the mother, before she renounced the vanities of the world to embrace Quakerism, was an accomplished performer on the spinet and mandolin, and busied herself in her spare time with the ladylike occupation of fine embroidering. When she accepted the austere discipline of her sect, her music was given up, and the embroidery consigned to the fire.

Elizabeth was a child of five when William Penn, a family friend, made them a visit, and told his thrilling tales of the new world and his beloved Indians. Even at that early age Elizabeth exhibited the type of mind that knows what it wants and flags it, a faculty she retained in maturity. As she listened spellbound to the great man's narration, she crept gradually closer to him, until at last he lifted her on his knee, and for her especial edification, told of the squaws and papooses, of little Indian babies swinging from tree boughs in birch-bark cradles made by their Indian mothers, of beautiful baby clothes made of the skins which their fathers hunted.

"Hast thou ever seen a papoose baby thyself?" inquired the practical English baby. "And hast thou got a moccasin shoe?"

Friend Penn had seen many papooses, and would send her a moccasin shoe. The delighted child could hardly be got to bed that night; hopping about, half undressed, she shouted, "Ho! ho! Friend Penn is going to send me an Indian moccasin," and demanded that her family rejoice with her. With an Indian moccasin, William Penn started into being a New Jersey town.

From that time on, the mind of the romantic little person was fixed on the American scene. Her dolls stared to the name of Pocahontas, and, as she preferred active to still life, kittens were urged into the rôle of papooses, swung in leather cradles of her own make from the bough of a tree. In miniature forests of her creation, William Penn addressed the assembled chiefs, made of sticks topped with feathers. Elizabeth's sisters were frankly bored by Indian games, and much preferred the familiar English ones, but with Quaker singleness of purpose Elizabeth held her ground.

"No! let us play that we all go to settle in America. Now suppose we are in the woods, with great big trees all around us, and squirrels running up and down them, and wolves growling."

This picture gave Sister Hannah the shivers: "I don't like wolves; they will bite thee. Father says they will bite."

"I should not be afraid," insisted the future pioneer, "I would run into the house and shut the door, when they came near enough for me to see their eyes. How I should love to go to America, such grand woods to run about in, and I should love to swing papooses in the trees."

Elizabeth had advanced to the age of eleven when John Estaugh, a young Irishman, came to preach at the London Yearly Meeting. The child was much impressed by his preaching, and he acquired merit in her eyes by reason of having been to America, where he had relatives. Elizabeth was still taking her meals in the nursery when John Haddon brought the youthful preacher home to dinner. Among other American curiosities he exhibited some ears of Indian corn, describing the beauty of a field of tasseled stalks swaying in the wind. John Haddon begged an ear for his little daughter, a treasure which she laid away with Friend Penn's moccasin. America became more than ever the land of her dreams, with the engaging young preacher in the foreground. "She often quoted his words afterwards, and began to read religious books with great diligence."

The next step in the development of a pioneer was the purchase of a tract of land in New Jersey. Haddon's neighbor, John Willis, had taken up land in that territory, and set up as a ship carpenter, buying his supplies from John Haddon. On the death of Willis, his son, who had no taste for pioneering, transferred the New Jersey tract to Haddon, an investment which may have been influenced by his daughter's interest. He entertained the idea of emigrating with his family, and had a house built on the property, but as other members were distinctly unsympathetic to Elizabeth's enthusiasm for wild life, he abandoned the plan. Desirous of making the property serviceable to any one who could make use of it, he proposed at a family gathering to bestow it on any relative who would develop and live on it. "Thy relatives," he was told, "are too well established in England, to wish to emigrate to the wilds of America."

Elizabeth, now seventeen years old, had been an eager listener to the offer and refusal of the gift; before the family parted for the night, she had a word to say: "Dear parents and sisters, it is now a long time I have had a strong impression on my mind that it is my duty to go to America. My feelings have been greatly drawn toward the poor brethren and sisters there. It has been clearly pointed out to me what I am to do; that a sign would be given when the way was opened, and tonight when I heard thy proposition to give the house and land to whoever would occupy it, I felt at once that thy words were the promised sign."

This speech was something of a poser for the family, especially for the genteel mother, who had been so proficient in ladylike accomplishments; she pointed out the responsibility of managing a large estate in a new wild land.

With filial respect the girl met all objections. "Young women have governed kingdoms," said she, "and surely it requires less wisdom to manage a farm. But let that not trouble us, dear Mother. He that feedeth the ravens will guide me in the work whereunto He has called me.

It is not to cultivate the farm, but to be a friend and physician to the people of that region."

The Quaker father would not quench the leadings of the spirit; all he asked was deliberation and caution: "Doubt not, my child, that we shall be as willing to give thee up to the Lord's disposal, however hard the trial may be. But when thou wert a very little girl thy imagination was much excited concerning America; therefore thou must be very careful that no desire for new adventures, founded on the will of the creature, mislead thee from the true light in this matter. I advise thee for some months to make it the subject of solemn meditation and prayer. Then if our lives be spared we will talk further concerning it."

The family dropped the subject, leaving Elizabeth entirely to the inward monitor. Solemn meditation and prayer, however, did not wholly absorb her time and energy; anticipating the answer to prayer, she crammed on agriculture, household management and the cure of ordinary diseases. When the period assigned for meditation had expired, she assured her family, "that the light shone with undiminished clearness, and she felt more strongly than ever that it was her appointed mission to comfort and strengthen the Lord's people in the new world."

The Lord's guidance and Elizabeth's determination was a combination before which the family hesitation and doubt gave way. "A poor widow of good sense and discretion" was discovered, who was willing to accompany the young girl as friend and housekeeper, and two trusty Quaker workmen completed the party. Whether Friend Penn's moccasin made a return trip to America, history sayeth not, but it is quite certain that John Estaugh's ear of Indian corn was not overlooked in the packing.

In the spring of 1700, just eighteen years after the landing of William Penn, Elizabeth, not yet twenty, set out for the New Jersey territory with her modest retinue. Her family and friends, who had no yearning for such adventure, regarded her as a martyr to principle; they parted from her in much love, not a tear shed on either side, Elizabeth "preserving a martyrlike cheerfulness and serenity to the end." The martyr crown on which her friends insisted does not seem to fit Elizabeth's head; this unusual young person was going to the life of which she had dreamed since babyhood, the Lord was favorable to her undertaking, her nerve and ability were adequate to seeing it through, martyrdom must have been far from her thought.

The estate on which she was to spend her long and useful life was three miles from the nearest neighbor. In a clearing, on the bank of a pleasant little stream stood the small house to which she came in the early summer, when trees and shrubs filled the world with color and fragrance, the birds chorusing as they went about their domestic concerns. The London-bred girl was not terrified by the isolation; she was up with the sun on that first morning in her own home, and found it all as delightful as she had dreamed; falling on her knees, she returned thanks: "Very beautiful hast thou made this earth. How bountiful are thy gifts, O Lord!"

In the make-up of this young woman romance and practicality were well balanced; she did not sit long to sentimentalize. There were five hundred acres of land to be made productive under her management, and her first step was to discover what crops could best be grown on it. When she was told that rye would give the best returns she promptly decided: "Then I shall eat rye bread." The long-treasured ear of Indian corn was also planted.

An attentive listener to the tales of William Penn, Elizabeth harbored no fear of the Indians; with a wisdom beyond that of many more mature settlers, she learned much of value from them regarding the healing virtues of indigenous herbs. There was no time for homesickness; she was as busy and as happy as the bees and birds, superintending her farm, or riding over the country to nurse the sick. She brought box hedging from England for her famous garden, and the yew trees which she planted two centuries ago are still thriving. When she needed bricks for her garden walks, she started a brick yard for their manufacture. Her brew house was probably the first medical laboratory in this country; here she prepared her simples, and made "a little wine for the stomach's sake." Long after she had died, New Jersey nurses recommended her salve as the "sovereignst remedy on earth." Herbs, vegetables and fruit from her garden were generously distributed to her less favored neighbors; her house was wide open to whoever claimed her hospitality; "she never turned a stranger from her door." When it was suggested to her that chance wanderers might prove undesirable guests, she answered, "Perfect love casteth out fear."

The long nights of Elizabeth's first winter had come, unhusked ears, the harvest of the gift ear of corn were hanging from the kitchen rafters, burning logs were roaring cheerily up the chimney, when the jingle of sleigh bells gave warning of guests, and two men came tramping up to the door. "Thou art welcome, Friend Estaugh," was Elizabeth's greeting, as she opened the door, "the more so for being entirely unexpected," for one of the men was the donor of the ear of corn.

The young man explained that only after his return to America had he learned that "the Lord called thee hither before me." There was much pleasant reminiscence, John Estaugh recalled how Elizabeth's father had talked to him of his little girl, who continually played that she was a settler in the woods. "I am a child still," said the girl, "and hast thou forgotten the ear of Indian corn which my father begged of thee for me? Since then I have seen it growing; and a goodly plant it is. All that and more," pointing to the ears hanging in the kitchen, "came from the corn left with my father. May the good seed sown by thy ministry be as fruitful." With an abundant harvest garnered, good wine and cider in the cellar, logs blazing in the chimney, and the pleasantest of young preachers to chat with, a martyr's crown has no place in the picture.

Elizabeth was no welsher; Providence had given her the desires of her heart, and she kept up her end; she was a whole public service commission in herself. As a heavy snow had fallen, her great ox teams went out to plow up miles of snow, opening up paths for her less opulent neighbors, the two young visitors lending a hand in the good work. Then a sled was loaded with medicines and delicacies for the sick, and John naturally accompanied the girl on her rounds. She was pleased with his kindness to the old, his gentleness to the little children; this engaging youth was quite up to the picture of him she had carried in her heart since the age of eleven.

When he preached the first-day sermon, Elizabeth found it so "marvelously adapted to the trials and temptations of her own soul that she almost deemed it was spoken on purpose for her." But John did not linger, he moved onward in his ministry, and Elizabeth heard no more of him until the following summer, when again he made her house a stopping place on his way to the Salem Quarterly Meeting. There were many other travelers to the Meeting, and the small house was filled to capacity that night, the stables as well. Next morning a large party mounted and took the road to Salem. It was not to his young hostess, but to an old lame woman that John gave assistance in mounting. "He is always kindest to the poor and neglected," reflected the observant Elizabeth. More sadly she reflected that John would be leaving for England after the Salem Meeting, and there was no saying how long he would be gone, nor what might happen. Elizabeth was not the kind to defer action, or to wait for fate to overtake her; always she went fearlessly out to meet it. As she halted and was fumbling with her saddle, the young man came to inquire what was wrong.

"Nothing, Friend John; I was merely looking to see if Joseph had buckled the girth securely." At that opportune moment the girth began to slip, and before John could put it right the entire company had ridden out of sight. Legend has it that Elizabeth then said: "Friend John, I have a subject of great importance on my mind, and one that nearly concerns thee. I am strongly impressed that the Lord hath sent thee to me as a partner for life. I tell thee my impressions frankly, but not without calm and deep reflection, for matrimony is a holy relation, and should be entered into with all sobriety. Thou art to leave this part of the country tomorrow, and not knowing when I should see thee again, I felt to tell thee what lay on my mind."

A deliberate young man was John, the proposal was

THE "BULL AND MOUTH," MEETING PLACE OF THE EARLY QUAKERS, THE SCENE OF MANY RIOTS

sudden, moreover he was poor and the girl was rich. "This thought is new to me, Elizabeth, and I have no light thereon. Thy company hath been right pleasant to me, and thy countenance ever reminds me of William Penn's title page 'Innocency with her open face.' I have observed, too, thy warm heartedness is tempered with a most excellent discretion, and thy speech is ever sincere. Assuredly such is the maiden I would ask of the Lord as a most precious gift. I came to this country solely on a religious visit, and it might distract my mind to entertain this subject at present. When I have discharged the duties of my mission I will speak further."

John certainly in his love-making verifies Elizabeth's description of him: "A pattern of Moderation in all things; not lifted up with any Enjoyments, nor cast down with Disappointments." She herself had verve enough for a large family, and moderation apparently appealed to her. As he was leaving next day for England, John went so far as to press her hand affectionately: "Farewell, Elizabeth; if it be the Lord's will I will see thee soon." A perfectly satisfactory arrangement to Elizabeth, no doubt, since she had been singularly successful in interpreting the Lord's will in matters that concerned her.

Notwithstanding his extreme moderation, John was no laggard lover. He paid his respects to Father Haddon in England, and had the family assurance that they would gladly welcome him as a member; with the parental blessing on the match, he was withheld by no vain pride as to the disparity of their fortunes. Within three months after Elizabeth's proposal, he was back in Haddonfield, rather a speedy round trip in those days.

In her own pleasant home John was married to Elizabeth, in the presence of Friends, who issued the following certificate as was the Quaker custom:

KNOW ALL MEN BY THESE PRESENTS THAT, Whereas John Estaugh and Elizabeth Haddon: of the Province of West New Jarsey and county of Gloucester: both Single Persons, the said Elizabeth being the Doughter of John Haddon of London In the Kingdom of England, haveing Several times Declared their Intentions of takeing each other in Maryage to Husband and Wife, at the monthly meetings of Newton, to which the belonge according to truthes order, and the said meeteings haveing received Sattisfaction Concerning their clearness both by due and orderly Enquire made here and allso by Certificates from Friends in England: as allso the consent of their Parents being hadd, So that the Sd. Meeteings have given their free Assent & concerrence therewith and thereunto &c.

These therefore may Certifye that upon the first day of the Tenth month in the Yeare One Thousand Seven hundred and two att a Publickue Meeteing att the house of the Said Elizabeth Haddon Apoynted and held on Purpose for the full accompleishing and Sollemnizeing of the said maryage they the said John and Elizabeth openly and sollemly in the presence of the Said Meeteing did take Each other in Maryage to Husband and Wife, the said John Sollemly promising in these Woords, Viz, Friends and Neighbors in the presence of God and you his people Whome I desire to be my Witnesses I Take this my Friend Elizabeth Haddon to be my Wife — promiseing through the Lords Assistance to be unto her A Loveing Husband till ye Lord by death Shall separate us and the Sd Elizabeth declareing as Followeth

Friends in the fear of the Lord and before you his people

whome I desire to be my witnesses I take this my Friend John Estaugh to be my husband promiseing through ye Lords Assistance to be unto him A faithfull and Loveing wife until the Lord by death shall Separate us. . . .

In Testimony whereof the Said John & Elizabeth have hereunto Sett their hands ye daye & yeare above said.

On the legend of Elizabeth Haddon's courtship, Longfellow founded his "Courtship of Miles Standish"; Priscilla, the Puritan maiden, was in fact Elizabeth the New Jersey Quaker.

Elizabeth was now in possession of everything which to her childish mind had seemed most desirable, a fine estate in the midst of great woods, sick and needy people on whom to expend her boundless energy, and the most engaging of young preachers for a life partner. A partner in every sense he was; he shared her predilection for dabbling in chemistry and medicine, and was skilful in ministering to the body as well as to the soul. To render unto the Lord a return for all his mercies, Elizabeth taxed herself generously. Her unbounded hospitality called for more extensive quarters, and a few years after her marriage she built a commodious stone mansion, elegantly though quietly furnished, a haven of rest for travel-worn Quakers; she was easily the most prominent citizen in that part of the world. Nor was John the only person sensible of her "most excellent discretion"; for half a century she held the most important post in the Society of Friends, clerk of the Meeting. A vote is never taken among Friends, nor is any vital matter decided until the consent of the Meeting is unanimous. Every member with an opinion expresses it, those without opinions do not register; the business in hand is threshed out until common ground is found. The clerk must enter a minute in the records giving "the sense of the Meeting," a duty which requires great discretion and a peculiar sensitiveness to mental atmosphere. Rarely in the history of the society has the record of a clerk been questioned.

In their calm unruffled Quaker way, husband and wife lived, as busy as nailers. John was made agent for the Pennsylvania Land Company, of London, a means of livelihood which left him free to give his best to his ministry. He traveled over the world on missionary journeys, "and when at home, as he had some skill in Chymistry and Physick, he freely bestowed much Labour and Time therein, for the Good of the People of the Neighborhood where he dwelt; and especially on the Poor, for whom he was much concerned; so that it may justly be said, the Blessing of those who were ready to perish came upon him."

He was sixty-seven, and in failing health, when, says his wife, he again "had a Concern to visit Friends at Tortola. This brought on him a deep Exercise, but when it was confirmed that it was really required of him to do so, he gave up to it. . . . He first wrote to them; but finding this would not excuse him, he durst no longer delay, but go he must. . . . We parted in the Aboundings of Love and Affection."

These West Indian trips were the heaviest trials of Elizabeth's happy life; the climate was unhealthy, the conditions unsanitary, but such calls were to the Quaker like the orders of a commander-in-chief to his lieutenants; they must be obeyed. It was John's last call to the colors. Friends in Tortola wrote his wife: "A shivering fit followed by fever seized him on the first day of the tenth month. He took great notice that it ended forty years since his marriage with thee; that during that time you had lived in much love, and parted in the same; and that leaving thee was his greatest concern of all outward enjoyments."

Elizabeth wrote a Testimony to her husband: "I'll venture to say, few, if any, in a married State, ever lived in sweeter Harmony than we did. Oh! what shall I say of him, but that he was a Man endowed with many good Gifts, which rendered him very agreeable to his Friends, and much more to me, his Wife. . . . My loss is as far beyond my Expressing, as is his Worth."

With happy memories of the past, Elizabeth had a future of twenty active, useful years. With never a papoose of her own to swing from the bough of a tree, she adopted her nephew, Ebenezer Hopkins, to share her happy old age. On crisp, pleasant winter nights, sleigh bells still jingled on the road to Haddon Hall, where young couples made love in decorous Quaker fashion, with the hearty approval of the hospitable Widow

Estaugh. She lived to the full her eighty-two years of life: "Her last illness brought great bodily pain, which she bore with much calmness of mind and sweetness of spirit. She departed this life as one falling asleep, full of days, like unto a shock of corn fully ripe."

The World as the Quakers Changed It

The early history of the Friends is one long record of invincible fortitude displayed in the presence of atrocious malevolence and unsparing ridicule. Theirs was a courage that the world calls passive and not active; the distinction is an idle one, for nobody who has seen the Friends working in the thick of a famine or a fever, or directing the operations of a life brigade on a stormy sea coast, . . . will ever doubt that they are the keenest of fighters. — SIR GEORGE TREVELYAN.

I always say that there is more real pluck in the ranks of the Quakers than in all our regiments of redcoats. — COBDEN.

No old saw has had its teeth so well worn by usage as that human nature never changes. Every living thing is certainly susceptible to change of habit, if not to change of nature. Wildcat is the synonym for aggressive ferocity, yet no other animal is so avid for human affection as tabby, the domesticated progeny of the fiercest of wild beasts. A comparison of our own times with the universal and incredible cruelty of the period in which Quakerism had its beginning should convince the most skeptical that, in the last few centuries, tabby's tamers have themselves undergone as great a taming process, though the work is far from complete.

New England will never be allowed to forget the atrocities committed during the witchcraft epidemic, yet it is only fair to say that, compared with the Old World, she has an almost spotless record. In an essay on "Crime and Punishment" by the Italian, Marquis Becarria, prefaced by Voltaire, it is estimated that the grand total of witches done to death by the combined Christian sects of Europe, by tortures of the most blood-curdling description, was one hundred thousand. The Jeremiahs of democracy might cheer up by reflecting that, as the world has grown more democratic, it has become a little less cruel.

The book is still to be written which shall trace the enormous influence of the Quakers through all its ramifications; statistics are of little value in estimating it, for it was out of all proportion to their numerical strength. They rolled in on society with the stealth and force of a tidal wave, and receded carrying away much rotten lumber of existing institutions.

Besse's "Collection of Sufferings" is geographically arranged, every section of the habitable globe furnishing a chapter. Scarce a prison in Great Britain and Ireland that did not lodge Quakers, and inflame them with a passion for prison reform. They suffered in Europe, Asia and the islands of the sea. Strange to say, although money was raised by English Friends to ransom Quaker slaves in Africa, the darkest continent contributes not a page to their sufferings. Quaker slaves enjoyed the respect of their owners, and the liberty they most prized, and were denied at home — the right of peaceable assembly. They held meetings, preached to their masters, made converts, and left a good report of the Mohammedans: "Nevertheless, though they be called Turks, ye seed of God is near unto them, and their kindnesse hath in some measure been shown to His servants." In the New World their itinerary covered every hamlet; in many of the colonies they were harshly dealt with, while in others the governors and chief citizens attended their meetings.

In the seventeenth-century struggle for liberty, the Quakers were those who dropped out of the Puritan ranks when the fight reached the height of violence. They had the sense to see that political revolution was not carrying them where they wanted to go, and the audacity to quit and take their own course. The first requisite to experience, says Bagehot, is an experiencing mind; the Quaker revolt against physical force was not the result of abstract theorizing, but the response of the most experiencing minds in England to the experience of violence. They were fed up on the English revolution and counter-revolution, and convinced that out of violence only violence comes; if experience teaches anything, it is that political revolution usually falls at last into the control of the most violent and least scrupulous, who establish a tyranny as oppressive as the one they set out to overthrow. Disraeli, father of the consummate politician, Lord Beaconsfield, says, there have been but two political parties in the world, the Outs and the Ins; the Outs all talk alike and the Ins all act alike. The

Quakers reacted immediately and practically to their intellectual conviction. All humane and decent-minded people express the hope, and even the belief, that, at some future time, war will be abolished. For us, said the Quakers, war is abolished now, and for them it was. The accepted creed of all mankind in their day, it has since become a debatable doctrine, its supporters increasingly on the defensive.

On the face of it, the readiness of the Quakers to endure the horrors of martyrdom for the privilege of wearing their hats when and where they pleased, seems the apotheosis of triviality. Though the underlying principle of the seventeenth-century fight was far from trivial, the pegs on which all factions hung their principles were equally absurd. Archbishop Laud, primate of all England, and virtually one of its rulers, in his fight against the rising power of Puritanism, unhesitatingly embroiled the nation in blood for the privilege of dictating in what garb, with what genuflections, and by what formulas all people should say their prayers. A letter of a henchman of the Archbishop, a member of the King's household and a soldier in the army which King Charles, at the Archbishop's instigation, led into the land of the oat-eaters to teach them the Episcopal ritual, manifests the spirit of the times (a few adjectives are omitted as a concession to delicacy): "We have had a most cold, wet and long time of it; but we have kept our soldiers warm with the hopes of rubbing, fubbing and scrubbing those scurvy, filthy, dirty, nasty, lousy, itchy, scabby, slovenly, snotty-nosed, logger-headed, foolish, insolent, proud, beggarly, impertinent, absurd, grout-headed, villainous, barbarous, bestial, false, lying, rogueish, devilish, long-eared, short-haired, damnable, atheistical, Puritanical crew of the Scotch Covenant. But now there is peace in Israel." Calvin and oatmeal porridge turned the missionary army homeward without carrying out the Archbishop's educational program. It is but fair to admit that Episcopalians and Puritans were equally skillful in the use of robust Anglo-Saxon invective.

While the bishops and the Puritans struggled for power, which each in turn abused, the Quaker forces entered the field, and brought into the fight the principles of toleration, human decency and Christian forbearance. Human nature changes little in one respect — the degenerating effect of power on character. The Quakers fought neither to have nor to hold power, but to emancipate men from inherited notions of the rights of power, to let in light on the darkness of human understanding. Enlightenment must come from within, not from without, and they therefore fell back on the Christian teaching, that the redemption of the world from darkness and chaos must be effected by individual salvation. Only by the self-discipline of the individual could the level of society be raised, and says John Milton, "There is not that thing in the world of more grave and urgent importance throughout the whole life of man than Discipline."

The Episcopacy, as well as the Puritans on both sides of the Atlantic, were determined not to leave this matter of grave and urgent importance to the Quakers themselves, and here they attacked them on ground from which they refused to be dislodged. For over two centuries a controversy has waged as to the rights and proprieties of the Quaker skirmish with the New England Puritans. Henry Cabot Lodge (and even, to some extent, John Fiske) has accepted the version of the Puritan ecclesiastics without a pinch of salt. A perusal of the records would leave little doubt as to the verdict, records so unbearably dull, however, that few would have the patience for it. The matter may be fairly summed up by quoting the opinions of the leaders on both sides.

John Cotton stands admittedly as the foremost of the Puritan guides, and was by no means the most extreme; compared with the malignant Hugh Peters or the Reverend Mr. Wilson, he presents a lovable character. At any rate, he was a revered teacher, and this is his teaching:

"The good that is brought to princes and subjects by the due punishment of apostate seducers and idolaters and blasphemers is manifold.

"First, it putteth away evill from the people and cutteth off a gangrene, which would spread to further ungodlinesse.

"Secondly, it driveth away wolves from worrying and scattering the sheep of Christ. For false teachers be wolves, and the very name of wolves holdeth forth what benefit would redound to the sheep *either by killing them or driving them away*.

"Thirdly, such executions upon such evill doers causeth all the country to heare and feare, and do no more such wickedness. Yea as these punishments are preventions of like wickedness in some, so they are wholesome medicines, to heale such as are curable of the eviles.

"Fourthly, the punishments executed upon false prophets and seducing teachers, doe bring down showers of blessing upon the civil state.

"Fifthly, it is an honour to God's justice that such judgments are executed."

To any but the astigmatic eye of a Calvinist theologian, this seems to be the same wholesome medicine prescribed by the great Doctor Laud for Cotton himself and his company of apostate seducers. The purgative medicine proved as ineffective as it was drastic. To the everlasting credit of the common sense of the common people of New England, the Salisbury mob administered an antidote for the fatal dose prescribed to the Quaker women.

Against Cotton's advocacy of the persecution which would maintain his caste in power, put Howgill's statement at the trial which sent him to his death. "It is a doctrine always held by us [the Quakers] that Christ's Kingdom could not be set up with carnal weapons; nor the gospel propagated by force of arms, nor the church of God built with violence; but the Prince of Peace was manifested amongst us, and we could learn war no more, but could love enemies and forgive them that did evil to us."

Or again, William Penn's incessant fight against the cruelty of bigotry: "Men may be angry for God's sake, and kill people too. Christ said it, and too many have practiced it. But what sort of Christians must they be, I pray, that can Hate in His name who bids us love, and kill for His sake that forbids killing, and commands love even to enemies? . . . Oh that we could see some as eager to turn people to God as they are to blow them up or set one against another."

Or George Fox's refusal to take legal action against the mob which had battered him within an inch of his life: "If the Lord did forgive them, he should not trouble about them."

These statements of the leaders are a fair exposition of the spirit animating the opposing parties, and a testimony to the mighty work which the Quakers wrought in changing public opinion. The Puritans honestly assumed that they were the appointed instruments for the destruction of God's enemies; the Quakers believed He could manage without their assistance. Their end was to enfranchise the consciences of men, and this end they held up against prelate and Puritan. Liberty or death was their cry; death they often got, but before their fight was finished we got liberty.

The right of free assembly was won by that "dogged

pertinacity" which the New Englanders have condemned as bad form, a resistance before which Church and State were helpless, and in which Masson, the biographer of John Milton, exults: "No other denomination so amazed and perplexed the authorities by their obstinacy as the Quakers. It was their boast that their worship, from its very nature, could not be stopped by 'men or devils.' From a meeting of Roman Catholics, they said, you have but to take away the Mass book, or the chalice, or the priest's garments, or even but to spill the water or blow out the candles, and the meeting is over. So in a meeting of Lutherans or Episcopalians, or a meeting of Presbyterians or Baptists or Socinians, there is always some implement or set of implements upon which all depends, be it the liturgy, or the gown or surplice, the Bible or the hourglass; remove these and make noise enough and there can be no service. Not so with a Quaker meeting. There men and women worship with their hearts, without implements, in silence as well as by speech. You may break in upon them, roar at them, drag them about; the meeting, if it be of any size, essentially still goes on till all the component individuals are murdered. Throw them out of doors in twos and threes and they but re-enter at the window and quietly resume their places. Pull their meeting house down, and they reassemble next day most punctually amid the broken walls and rafters. Shovel sand and dirt down upon them, and there they sit, a sight to see, musing immovably among the rubbish. This is no description from fancy; it was the actual practice of the Quakers all over the country. They held their meetings regularly, perseveringly and without the least concealment, keeping the doors of their meeting house purposely open that all might enter, informers, constables or soldiers, and do whatever they chose. In fact the Quakers behaved magnificently. By their peculiar method of open violation of the law and passive resistance only, they rendered a service to the common cause of all Nonconformist sects which has never been sufficiently acknowledged. The authorities had begun to fear them as a kind of supernatural folk, and knew not what to do with them, but cram them into gaols and let them lie there. In fact the gaols of those days were less places of punishment for criminals than receptacles for a great proportion of what was bravest and most excellent in the manhood and womanhood of England."

"We shall engage by God's assistance," said William Penn, "to lead peaceable, just and industrious lives among men, to the good example of all. But if after all we have said, suffering should be our inheritance of this generation, be it known to them all — That meet we must and meet we cannot but encourage all to do, (whatever we sustain)."

Out of the mouths of many witnesses it seems to be established that at fearful cost to themselves, the right of free assembly was the gift of the Quakers to our race. Nor were they doubtful that in their fight against religion

WORSHIPPING IN SPIRIT, A TYPICAL QUAKER MEETING

(*From a Painting by J. Walter West, R.W.S.*)

by compulsion, they had won a permanent victory for posterity. "Though this body of clay must return to the dust," said a youthful martyr, "yet I leave this testimony, that I have served God in my generation: and that spirit which hath lived and acted and ruled in me, shall yet break forth in thousands."

It did indeed break forth in strange places; long before the radio carried words, ideas moved through space. Contemporaneous with George Fox, a French Carmelite monk developed what he called "the practice of the presence of God." Like the Quaker, he habitually retired into the Kingdom of Heaven within, and returned with an assurance of power. His ecclesiastical overlords investigated good Brother Lawrence, uncertain whether to silence or canonize him. Like Admiral Penn they realized that personal communion with the unseen power would do away with the middleman and "make an end of the priests till the end of the world." As the monk remained an obedient son of the Church, he came to no harm, and was noted for his spiritual power. Spiritual power can no more be gainsaid than electricity. An illiterate philosopher expatiating on the power of God to a Hyde Park audience was heckled by a skeptic:

"I say, 'ow do you know there is a God?"

"'Ow do I know? I've 'ad the experience of the power."

"But I've 'ad the experience that there ain't no God."

"My friend, you can 'ave an experience that there is

somethink, but nobody can 'ave an experience that there isn't anythink."

Not by political power, but by the power of God, the Quakers started out to change the world, yet their influence on American institutions was considerable. In the beginnings of our history Pennsylvania, New Jersey, and Delaware were privately owned by Quakers. In North Carolina they had a flourishing settlement, and one of the early and influential governors of that colony was a Quaker. In Rhode Island they held the governorship for thirty-six terms, and they were elected to many of the chief offices in the province. The wisdom and ability with which they administered the affairs of Pennsylvania for seventy-five years, made that province, according to Lord Acton, "an almost solitary example of freedom" at that time. As Ins they practiced what as Outs they had preached.

Suddenly they abandoned the field of politics, and reverted to their original position that politics could not be made to square with the Christian life till men were more enlightened. When the injustice and cupidity of other Pennsylvania settlers had exasperated the Indians into an alliance with the French, when Pennsylvania, the Holy Experiment by which Penn endeavored to prove to the world that justice and mercy give better results than brute force, was offering a bounty for the scalp of a male Indian, and a lesser tariff for the scalp of a female, or a child, the Quakers were ready to quit. Although security and prosperity had resulted from their "just and lenient measures," the party which had despoiled and enraged the Indians, saddled the responsibility for their outbreaks on Quaker pacifism, and clamored to civilize the red man with a gun. Some zealous Calvinists went so far as to say, that Jehovah, in a jealous rage at the leniency shown to the heathen, had permitted the savage onslaughts.

Unpopular as their pacifism was, their probity was so highly esteemed that they were still elected to a majority in the Pennsylvania Assembly. By advice of the Society, Quakers resigned from all public offices, and yielded the political control of the province they had founded, and so admirably managed, to the enemy invader. Their policy of nonresistance in this instance has been most severely criticized by the Quakers themselves. They were in a tight place, as a controlling majority of pacifists in an Assembly representing a warlike majority of the populace bent on supporting England in the wars with her European neighbors.

While they made a creditable showing in statecraft, it was by their educational campaign that they hoped to change the thoughts of men. During their forty years of wandering in the waste places of bigotry and cruelty, they pushed their ideas into every corner of the world, and into every class of society. Thousands were reached by their message for one who was attracted to their form of worship, divested as it was of all ecclesiastical arts. Their preachers were unpaid, there was no tax on the faithful except for the relief of the persecuted, and therefore no financial urge to increase their numbers. They were quite content to "publish the Truth" at their own expense, and to "tender" the hearts of men, let them worship where and how they would. Like the famous Johnny Appleseed, wherever they wandered they dropped the seed, preaching that war, and all other forms of violence, proceeded from the lust for power and revenge (lust which must be individually conquered); that the devil cannot be fought with fire.

Slavery, a recognized institution in the seventeenth century, they abolished, as they had abolished war, though more gradually. In 1688 the German Quakers of Pennsylvania made their first public protest against the holding of human chattels, in a naïve appeal to their own sect; they asked to be informed:

"Is there any that would be done or handled in this manner, *viz.* to be sold or made a slave of for all the time of his life? How fearful and faint-hearted are many on the sea when they see a strange vessel, being afraid it should be a Turk? . . . Now what is this better than Turks do? Now, though they are black, we cannot conceive that there is more liberty to have them slaves, than it is to have white ones."

For nearly a century after this appeal an intensive educational work was carried on among their own members, until in Independence year, 1776, they made their stand; after that time no slaveholder could continue a member of the Society of Friends. A committee was appointed to decide the amount of earned but unpaid increment to which the freedmen were entitled.

It was in their man-to-man canvass that the most valuable and least traceable work of the Quakers was done; we get hints of it only in the sketchiest of stories scattered through the records of the martyrs. Here and there in the lists of convicts appears the name of Leonard Fell, one of the knights-errant of the sect. On one occasion Leonard's missionary journey was interrupted by a gentleman of the road, who met with no remonstrance as he divested the Quaker of his possessions, including his horse. Leonard was accustomed to hold-ups by the clergy and magistrates, and yielded gracefully. Before he made off with the booty, Leonard in a concern for the robber's soul, begged him to desist from his evil life. The highwayman threatened to knock out his brains if he persisted in giving ethical instruction.

"Friend," continued the preacher mildly, "though I would not give my life to save my horse or my money, I would give it to save thy soul." The robber melted to the point of restitution.

During the French and English wars, an English vessel in which a Quaker, named Fox, was part owner, captured a French ship, and against the protests of Fox, the spoils were divided. Fox deposited his share in the bank, and after the treaty of peace advertised for the rightful owners, to whom he returned principal and interest. From this incident sprang up an acquaintance between the English Quakers and like-minded French.

Ascending the social ladder, we find the Friends making a sortie on Peter the Great and Prince Menzikoff, while the Czar was studying the ways of the English. Friends waited on the Emperor to call his attention to their ways. He was unable to understand, "of what use can you be in any kingdom, seeing you will not bear arms or fight." Thomas Story enlightened him. "Many of us fought with courage and magnanimity, in days of ignorance. I myself have worn a sword and other arms, and knew how to use them. . . . When it pleased God to reveal in our hearts the life and power of Jesus Christ, we were then reconciled unto God, one unto another, unto our enemies, and to all men. . . . He hath left us no right to fight and destroy, but to convert." Moreover, as their religion prohibited idleness, they engaged in useful occupations, adding to the national prosperity, and following the example of their Master, they paid taxes to the civil government. It was an adroit argument of William Penn, that, if they could not fight for a prince, neither could they fight against him, a point worthy of consideration in that time of upheaval.

The Czar was presented with a copy of Barclay's scholarly Apology for the faith in Latin, but learning that German was the only foreign language with which he was familiar, they hastened back to leave a copy of the Apology in that tongue. They refused money for the literature: "All that we desired was, that, in case any of our friends should come into his country, and preach those principles, and be persecuted for the same, he would be pleased to afford them protection and relief."

At Deptford, William Penn continued the Czar's education, and evidently a lasting impression was made on the great Peter; fifteen years later, when, as an ally of the Danes, he quartered his army at Frederickstadt, he inquired if there was a Quaker meeting in that town. There was a Meeting house, but his soldiers had been billeted in it. The Emperor ordered it cleared of soldiers, and with his aides attended the meetings. "Whoever could live according to that doctrine," he thought, "would be happy." It does not appear that he chose that path to happiness, but we do know that a sect holding similar doctrines found a refuge in Russia, and flourished there unmolested until very recently, when they moved to this side of the Atlantic. It is impossible to estimate the modifications of public opinion wrought by such assiduous propaganda, either among highwaymen and fellow-convicts or among crowned heads.

The importance of these unwearying appeals to the individual to cut loose from tradition, and think independently, can hardly be overstressed. The conviction that the universal conscience when awakened was on the side of right was rooted in the belief in religion as an experience of spiritual life. "You will say Christ saith this," argued Fox, "and the apostles say this; but what canst thou say? Art thou a child of Light, and hast thou walked in the Light, and what thou speakest is it inwardly from God? "

From the belief in the universality of the Light came the principles of equality and fraternity. We read in John Richardson's Journal: " We were at a Yearly Meeting in Treddhaven in Maryland . . . to which meeting for worship came William Penn, Lord Baltimore and his lady, with their retinue; but it was late when they came, and the strength and glory of the heavenly power was going off from the meeting; so that the lady was much disappointed, as I understand by William Penn, for she told him, 'she did not want to hear him preach, and such as he, for he was a scholar and a wise man; and she did not question but he could preach, but she wanted to hear some of our mechanics preach, as husbandmen, shoemakers, and suchlike rustics, for she thought they could not preach to any purpose.' William Penn told her, some of these were rather the best preachers we had amongst us." George Fox the shoemaker, Penn considered rather the best, and by far the most influential preacher in all England at that time. Liberty, equality and fraternity were the inevitable corollaries of the religion he preached, and by which he was changing the opinions of men.

Fox's insistence on sex equality, some of his early disciples regarded as so " monstrous," that they withdrew from the Society; yet the idea gained ground slowly, and was undoubtedly a factor in changing the status of women. Women derisively called "she preachers" won their way through to respect. Judith Zinspenning was the most prominent minister among the Dutch Quakers. She became a mother in Israel without detriment to her domestic responsibilities; she married Jacob Sewel, and was the mother of Sewel the Quaker historian. Her ministry was acceptable outside her sect: "It is true, friend, we do not allow women to speak in the Church, yet we bear that respect to you that we give you the liberty of speaking."

The Quakers were innovators regarding the right of free thought, free speech and free assembly, the rights of women, the rights of the backward races, and a slowly changing world has come gradually nearer to the ideas which they advanced. Dr. Ellis is well on the side of truth when he declares that their "dogged pertinacity" in promulgating their ideas drove the Puritan rulers of New England to a frenzy; he stops short of telling that the violence of that frenzy, and their heroic resistance rallied the liberty-loving element to rebel against the savagery which stains the memory of the Founding Fathers. It is no exaggeration to say, that as no other religious group came within hailing distance of the Quakers in toleration, so no other sect fought its way through to toleration so patiently and gallantly.

In "The Emancipation of Massachusetts," Brooks Adams, a son of the Old Colony, makes a most readable defense for the disturbers of its peace. Mr. Adams pooh-poohs even the occasional antics, which other critics have overemphasized, and concludes: "The horrors of the Inquisition, the Massacre of St. Bartholomew, the atrocities of Laud, the abominations of the Scotch Kirk, the persecution of the Quakers, had one object — the enslavement of the mind. Freedom of thought is the greatest triumph over tyranny that brave men have ever won; for this they fought the wars of the Reformation; for this they have left their bones to whiten upon unnumbered fields of battle; for this they have gone by thousands to the dungeon, the scaffold, and the stake. We owe to their heroic devotion the most priceless of our treasures, our perfect liberty of thought and speech[1]; and all who love their country's freedom may well reverence the memory of those marytred Quakers by whose death and agony the battle in New England has been won." A battle in which the victor suffered all the casualties, and left no new wrongs for old.

The social states of human kinds
Are made by multitudes of minds,
And after multitudes of years
A little human growth appears
Worth having, even to the soul
Who sees most plain it's not the whole.
— MASEFIELD in *The Everlasting Mercy*.

[1] This was written in 1887.

BIBLIOGRAPHY

Lord Acton, *History of Freedom.*
Brooks Adams, *Emancipation of Massachusetts.*
C. F. Adams, *Three Episodes of Massachusetts History.*
Margaret E. Hirst, *Quakers in Peace and War.*
William Penn, *Janney.*
Sharpless, *Quaker Experiment in Government.*
Sewel, *History of the Christian People Called Quakers.*
Besse, *Sufferings of the Quakers.*
Emmott, *A Short History of Quakerism.*
William Penn, *Works of.*
Rufus Jones, *Works of.*
William James, *Varieties of Religious Experience.*
George Fox's *Journal.*